Summary of Contents: Volume I

Summary of Contents: Volume II

W9-DHX-479

The PHP Anthology

Volume II: Applications

by Harry Fuecks

The PHP Anthology: Volume II: Applications

by Harry Fuecks

Copyright © 2003 SitePoint Pty. Ltd.

Editor: Georgina Laidlaw
Technical Editor: Kevin Yank
Cover Design: Julian Carroll
Printing History:
   First Edition: December 2003, February 2004

Notice of Rights

Notice of Liability

Trademark Notice

Published by SitePoint Pty. Ltd.

424 Smith Street Collingwood
VIC Australia 3066.

Web: www.sitepoint.com
Email: business@sitepoint.com

ISBN 0-9579218-4-5
Printed and bound in the United States of America

About The Author

Harry is a technical writer, programmer, and system engineer. He has worked in corporate IT since 1994, having completed a Bachelor's degree in Physics. He first came across PHP in 1999, while putting together a small Intranet. Today, he's the lead developer of a corporate Extranet, where PHP plays an important role in delivering a unified platform for numerous back office systems.

In his off hours he writes technical articles for SitePoint and runs phpPatterns (http://www.phppatterns.com/), a site exploring PHP application design.

Originally from the United Kingdom, he now lives in Switzerland. In May, Harry became the proud father of a beautiful baby girl who keeps him busy all day (and night!)

About SitePoint

SitePoint specializes in publishing fun, practical and easy-to-understand content for Web Professionals. Visit http://www.sitepoint.com/ to access our books, newsletters, articles and community forums.

For Natalie and Masha

Table of Contents

Preface

If I had one goal in mind while writing *The PHP Anthology*, it was to demonstrate just how easy it is to create intricate and powerful Web applications with an object oriented approach. In many cases, the more common procedural approach would result in unmanageable and bug-ridden "spaghetti code."

In *The PHP Anthology, Volume I: Foundations*, I laid the groundwork by introducing that approach and demonstrating its application to some relatively simple issues in Web development. With Volume II, I hope to blow your socks off by tackling some traditionally *complex* problems with those same principles—to great effect.

In examining the solutions here, you'll see how putting together your application with well designed classes is much like stacking building blocks, each fitting perfectly atop the other. Thanks to the principles of object oriented programming (OOP), different "blocks" of code needn't be concerned with the specifics of the other blocks in the structure.

One particular example in Chapter 3 looks at converting HTML content to Adobe's Portable Document Format (PDF), using no less than *eight* separate classes in conjunction to fetch content from a database, parse the HTML, and, finally, output the PDF. The solution involves a number of steps, but, by breaking it down into manageable components in the form of classes, the complexity is reduced to the simple interactions between them.

Other issues tackled in this volume, either head-on, or as a side-effect of specific solutions, include:

❏ Layered application structure and the principles of **N-Tier design**

❏ Providing and consuming **Web services** using XML-RPC and SOAP

❏ Professional **development techniques**, such as API documentation and unit testing

❏ Software **design patterns**, and how to apply them in PHP

When dealing with these more advanced subjects, my goal is not to provide all the answers (many are worthy of books in themselves), but to open doors to new concepts for you to explore further on your own.

My hope is that this book will enrich your understanding of PHP and motivate you to raise your development practices to a professional level, allowing you to change your job description from "PHP hacker" to "PHP developer."

Who should read this book?

This book, *The PHP Anthology, Volume II: Applications*, builds on the first book, *The PHP Anthology, Volume I: Foundations*, to provide practical solutions that are commonly required in many of today's online applications. So, if you build Websites and Web applications with PHP, then this book is for you.

For less experienced PHP developers, reading *The PHP Anthology, Volume I: Foundations* before you start this book is a good idea, as many of the solutions presented here build on knowledge introduced in that volume. It should be possible for the PHP veteran to begin with this second book, referring to the code archive to fill in any gaps.

What's covered in this book?

In summary, here's what you'll find in each of the chapters in this volume:

Chapter 1: Access Control
Beginning with basic HTTP authentication, then moving on to application level authentication, this chapter looks at ways to control access to your site. Later solutions look at implementing a user registration system and creating a fine-grained access control system with users, groups and permissions.

Chapter 2: XML
With XML rapidly becoming an essential part of almost all Web-based applications, this chapter begins by exploring the SAX and DOM APIs to help parse an RSS feed, before examining the generation of your own RSS feed with DOM. Following that, we'll see how XPath can be used to reduce the coding effort involved in parsing XML, then move on to XML transformations with XSLT. Finally, this chapter shows how Web services can be built using PHP, XML-RPC and SOAP.

Chapter 3: Alternative Content Types
With the wide range of media now in use on the Internet, there's often a need to be able to use PHP to render content types other than (X)HTML. This chapter begins by looking at PDF generation using pure PHP, and how to convert content that contains embedded HTML markup into PDF form.

Following that, we'll look at generating SVG images with PHP, and learn how to "WAP enable" a Website quickly and efficiently. Finally, this chapter looks at how XUL can be applied to build more powerful administrative interfaces to your application, reducing load on your server and speeding administrative tasks.

Chapter 4: Stats and Tracking

Here, we look at the all-important process of gathering statistical information about visitors to your site. We'll experiment with various mechanisms you can use to capture data, and help you lay the foundations that can become critical in improving the experience you offer site users.

Chapter 5: Caching

This chapter takes the fundamental view that "HTML is fastest," and shows you how you can take advantage of caching on both the client and server sides to reduce bandwidth usage and dramatically improve performance.

Chapter 6: Development Technique

The goal of this chapter is to examine some of the techniques that have proved themselves in helping development projects succeed. The discussion covers common optimizations you might apply to your code, a summary of N-Tier application design, how to add API documentation to your work, and how to reduce bugs with unit testing.

Chapter 7: Design Patterns

The notion of software Design Patterns has been widely accepted as a useful approach to application design. This chapter introduces them as a concept, then illustrates their implementation with five common patterns applied to "real" problems in PHP: The Factory Method, The Iterator Pattern, The Strategy Pattern, The Adapter Pattern, and the Observer Pattern.

The Book's Website

Located at http://www.sitepoint.com/books/phpant1/, the Website supporting this book will give you access to the following facilities:

The Code Archive

As you progress through this book, you'll note a number of references to the code archive. This is a downloadable ZIP archive that contains complete code for all the examples presented in the book.

Besides the PHP scripts themselves, the archive contains a number of shared libraries, which are bundled in the SPLIB directory. In order for the scripts that rely on these libraries to work as intended, you'll need to add this directory to PHP's include_path (see "How do I include one PHP script in another?" in Volume I, Chapter 1 for full details on include_path). Doing this will also make it easier to use these libraries in your own projects.

For full instructions on how to install and use the code archive, consult the readme.txt file in the archive.

Updates and Errata

No book is perfect, and we expect that watchful readers will be able to spot at least one or two mistakes before the end of this one. The Errata page on the book's Website will always have the latest information about known typographical and code errors, and necessary updates for new releases of PHP and the various Web standards.

The SitePoint Forums

If you'd like to communicate with me or anyone else on the SitePoint publishing team about this book, you should join SitePoint's online community[2]. As I mentioned above, the PHP forums[3], in particular, can offer an abundance of information above and beyond the solutions in this book.

In fact, you should join that community even if you *don't* want to talk to us, because there are a lot of fun and experienced Web designers and developers hanging out there. It's a good way to learn new stuff, get questions answered in a hurry, and just have fun.

The SitePoint Newsletters

In addition to books like this one, SitePoint publishes free email newsletters including *The SitePoint Tribune* and *The SitePoint Tech Times*. In them, you'll read about the latest news, product releases, trends, tips, and techniques for all aspects of Web development. If nothing else, you'll get useful PHP articles and tips, but if you're interested in learning other technologies, you'll find them especially

---

[2] http://www.sitepointforums.com/
[3] http://www.sitepointforums.com/forumdisplay.php?forumid=34

valuable. Go ahead and sign up to one or more SitePoint newsletters at http://www.sitepoint.com/newsletter/—I'll wait!

Your Feedback

If you can't find your answer through the forums, or if you wish to contact us for any other reason, the best place to write is <books@sitepoint.com>. We have a well-manned email support system set up to track your inquiries, and if our support staff is unable to answer your question, they send it straight to me. Suggestions for improvements as well as notices of any mistakes you may find are especially welcome.

Acknowledgements

First and foremost, I'd like to thank the SitePoint team for doing such a great job in making this book possible, for being understanding as deadlines inevitably slipped past, and for their personal touch, which makes it a pleasure to work with them.

Particular thanks go to Kevin Yank, whose valuable technical insight and close cooperation throughout the process has tied up many loose ends and helped make *The PHP Anthology* both readable and accessible. Thanks also to Julian Szemere, whose frequent feedback helped shape the content of this anthology, and to Georgina Laidlaw, who managed to make some of my "late at night" moments more coherent.

A special thanks to the many who contribute to SitePoint Forums[5]. There's a long list of those who deserve praise for their selflessness in sharing their own practical experience with PHP. It's been fascinating to watch the PHP forums grow over the last three years, from discussing the basics of PHP's syntax, to, more recently, the finer points of enterprise application architecture. As a whole, I'm sure SitePoint's PHP community has made a very significant contribution to making PHP a popular and successful technology.

Finally, returning home, I'd like to thank Natalie, whose patience, love, and understanding throughout continue to amaze me. Halfway through writing this book, our first child, Masha, was born; writing a book at the same time was not always easy.

---

[5] http://www.sitepointforums.com/

1

Access Control

One of the side effects of building your site with PHP, as opposed to plain HTML, is that you'll be building dynamic Web applications rather than static Web pages. Your site will let you "do" things that weren't possible with plain HTML. But how can you ensure that only you, or those to whom you give permission, are able to "do things," and prevent the Internet's raging hordes from running riot on your site?

In this chapter, we'll be looking at the mechanisms you can employ with PHP to build authentication systems and control access to the parts of your site you regard as private.

One word of warning before I go any further: any system you build, which involves the transfer of data from a Web page over the Internet, will send that information in clear text by default.[1] What this means is that if someone is "listening in" on the network between the client's Web browser and the Web server, which is possible using a tool known as a **packet sniffer**, they will be able to read the user name and password sent via your form. The chances of this happening are fairly small, as typically only trusted organizations like ISPs have the access require to intercept packets. However, there is still a risk, and it's one you should take seriously.

---

[1] Web servers that require **Secure Socket Layer** (SSL) connections will safely encrypt the data during transit. This is the best way to protect sensitive data in today's Web applications.

In addition to strategies for building access control systems for your site, in this chapter you'll find plenty of references to useful information (there are more in Appendix C). I can't stress enough the importance of a little healthy paranoia in building Web-based applications. The SitePoint Forums frequently receive visits from would-be Website developers who got their fingers burned when it came to site security.

This chapter requires the following MySQL tables, in addition to the user table from Volume I, Chapter 9. Note that you'll find the SQL code to create all of these, along with sample data, in the code archive in the sql/ directory.

First, you'll need a table for storing temporary sign up information:

```
CREATE TABLE signup (
  signup_id    INT(11)      NOT NULL AUTO_INCREMENT,
  login        VARCHAR(50) NOT NULL DEFAULT '',
  password     VARCHAR(50) NOT NULL DEFAULT '',
  email        VARCHAR(50) DEFAULT NULL,
  firstName    VARCHAR(50) DEFAULT NULL,
  lastName     VARCHAR(50) DEFAULT NULL,
  signature    TEXT         NOT NULL,
  confirm_code VARCHAR(40) NOT NULL DEFAULT '',
  created      INT(11)      NOT NULL DEFAULT '0',
  PRIMARY KEY (signup_id),
  UNIQUE KEY confirm_code (confirm_code),
  UNIQUE KEY user_login (login),
  UNIQUE KEY email (email)
)
```

You'll need a table for storing groups[2]:

```
CREATE TABLE collection (
  collection_id INT(11)      NOT NULL auto_increment,
  name          VARCHAR(50) NOT NULL default '',
  description   TEXT         NOT NULL,
  PRIMARY KEY (collection_id)
)
```

Next, there's a lookup table between users and groups:

```
CREATE TABLE user2collection (
  user_id       INT(11)      NOT NULL default '0',
  collection_id INT(11)      NOT NULL default '0',
```

---

[2]Note that I've called this table collection. The name "group" would cause problems, as GROUP is a keyword in SELECT query syntax.

```
    PRIMARY KEY (user_id, collection_id)
)
```

Don't forget this table for storing permissions:

```
CREATE TABLE permission (
  permission_id INT(11)     NOT NULL AUTO_INCREMENT,
  name          VARCHAR(50) NOT NULL DEFAULT '',
  description   TEXT        NOT NULL,
  PRIMARY KEY (permission_id)
)
```

And finally, you'll need this lookup table between groups and permissions:

```
CREATE TABLE collection2permission (
  collection_id INT(11)     NOT NULL DEFAULT '0',
  permission_id INT(11)     NOT NULL DEFAULT '0',
  PRIMARY KEY (collection_id, permission_id)
)
```

How do I use HTTP authentication with PHP?

Hypertext Transfer Protocol[1] (HTTP) defines its own authentication mechanisms, namely "Basic" and "Digest" authentication, which are defined in RFC 2617[2]. If you run PHP on an Apache server, you can take advantage of the **basic authentication** mechanism (digest authentication is on the list of features yet to be released) using PHP's `header` function and a couple of predefined variables. A general discussion of these features is provided in the PHP Manual[3].

Heads Up

The first thing to understand is what actually happens when your browser sends a request to a Web server to give it a Web page. HTTP is the protocol for communication between a browser and a Web server. When your Web browser sends a request to a Web server, it uses an HTTP request to tell the server which page it wants. The server then replies with an HTTP response that describes the type and characteristics of the document being sent, then delivers the document itself.

---

[1] ftp://ftp.isi.edu/in-notes/rfc2616.txt
[2] ftp://ftp.isi.edu/in-notes/rfc2617.txt
[3] http://www.php.net/features.http-auth

For example, a client might send the following request to a server:

```
GET /subcat/98 HTTP/1.1
Host: www.sitepoint.com
```

Here's what it might get back from the server:

```
HTTP/1.1 200 OK
Date: Tue, 25 Feb 2003 15:18:24 GMT
Server: Apache/1.3.27 (Unix) PHP/4.3.1
X-Powered-By: PHP/4.3.1
Connection: close
Content-Type: text/html

<!DOCTYPE html PUBLIC "-//W3C//DTD XHTML 1.0 Strict//EN"
"http://www.w3.org/TR/xhtml1/DTD/xhtml1-strict.dtd">
<html xmlns="http://www.w3.org/1999/xhtml">
<head>
<title>SitePoint : Empowering Web Developers Since 1997</title>
…
```

Don't believe me? Try it for yourself:

File: **1.php**

```php
<?php
// Connect to sitepoint.com
$fp = fsockopen('www.sitepoint.com', '80');

// Send the request
fputs($fp,
  "GET /subcat/98 HTTP/1.1\r\nHost: www.sitepoint.com\r\n\r\n");

// Fetch the response
$response = '';
while (!feof($fp)) {
  $response .= fgets($fp, 128);
}
fclose($fp);

// Convert HTML to entities
$response = htmlspecialchars($response);

// Display the response
echo nl2br($response);
?>
```

Authentication headers are additional headers used by a server to instruct the browser that it must send a valid user name and password in order to view the page.

In response to a normal request for a page secured with basic HTTP authentication, a server might respond with headers like these:

```
HTTP/1.1 401 Authorization Required
Date: Tue, 25 Feb 2003 15:41:54 GMT
Server: Apache/1.3.27 (Unix) PHP/4.3.1
X-Powered-By: PHP/4.3.1
WWW-Authenticate: Basic realm="PHP Secured"
Connection: close
Content-Type: text/html
```

No further information is sent, but notice the status code HTTP/1.1 401 Authorization Required and the WWW-Authenticate header. Together, these indicate that the page is protected by HTTP authentication, and is not available to an unauthorized user. How a visitor's browser goes about dealing with this information may vary, but, usually, the user will see a small pop-up dialog box like that shown in Figure 1.1.

Figure 1.1. Let Me In!

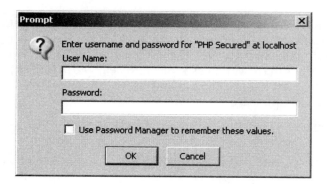

The dialog prompts site visitors to enter their user names and passwords. If visitors using Internet Explorer enter these login details incorrectly three times, the browser will display the "Unauthorized" message instead of displaying the prompt again. In other browsers, such as Opera, users may be able to continue trying indefinitely.

Notice that the realm value specified in the WWW-Authenticate header is displayed in the dialog box. A **realm** is a "security space" or "zone" within which a particular set of login details are valid. Upon successful authentication, the browser will remember the correct user name and password combination and automatically re-send it in any future request to that realm. When the user navigates to another realm, however, the browser displays a fresh prompt once again.

In any case, the user must provide a user name and password to get the page. The browser then sends those credentials with a second page request like this:

```
GET /admin/ HTTP/1.1
Host: www.sitepoint.com
Authorization: Basic jTSAbT766yNOhGjUi
```

The Authorization header contains the user name and password encoded with **base64 encoding** which, it is worth noting, is *not* secure—but at least makes it unreadable for humans.

The server will check to ensure that the credentials are valid. If they are not, the server will send the Authorization Required response again, as shown previously. If the credentials are valid, the server will send the requested page as normal.

Not by the Hairs of my Chin...

Now that you have a rough idea of how HTTP authentication works, how might you secure a PHP page with it? When PHP receives an Authorization header from a Web browser, it automatically decodes the user name and password combination and stores the values in the variables $_SERVER['PHP_AUTH_USER'] and $_SERVER['PHP_AUTH_PW'] for the user name and password, respectively. Here's how you could secure a simple page:

File: **2.php**

```php
<?php
// An array of allowed users and their passwords
$users = array(
  'harryf' => 'secret',
  'littlepig' => 'chinny'
);

// If there's no Authentication header, exit
if (!isset($_SERVER['PHP_AUTH_USER'])) {
  header('HTTP/1.1 401 Unauthorized');
  header('WWW-Authenticate: Basic realm="PHP Secured"');
```

```
   exit('This page requires authentication');
}

// If the user name doesn't exist, exit
if (!isset($users[$_SERVER['PHP_AUTH_USER']])) {
  header('HTTP/1.1 401 Unauthorized');
  header('WWW-Authenticate: Basic realm="PHP Secured"');
  exit('Unauthorized!');
}

// Is the password doesn't match the username, exit
if ($users[$_SERVER['PHP_AUTH_USER']] != $_SERVER['PHP_AUTH_PW'])
{
  header('HTTP/1.1 401 Unauthorized');
  header('WWW-Authenticate: Basic realm="PHP Secured"');
  exit('Unauthorized!');
}

echo 'You\'re in';
?>
```

First, the script checks to see if an authentication has been sent by the browser; if it hasn't, the script sends the Authorization Required headers and terminates. If login details *were* submitted, it checks that the submitted user name actually exists. If we hadn't checked this, we'd get a PHP notice stating that the array key didn't exist when performing the third check on particular PHP configurations (see Volume I, Chapter 10). The third check ensures that the user name and password combination in the $users array matches the details sent by the Web browser.

Note that we could also have checked the user name and password against a table in a database—something we'll look at in "How do I authenticate users with sessions?".

 Tip

When to Send Headers

In PHP, the moment your script outputs anything that's meant for display, the Web server finishes sending the headers and begins to send the content itself. You cannot send further HTTP headers once the body of the HTTP message—the Web page itself—has begun to be sent. This means that if you use the header function or session_start after the body has begun, you'll get an error message like this:

```
Warning: Cannot add header information - headers already
sent by (output started at...
```

> Remember, any text or whitespace outside the **<?php … ?>** tags causes output to be sent to the browser. If you have whitespace before a **<?php** tag or after a **?>** tag, you won't be able to send headers to the browser past that point.

This type of authentication is handy in that it's easy to implement, but it's none too pretty in terms of the user experience. It does present a useful authentication mechanism for use with Web services, however—something we'll see in Chapter 2.

Note that PEAR provides the Auth_HTTP[4] package, which you should consider if you're planning to use HTTP authentication in earnest, as it will help you avoid making critical errors. For a detailed discussion of PEAR, consult Appendix D.

How do I authenticate users with sessions?

Sessions are a mechanism that allows PHP to **preserve state** between executions. In simple terms, sessions allow you to store variables from one page and use them on another. So if a visitor tells you his name is "Bob" (via a form) on one page, sessions will help you remember his name and allow you to, for instance, place on all the other pages of your site personal messages such as, "Where would you like to go today, Bob?" (don't be surprised if Bob leaves pretty quickly, though).

The basic mechanism of sessions works like this: first, PHP generates a unique, thirty-two character string to identify the session. It then passes the value to the browser; simultaneously, it creates a file on the server and includes the session ID in the filename. There are two methods by which PHP can inform a browser of its session ID: by adding the ID to the query string of all relative links on the page, or by sending it as a cookie. Within the file that's stored on the server, PHP saves the names and values of the variables it has been told to store for the session.

When the browser makes a request for another page, it tells PHP which session it was assigned via the URL query string, or by returning the cookie. PHP then looks up the file it created when the session was started, and so has access to the data stored within the session.

---

[4] http://pear.php.net/AUTH_HTTP

Once the session has been established, it will continue until it is specifically destroyed by PHP (in response to a user clicking "Log out," for example), or the session has been inactive for longer than a given period of time (24 minutes by default), at which point it becomes flagged for garbage collection and will be deleted the next time PHP checks for outdated sessions.

The following HTTP response headers show a server passing a session cookie to a browser, as a result of the `session_start` function in a PHP script:

```
HTTP/1.1 200 OK
Date: Wed, 26 Feb 2003 02:23:08 GMT
Server: Apache/1.3.27 (Unix) PHP/4.3.1
X-Powered-By: PHP/4.3.1
Set-Cookie: PHPSESSID=ce558537fb4aefe349bb8d48c5dcc6d3; path=/
Connection: close
Content-Type: text/html

<!DOCTYPE html PUBLIC "-//W3C//DTD XHTML 1.0 Strict//EN"
"http://www.w3.org/TR/xhtml1/DTD/xhtml1-strict.dtd">
<html xmlns="http://www.w3.org/1999/xhtml">
…
```

Note that I've said sessions are stored on the server as files. It's also possible to store sessions using other means, such as a database or even shared memory. This can be useful for displaying "Who is Online" type information as well as load balancing multiple Web servers using a single session repository, allowing visitors to (unknowingly) swap servers while maintaining their session.

Session Security

Sessions are very useful, but there are some important security considerations you should take into account when using them in your applications:

❏ By default, all a browser has to do to gain control of a session is pass a valid session ID to PHP. In an ideal world, you could store the IP address that registered the session, and double check it on every new request that used the associated session ID. Unfortunately, some ISPs, such as AOL, assign their users a new IP on almost every page request, so this type of security mechanism would soon start throwing valid users out of the system. As such, it's important to design your application in a manner that assumes that one of your users will eventually have his or her session "hijacked." The user's account is only exposed as long as the session hasn't expired, so your focus should be on preventing the hijackers from doing serious damage while they're in the system.

This means, for example, that for logged-in users to change their accounts' passwords, they should be asked to provide their old passwords—obviously, hijackers won't know these. Also, be careful with the personal information you make available to users (such as credit card details), and if you give users the opportunity to make significant changes to their accounts, for instance, changing a shipping address, be sure to send a summary notification to their email address (this will alert users whose sessions have been hijacked).

To keep the session ID *completely* hidden, you'll need to use SSL to encrypt the conversation. What's more, you should only use the cookie method of passing the session ID. If you pass it in the URL, you may give away the session ID upon referring the visitor to another site, thanks to the `referrer` header in the HTTP request.

☐ The files PHP creates for the purpose of storing session information are, by default, stored in the temporary directory of the operating system under which PHP is running. On Unix based systems such as Linux, this will be `/tmp`. And, if you're on a shared server, this will mean that other users on the server can read the files' contents. They may not be able to identify *which* virtual host and PHP script are the owners of the session but, depending on the information you place there, they may be able to guess.

This is a serious cause for concern on shared PHP systems; the most effective solution is to store your sessions in a database, rather than the server's temporary directory. We'll look more closely at custom session handlers later in this chapter, but a partial solution is to set the `session.save_path` option to a directory that's not available to the public. You'll need to contact your hosting company in order to have set the correct permissions for that directory, so that the 'nobody' or 'wwwuser' user with which PHP runs has access to read, write, and delete files in that directory.

Session IDs and Cross-Site Scripting

One final warning: using a common Web security exploit, **cross-site scripting** (XSS), it's possible for an attacker to place JavaScript on your site that will cause visitors to give away their session ID to a remote Website, thereby allowing their sessions to be hijacked. If you allow your visitors to post *any* HTML, make sure you check and validate it very carefully (see Appendix C for more on XSS and Volume I, Chapter 5 for an HTML filtering mechanism).

Remember the golden rules: *never rely on client side technologies (such as JavaScript) to handle security* and *never trust anything you get from a browser*.

Getting Started

I hope that introduction hasn't made you so paranoid about using sessions that you'll never touch them. In general, sessions offer a mechanism that is both simple to use and powerful—it's an essential tool for building online applications.

The first development trick you need to know is that you should always access session variables using their predefined global variable $_SESSION, not the functions session_register and session_unregister. These functions fail to work correctly when PHP's register_globals setting has been disabled, which is the way you should be programming with PHP (see Appendix A for details).

To start off slowly, here's a simple example of how sessions can be used:

File: **3.php**

```php
<?php
session_start();

// If session variable doesn't exist, register it
if (!isset($_SESSION['test'])) {
  $_SESSION['test'] = 'Hello World!';
  echo '$_SESSION[\'test\'] is registered.<br />' .
      'Please refresh page';
} else {
  // It's registered so display it
  echo '$_SESSION[\'test\'] = ' . $_SESSION['test'];
}
?>
```

The first order of business in a script that uses sessions is to call session_start to load any existing session variables.

This script registers the session variable the first time the page is displayed. The next time (and all times thereafter, until the session times out through inactivity), the script will display the value of the session variable.

That's a simple example of how sessions can be used. We'll use them to store the value of a user name and password shortly, but first, we need to put together some classes that will collaborate to deal with both sessions and authentication. Don't panic! The classes themselves may get fairly complex, but using them from an external script will be easy.

First, let's develop a class for sessions. All code will use this class to access sessions, rather than using the $_SESSION variable directly. This has the advantage that if we ever want to switch to an alternative session handling mechanism, such as one we've built ourselves, we simply need to modify the class, rather than rewriting a lot of code. We can provide an interface to the $_SESSION variable with a few simple methods:

File: **Session/Session.php (in SPLIB)**

```php
<?php
/**
 * A wrapper around PHP's session functions
 * <code>
 * $session = new Session();
 * $session->set('message','Hello World!');
 * echo ( $session->get('message'); // Displays 'Hello World!'
 * </code>
 * @package SPLIB
 * @access public
 */
class Session {
  /**
   * Session constructor<br />
   * Starts the session with session_start()
   * <b>Note:</b> that if the session has already started,
   * session_start() does nothing
   * @access public
   */
  function Session()
  {
    session_start();
  }

  /**
   * Sets a session variable
   * @param string name of variable
   * @param mixed value of variable
   * @return void
   * @access public
   */
  function set($name, $value)
  {
    $_SESSION[$name] = $value;
  }

  /**
```

```php
 * Fetches a session variable
 * @param string name of variable
 * @return mixed value of session varaible
 * @access public
 */
function get($name)
{
  if (isset($_SESSION[$name])) {
    return $_SESSION[$name];
  } else {
    return false;
  }
}

/**
 * Deletes a session variable
 * @param string name of variable
 * @return void
 * @access public
 */
function del($name)
{
  unset($_SESSION[$name]);
}

/**
 * Destroys the whole session
 * @return void
 * @access public
 */
function destroy()
{
  $_SESSION = array();
  session_destroy();
}
}
?>
```

Next, we build an authentication class, called Auth, which will use the MySQL class we saw in earlier chapters, as well as the above Session class.

We begin by defining a few constants that will make it easy to customize this class for different environments:

File: **AccessControl/Auth.php (in SPLIB) (excerpt)**

```php
// Name to use for login variable e.g. $_POST['login']
@define('USER_LOGIN_VAR', 'login');
// Name to use for password variable e.g. $_POST['password']
@define('USER_PASSW_VAR', 'password');

# Modify these constants to match your user login table
// Name of users table
@define('USER_TABLE', 'user');
// Name of login column in table
@define('USER_TABLE_LOGIN', 'login');
// Name of password column in table
@define('USER_TABLE_PASSW', 'password');
```

The first two constants are for the names of the user name and password fields of the login form we'll build in a moment. The next three provide details of the table in which user information is stored.

Next come the properties and constructor for the class:

File: **AccessControl/Auth.php (in SPLIB) (excerpt)**

```php
/**
 * Authentication class<br />
 * Automatically authenticates users on construction<br />
 * <b>Note:</b> requires the Session/Session class be available
 * @access public
 * @package SPLIB
 */
class Auth {
  /**
   * Instance of database connection class
   * @access private
   * @var object
   */
  var $db;

  /**
   * Instance of Session class
   * @access private
   * @var Session
   */
  var $session;

  /**
   * Url to re-direct to in not authenticated
```

```
   * @access private
   * @var string
   */
  var $redirect;

  /**
   * String to use when making hash of username and password
   * @access private
   * @var string
   */
  var $hashKey;

  /**
   * Are passwords being encrypted
   * @access private
   * @var boolean
   */
  var $md5;

  /**
   * Auth constructor
   * Checks for valid user automatically
   * @param object database connection
   * @param string URL to redirect to on failed login
   * @param string key to use when making hash of user name and
   *                password
   * @param boolean if passwords are md5 encrypted in database
   *                (optional)
   * @access public
   */
  function Auth(&$db, $redirect, $hashKey, $md5 = true)
  {
    $this->db       = &$db;
    $this->redirect = $redirect;
    $this->hashKey  = $hashKey;
    $this->md5      = $md5;
    $this->session  = &new Session();
    $this->login();
  }
```

The $db parameter accepts an instance of the MySQL class, which we created in Volume I, Chapter 3.

The $redirect parameter specifies a URL to which visitors will be redirected if they aren't logged in, or if their user name or password is incorrect. This might be a login form, for example.

The $hashKey parameter is a seed we provide to double check the user names and passwords of users who are already logged in. I'll explain this in more detail later.

The $md5 parameter tells the class whether we've used MD5 encryption to store the passwords in the database.

MD5 Digests

MD5 is a simple **message digest** algorithm (often referred to as one-way encryption) that translates any string (such as a password) into a short series of ASCII characters, called an MD5 digest. A particular string will always produce the same digest, but it is practically impossible to guess a string that will produce a given digest. By storing only the MD5 digest of your users' passwords in the database, you can verify their login credentials without actually storing the passwords on your server! The built-in PHP function md5 lets you calculate the MD5 digest of any string in PHP.

The constructor goes on to create a new instance of the Session class, which it stores in an instance variable, and finally calls the login method to validate the user against the database.

Here's the login method:

File: **AccessControl/Auth.php (in SPLIB) (excerpt)**

```php
/**
 * Checks username and password against database
 * @return void
 * @access private
 */
function login()
{
  // See if we have values already stored in the session
  if ($this->session->get('login_hash')) {
    $this->confirmAuth();
    return;
  }

  // If this is a fresh login, check $_POST variables
  if (!isset($_POST[USER_LOGIN_VAR]) ||
      !isset($_POST[USER_PASSW_VAR])) {
    $this->redirect();
  }

  if ($this->md5) {
```

```
    $password = md5($_POST[USER_PASSW_VAR]);
  } else {
    $password = $_POST[USER_PASSW_VAR];
  }

  // Escape the variables for the query
  $login = mysql_escape_string($_POST[USER_LOGIN_VAR]);
  $password = mysql_escape_string($password);

  // Query to count number of users with this combination
  $sql = "SELECT COUNT(*) AS num_users
          FROM " . USER_TABLE . "
          WHERE
            " . USER_TABLE_LOGIN . "='$login' AND
            " . USER_TABLE_PASSW . "='$password'";

  $result = $this->db->query($sql);
  $row = $result->fetch();

  // If there isn't is exactly one entry, redirect
  if ($row['num_users'] != 1) {
    $this->redirect();
  // Else is a valid user; set the session variables
  } else {
    $this->storeAuth($login, $password);
  }
}
```

The login method first checks to see whether values for the user name and password are currently stored in the session; if they are, it calls the **confirmAuth** method (see below). If user name and password values are not stored in the session, the method checks to see if they're available in the $_POST array and, if they're not, it calls the **redirect** method (see below).

Assuming it has found the $_POST values, the script performs a query against the database to see if it can find a record to match the submitted user name and password. There must be exactly one matching record, otherwise the visitor will be redirected. Finally, assuming the script has got this far, it registers the user name and password as session variables using the storeAuth method (see below), which makes them available for future page requests.

One thing to note about the login method is that it *assumes magic_quotes_gpc is switched off*, as it uses mysql_escape_string to prepare submitted values for incorporation into database queries. In the scripts that utilize this class, we'll include the script that nullifies the effect of magic quotes (see "How do I write portable PHP code?" in Volume I, Chapter 1).

Let's now look at the methods that `login` uses.

File: **AccessControl/Auth.php (in SPLIB) (excerpt)**

```php
/**
 * Sets the session variables after a successful login
 * @return void
 * @access protected
 */
function storeAuth($login, $password)
{
    $this->session->set(USER_LOGIN_VAR, $login);
    $this->session->set(USER_PASSW_VAR, $password);

    // Create a session variable to use to confirm sessions
    $hashKey = md5($this->hashKey . $login . $password);
    $this->session->set('login_hash', $hashKey);
}
```

The `storeAuth` method is used to add the user name and password to the session, along with a hash value. This is comprised of a seed value defined using the `Auth` class (remember the `$hashKey` parameter required by the constructor?), as well as the user name and password values. As we'll see in the `confirmAuth` method below, instead of laboriously checking the database to verify the login credentials whenever a user requests a page, the class simply checks that the current user name and password produce a hash value that's the same as that stored in the session. This prevents potential attackers from attempting to change the stored user name after login if your PHP configuration has `register_globals` enabled.

As I've just described, the `confirmAuth` method is used to double check credentials stored in the session once a user is logged in. Notice how we reproduce the hash built by the `storeAuth` method. If this fails to match the original hash value, the user is immediately logged out.

File: **AccessControl/Auth.php (in SPLIB) (excerpt)**

```php
/**
 * Confirms that an existing login is still valid
 * @return void
 * @access private
 */
function confirmAuth()
{
```

```
  $login = $this->session->get(USER_LOGIN_VAR);
  $password = $this->session->get(USER_PASSW_VAR);
  $hashKey = $this->session->get('login_hash');
  if (md5($this->hashKey . $login . $password) != $hashKey)
  {
    $this->logout(true);
  }
}
```

The `logout` method is the only public method in the `Auth` class. It's used to remove the login credentials from the session and return the user to the login form:

File: **AccessControl/Auth.php** (in **SPLIB**) (excerpt)

```
/**
 * Logs the user out
 * @param boolean Parameter to pass on to Auth::redirect()
 *                (optional)
 * @return void
 * @access public
 */
function logout($from = false)
{
  $this->session->del(USER_LOGIN_VAR);
  $this->session->del(USER_PASSW_VAR);
  $this->session->del('login_hash');
  $this->redirect($from);
}
```

The `redirect` method is used to return the visitor to the login form (or whatever URL we specified upon instantiating the `Auth` class):

File: **AccessControl/Auth.php** (in **SPLIB**) (excerpt)

```
/**
 * Redirects browser and terminates script execution
 * @param boolean adverstise URL where this user came from
 *                (optional)
 * @return void
 * @access private
 */
function redirect($from = true)
{
  if ($from) {
    header('Location: ' . $this->redirect . '?from=' .
           $_SERVER['REQUEST_URI']);
  } else {
    header('Location: ' . $this->redirect);
```

```
    }
    exit();
}
```

Unless you tell it not to, this method will send the `from` variable via the query string to the script to which the browser is redirected. This allows the login form to return the users to the location from which they came; it saves the users from having to navigate back to that point, which might be useful if, for example, a session times out. Note that in the `logout` method we specified that `redirect` should *not* provide the `from` variable. If it did, the script might return users to the URL they used to log out, putting them in a loop from which they couldn't log in.

One important note to make here is that the redirection URL (which is set by the constructor) should be *absolute*, not relative. According to the HTTP specification, an absolute URL must be provided when a `Location` header is used. Later on, when we put this class into action, I'm going to break that rule and use a relative URL, because I can't guess the script's location on your server. This works because most recent browsers understand it (even though they shouldn't). On a live site, make sure you provide a full, absolute URL.

Finally, and most importantly, we use `exit` to terminate all further processing. This prevents the calling script sending the protected content that follows the authentication code. Although we've sent a header that should redirect the browser, we can't rely on the browser to do what it's told. If the request were sent by, for instance, a Perl script *pretending* to be a Web browser, whoever was using the script would, no doubt, have total control over its behavior and could quite easily ignore the instruction to redirect elsewhere. Hence, the `exit` statement is critical.

Overall, this approach helps save us from our own mistakes; if a given user is not valid, script execution halts and the user is redirected to another "safe" page. The alternative approach might be to build conditional statements into a page, like this:

```
if ($auth->login()) {
  echo 'You are logged in';
} else {
  echo 'Invalid login';
}
```

However, this isn't really a good idea. In a more complex scenario, which involves multiple file inclusions, and has classes take responsibility for different parts of the application, it's possible that you may unwittingly allow unauthorized visitors access. The approach of redirection is simple, reliable, and less likely to lead to such nasty surprises.

Authentication in Action

Now that you've seen the internals of the Session and Auth classes, let's take a look at some code that makes use of them. First, here's the script that will act as the login form:

File: **4.php**

```php
<?php
// If $_GET['from'] comes from the Auth class
if (isset($_GET['from'])) {
  $target = $_GET['from'];
} else {
  // Default URL: usually index.php
  $target = '5.php';
}
?>
<!DOCTYPE html PUBLIC "-//W3C//DTD XHTML 1.0 Transitional//EN"
  "http://www.w3.org/TR/xhtml1/DTD/xhtml1-transitional.dtd">
<html xmlns="http://www.w3.org/1999/xhtml">
<head>
<title> Login Form </title>
<meta http-equiv="Content-type"
  content="text/html; charset=iso-8859-1" />
<style type="text/css">
body, a, td, input
{
    font-family: verdana;
    font-size: 11px;
}
h1
{
    font-family: verdana;
    font-size: 15px;
    color: navy;
}
</style>
</head>
<body>
<h1>Please log in</h1>
<form action="<?php echo $target; ?>" method="post">
<table>
```

```
<tr valign="top">
<td>Login Name:</td>
<td><input type="text" name="login" /></td>
</tr>
<tr valign="top">
<td>Password:</td>
<td><input type="password" name="password" /></td>
</tr>
<tr valign="top">
<td></td>
<td><input type="submit" value=" Login " /></td>
</tr>
</table>
</form>
</body>
</html>
```

At the beginning of the script, we check for the $_GET['from'] query string variable. If it exists, we use it as the action of the form (i.e. the page to which the form is submitted), so that a successful login will send the user to the requested page. Otherwise, a default target page is used (5.php in this example).

Later in this chapter, we'll reproduce this form using QuickForm, which may make an interesting comparison.

Next, let's look at the secure page:

File: **5.php**

```php
<?php
// Include Magic Quotes stripping script
require_once 'MagicQuotes/strip_quotes.php';

// Include MySQL class
require_once 'Database/MySQL.php';

// Include Session class
require_once 'Session/Session.php';

// Include Auth class
require_once 'AccessControl/Auth.php';

$host    = 'localhost'; // Hostname of MySQL server
$dbUser  = 'harryf';    // Username for MySQL
$dbPass  = 'secret';    // Password for user
$dbName  = 'sitepoint'; // Database name
```

```php
// Instantiate MySQL connection
$db = &new MySQL($host, $dbUser, $dbPass, $dbName);

// Instantiate the Auth class
$auth = &new Auth($db, '4.php', 'secret');

// For logging out
if (isset($_GET['action']) && $_GET['action'] == 'logout') {
  $auth->logout();
}
?>
<!DOCTYPE html public "-//W3C//DTD XHTML 1.0 Transitional//EN"
  "http://www.w3.org/TR/xhtml1/DTD/xhtml1-transitional.dtd">
<html xmlns="http://www.w3.org/1999/xhtml">
<head>
<title> Welcome </title>
<meta http-equiv="Content-type"
  content="text/html; charset=iso-8859-1" />
<style type="text/css">
body, a, td, input
{
    font-family: verdana;
    font-size: 11px;
}
h1
{
    font-family: verdana;
    font-size: 15px;
    color: navy
}
</style>
</head>
<body>
<h1>Welcome</h1>
<p>You are now logged in</p>
<?php
if (isset($_GET['action']) && $_GET['action'] == 'test') {
  echo '<p>This is a test page. You are still logged in';
}
?>
<p><a href="<?php echo $_SERVER['PHP_SELF'];
  ?>?action=test">Test page</a></p>
<p><a href="<?php echo $_SERVER['PHP_SELF'];
  ?>?action=logout">Logout</a></p>
```

```
</body>
</html>
```

The only way the user can view this page is to have provided a correct user name and password. The moment that the Auth class is instantiated, it performs the security check. If valid user name and password values have been submitted via a form, they are stored by Auth in a session variable, allowing the visitor to continue surfing without having to log in again.

As promised, using the Auth class is very easy. To secure a page with it, all you need to do is place this at the start:[3]

```
// Instantiate the Auth class
$auth = &new Auth(&$db, $loginUrl);
```

As previously mentioned, $loginUrl is the URL to which the Auth class should redirect people who aren't already logged in.

Room for Improvement

The basic mechanics of the Auth class are solid, but it's missing the more involved elements that will be necessary to halt the efforts of any serious intruders.

It's a good idea to implement a mechanism to keep an eye on the number of failed login attempts made from a single client. If your application always responds immediately to any login attempt, it will be possible for a potential intruder to make large numbers of requests in a very short time, trying different user name and password combinations. The solution is to build a mechanism that counts the number of failed attempts using a session variable. Every time the number of failures is divisible by three (i.e. three incorrect passwords are entered), use PHP's sleep function to delay the next attempt by, for example, ten seconds. You may also decide that, after a certain threshold value (for example, fifteen failed attempts), you block all further access from that IP address for a given period (such as an hour). Of course, changing an IP address is much easier than changing a phone number, but you will at least stall would-be intruders, and may perhaps make their life difficult enough to persuade them to go elsewhere.

Another important ingredient for a good security system is an "event logging" mechanism that keeps track of suspicious access. In Chapter 4, you'll find the basic mechanics of logging visitor information, including how to track IP addresses,

---

[3]Of course, you must also include the Auth.php file that contains the class definition with require_once.

while the observer pattern found in Chapter 7 could be used to "watch" the Auth class for the number of failed attempts.

You may want to tie the logging to some kind of alert mechanism that will warn you if someone attacks your site, giving you the chance to respond immediately. In critical environments, consider using an SMS gateway as your alerting system so that you'll receive notification even when you're not online.

How do I build a user registration system?

Having an authentication system is fine, but how do you fill it with users in the first place? If only yourself and a few friends will access your site, you can probably create accounts for all users through your database administration interface. However, for a site that's intended to become a flourishing community to which anyone and everyone is free to sign up, you'll want to automate this process. You'll want to allow visitors to register themselves, but you'll probably still need some level of "screening" so that you have at least a little information about the people who have signed up (such as a way to confirm their identity). A common and effective screening approach is to have the registrants confirm their email address.

The purpose of the screening mechanism is to give you the ability to make it difficult for users who have "broken the rules" and lost their account privileges to create new accounts. You have (at least one of) their email addresses—if they try to register again using that address, you can deny them access. Be warned, though; a new type of Internet service is becoming popular. Pioneered by Mailinator[5], these services provide users with temporary email addresses they can use for registrations.

Here, we'll put together a registration system that validates new registrants using their email addresses; they'll receive an email that asks them to confirm their registration via a URL.

More Classes!

A registration system is yet another great opportunity to build more classes! This time, though, it will be even more interesting, as we use the

---

[5] http://www.mailinator.com/

PEAR::HTML_QuickForm package (Volume I, Chapter 9) and `phpmailer` (Volume I, Chapter 8) to do some of the work for the registration system. The rest will be handled by classes I've built myself, but the end result will be easy for you to customize and reuse in your own applications.

First of all, we need to visualize the process of (successfully) signing up a new user:

1. The user fills in the registration form.

2. On the user's completion of the form, we insert a record into the `signup` table and send a confirmation email.

3. The visitor follows the link in the email and confirms the account.

4. We copy the details from the `signup` table to the `user` table. The account is now active.

We use two tables for handling signups, to separate the "dangerous" data from the "safe" data. You'll want to have a cron job or similar to check the `signup` table on a regular basis and delete any entries that are older than, say, twenty-four hours. Separating the tables makes it easier to purge the contents of the `signup` table (avoiding unfortunate errors), and keep the `user` table trim so there's no unnecessary impact on performance during user authentication.

The first thing we need is a class to handle the key steps in the signup process. To begin, we must define a set of constants for the table and column names used by the class. This will allow you to override their values in your scripts, should you use a different table structure.

File: **AccessControl/SignUp.php (in SPLIB) (excerpt)**

```
# Modify these constants to match your user login and signup
# tables
// Name of users table
@define('USER_TABLE', 'user');
// Name of signup table
@define('SIGNUP_TABLE', 'signup');
// Name of login column in table
@define('USER_TABLE_LOGIN', 'login');
// Name of password column in table
@define('USER_TABLE_PASSW', 'password');
// Name of email column in table
@define('USER_TABLE_EMAIL', 'email');
// Name of firstname column in table
```

```
@define('USER_TABLE_FIRST', 'firstName');
// Name of lastname column in table
@define('USER_TABLE_LAST', 'lastName');
// Name of signature column in table
@define('USER_TABLE_SIGN', 'signature');
// Name of ID column in signup
@define('SIGNUP_TABLE_ID', 'signup_id');
// Name of confirm_code column in signup
@define('SIGNUP_TABLE_CONFIRM', 'confirm_code');
// Name of created column in signup
@define('SIGNUP_TABLE_CREATED', 'created');
```

With the constants out of the way, we can proceed to the member variables and constructor for the SignUp class:

File: **AccessControl/SignUp.php (in SPLIB) (excerpt)**

```
/**
 * SignUp Class<br />
 * Provides functionality for for user sign up<br />
 * <b>Note:</b> you will need to modify the createSignup() method
 * if you are using a different database table structure
 * <b>Note:</b> this class requires
 * @link http://phpmailer.sourceforge.net/ PHPMailer
 * @access public
 * @package SPLIB
 */
class SignUp {
  /**
   * Database connection
   * @access private
   * @var object
   */
  var $db;

  /**
   * The name / address the signup email should be sent from
   * @access private
   * @var array
   */
  var $from;

  /**
   * The name / address the signup email should be sent to
   * @access private
   * @var array
   */
```

```
var $to;

/**
 * The subject of the confirmation email
 * @access private
 * @var string
 */
var $subject;

/**
 * Text of message to send with confirmation email
 *
 * @var string
 */
var $message;

/**
 * Whether to send HTML email or not
 * @access private
 * @var boolean
 */
var $html;

/**
 * Url to use for confirmation
 * @access private
 * @var string
 */
var $listener;

/**
 * Confirmation code to append to $this->listener
 * @access private
 * @var string
 */
var $confirmCode;

/**
 * SignUp constructor
 * @param object instance of database connection
 * @param string URL for confirming the the signup
 * @param string name for confirmation email
 * @param string address for confirmation email
 * @param string subject of the confirmation message
 * @param string the confirmation message containing
 *                    <confirm_url/>
```

```
 * @access public
 */
function SignUp(&$db, $listener, $frmName, $frmAddress, $subj,
              $msg, $html)
{
  $this->db              = &$db;
  $this->listener        = $listener;
  $this->from[$frmName]  = $frmAddress;
  $this->subject         = $subj;
  $this->message         = $msg;
  $this->html            = $html;
}
```

When we instantiate the class in the constructor above, we need to pass it a connection to the database; we do this using the MySQL class. Then, we tell it the URL to which registrants should be directed when they confirm their signup. We also give it a 'From' name and address for the signup email (e.g. Your Name <you@yoursite.com>), as well as the subject and message for the email itself. Finally, we need to identify whether or not this is an HTML email, so that phpmailer can format the message correctly.

Whether it's HTML or not, the message should contain at least one special tag, <confirm_url/>. This acts as a "placeholder" in the message, identifying the location at which the confirmation URL that's built by the SignUp class should be inserted.

Moving on, the createCode method is called internally within the class, and is used to generate the confirmation code that will be sent via email:

File: **AccessControl/SignUp.php (in SPLIB) (excerpt)**

```
/**
 * Creates the confirmation code
 * @return void
 * @access private
 */
function createCode($login)
{
  srand((double)microtime() * 1000000);
  $this->confirmCode = md5($login . time() . rand(1, 1000000));
}
```

The createSignup method is used to insert records into the signup table:

```php
/**
 * Inserts a record into the signup table
 * @param array contains user details. See constants defined for
 *                 array keys
 * @return boolean true on success
 * @access public
 */
function createSignup($userDetails)
{
    $login     = mysql_escape_string(
                     $userDetails[USER_TABLE_LOGIN]);
    $password  = mysql_escape_string(
                     $userDetails[USER_TABLE_PASSW]);
    $email     = mysql_escape_string(
                     $userDetails[USER_TABLE_EMAIL]);
    $firstName = mysql_escape_string(
                     $userDetails[USER_TABLE_FIRST]);
    $lastName  = mysql_escape_string(
                     $userDetails[USER_TABLE_LAST]);
    $signature = mysql_escape_string(
                     $userDetails[USER_TABLE_SIGN]);

    // First check login and email are unique in user table
    $sql = "SELECT * FROM " . USER_TABLE . "
            WHERE
              " . USER_TABLE_LOGIN . "='$login' OR
              " . USER_TABLE_EMAIL . "='$email'";
    $result = $this->db->query($sql);

    if ($result->size() > 0) {
        trigger_error('Unique username and email address required');
        return false;
    }

    $this->createCode($login);
    $toName = $firstName . ' ' . $lastName;
    $this->to[$toName] = $email;

    $sql = "INSERT INTO " . SIGNUP_TABLE . " SET
              " . USER_TABLE_LOGIN . "='$login',
              " . USER_TABLE_PASSW . "='$password',
              " . USER_TABLE_EMAIL . "='$email',
              " . USER_TABLE_FIRST . "='$firstName',
              " . USER_TABLE_LAST . "='$lastName',
              " . USER_TABLE_SIGN . "='$signature',
```

```
            " . SIGNUP_TABLE_CONFIRM . "='$this->confirmCode',
            " . SIGNUP_TABLE_CREATED . "='" . time() . "'";

   $result = $this->db->query($sql);

   if ($result->isError()) {
     return false;
   } else {
     return true;
   }
 }
}
```

When the registration form is submitted, we'll use this method to create a record of the signup. Note that when the system checks to see whether the submitted user name or email address already exists in the database, a match will trigger an error. You could "catch" this error by defining your own custom error handler (see Volume I, Chapter 10 for more information).

We add slashes to the incoming fields to make sure there are no injection attacks (see Volume I, Chapter 3). Because we're using QuickForm, any slashes added by magic quotes are automatically removed; but when you're not using Quick-Form, be sure to include the script from "How do I write portable PHP code?" in Volume I, Chapter 1, which strips quotes from your form code.

Next, we use the `sendConfirmation` method to send a confirmation email to the person who's just signed up:

File: **AccessControl/SignUp.php (in SPLIB) (excerpt)**

```
/**
 * Sends the confirmation email
 * @return boolean true on success
 * @access public
 */
function sendConfirmation()
{
  $mail = new phpmailer();
  $from = each($this->from);
  $mail->FromName = $from[0];
  $mail->From = $from[1];
  $to = each($this->to);
  $mail->AddAddress($to[1], $to[0]);
  $mail->Subject = $this->subject;
  if ($this->html) {
    $replace = '<a href="' . $this->listener . '?code=' .
              $this->confirmCode . '">' . $this->listener .
```

```
                     '?code=' . $this->confirmCode . '</a>';
  } else {
    $replace = $this->listener . '?code=' . $this->confirmCode;
  }
  $this->message = str_replace('<confirm_url/>',
                                 $replace,
                                 $this->message);
  $mail->IsHTML($this->html);

  $mail->Body = $this->message;
  if ($mail->send()) {
    return TRUE;
  } else {
    return FALSE;
  }
}
```

Finally, the `confirm` method is used to examine confirmations via the URL sent
in the email:

File: **AccessControl/SignUp.php (in SPLIB) (excerpt)**

```
/**
 * Confirms a signup against the confirmation code. If it
 * matches, copies the row to the user table and deletes
 * the row from signup
 * @return boolean true on success
 * @access public
 */
function confirm($confirmCode)
{
  $confirmCode = mysql_escape_string($confirmCode);
  $sql = "SELECT * FROM " . SIGNUP_TABLE . "
          WHERE " . SIGNUP_TABLE_CONFIRM . "='$confirmCode'";
  $result = $this->db->query($sql);
  if ($result->size() == 1) {
    $row = $result->fetch();

    // Copy the data from Signup to User table
    $sql = "INSERT INTO " . USER_TABLE . " SET
            " . USER_TABLE_LOGIN . "='" .
              mysql_escape_string($row[USER_TABLE_LOGIN]) . "',
            " . USER_TABLE_PASSW . "='" .
              mysql_escape_string($row[USER_TABLE_PASSW]) . "',
            " . USER_TABLE_EMAIL . "='" .
              mysql_escape_string($row[USER_TABLE_EMAIL]) . "',
            " . USER_TABLE_FIRST . "='" .
```

```
            mysql_escape_string($row[USER_TABLE_FIRST]) . "',
        " . USER_TABLE_LAST . "='" .
            mysql_escape_string($row[USER_TABLE_LAST]) . "',
        " . USER_TABLE_SIGN . "='" .
            mysql_escape_string($row[USER_TABLE_SIGN]) . "'";

    $result = $this->db->query($sql);
    if ($result->isError()) {
      return FALSE;
    } else {
      // Delete row from signup table
      $sql = "DELETE FROM " . SIGNUP_TABLE . "
            WHERE " . SIGNUP_TABLE_ID . "='" .
            $row[SIGNUP_TABLE_ID] . "'";
      $this->db->query($sql);
      return TRUE;
    }
  } else {
    return FALSE;
  }
}
}
```

If an account is successfully confirmed, the row is copied to the user table (note that I had to re-escape the values stored in the signup table in case they contained SQL injections that were escaped when originally inserted), and the old row in the signup table is deleted. You will need to edit this method if your table structures do not match the ones used here.

Putting this class into action, we'll modify the registration form we built in Volume I, Chapter 9 with QuickForm. For the sake of clarity, I've kept the registration form to a single procedural listing, but in practice, to help keep code both maintainable and readable, it would be better to restructure it using classes. This time, I've also used QuickForm's templating features to modify the look of the page; you'll find the details in the code for this chapter. Here, we'll concentrate on the code that's specific to the sign up process:

First, we have to include the five classes we'll be using:

File: **6.php (excerpt)**

```php
<?php
// Include the MySQL class
require_once 'Database/MySQL.php';

// Include the Session class
```

```
require_once 'Session/Session.php';

// Include the SignUp class
require_once 'AccessControl/SignUp.php';

// Include the QuickForm class
require_once 'HTML/QuickForm.php';

// Include the phpmailer class
require_once 'ThirdParty/phpmailer/class.phpmailer.php';
```

Once we set up the variables we need, we can instantiate our own classes:

File: **6.php (excerpt)**

```
// Settings for SignUp class
$listener = 'http://localhost/sitepoint/AccessControl/6.php';
$frmName = 'Your Name';
$frmAddress = 'noreply@yoursite.com';
$subj = 'Account Confirmation';
$msg = <<<EOD
<html>
<body>
<h2>Thank you for registering!</h2>
<div>The final step is to confirm
your account by clicking on:</div>
<div><confirm_url/></div>
<div>
<b>Your Site Team</b>
</div>
</body>
</html>
EOD;

// Instantiate the MySQL class
$db = &new MySQL($host, $dbUser, $dbPass, $dbName);

// Instantiate the Session class
$session = new Session;

// Instantiate the signup class
$signUp = new SignUp($db, $listener, $frmName,
                     $frmAddress, $subj, $msg, TRUE);
```

The following code checks to see if we have an incoming confirmation:

File: **6.php (excerpt)**

```
// Is this an account confirmation?
if (isset($_GET['code'])) {
  if ($signUp->confirm($_GET['code'])) {
    $display = 'Thank you. Your account has now been confirmed.' .
              '<br />You can now <a href="4.php">login</a>';
  } else {
    $display = 'There was a problem confirming your account.' .
              '<br />Please try again or contact the site ' .
              'administrators';
  }

// Otherwise display the form
} else {
  // ...form creation code omitted...
```

If not, execution moves on to building the body of the form, which I'll omit here, as it was covered in Volume I, Chapter 9. If you don't have that volume, you can refer to the code archive.

Towards the end of the script appears the code that inserts a value into the signup table and, if all went well, sends the confirmation email:

File: **6.php (excerpt)**

```
// If the form is submitted...
if ($form->validate()) {
  // Apply the encryption filter to the password
  $form->applyFilter('password', 'encryptValue');

  // Build an array from the submitted form values
  $submitVars = array(
      'login' => $form->getSubmitValue('login'),
      'password' => $form->getSubmitValue('password'),
      'email' => $form->getSubmitValue('email'),
      'firstName' => $form->getSubmitValue('firstName'),
      'lastName' => $form->getSubmitValue('lastName'),
      'signature' => $form->getSubmitValue('signature')
  );

  // Create signup
  if ($signUp->createSignup($submitVars)) {
    // Send confirmation email
    if ($signUp->sendConfirmation()) {
      $display = 'Thank you. Please check your email to ' .
                'confirm your account';
```

```
    } else {
      $display = 'Unable to send confirmation email.<br />' .
                'Please contact the site administrators';
    }
  } else {
    $display = 'There was an error creating your account.' .
              '<br />Please try again later or ' .
              'contact the site administrators';
  }
} else {
  // If not submitted, display the form
  $display = $form->toHtml();
}
}
```

The finished registration form now looks like the one shown in Figure 1.2.

Figure 1.2. Sign on the Dotted Line

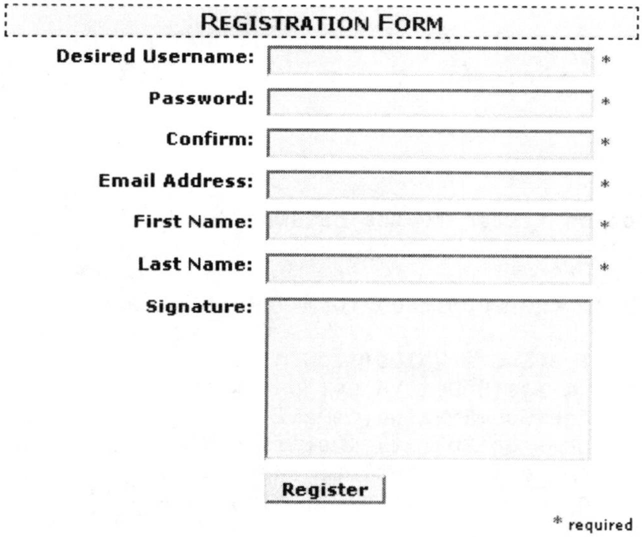

Missing Pieces

So that you don't get bored, there are a couple of remaining pieces for you to fill in. Currently, the **createSignup** method triggers an error if there already exists a registered user with the login name or email provided by the new registrant. If you're happy with QuickForm, you might want to split this check into a separate method that QuickForm can apply as a rule for each field in the form. This should reduce frustration when users find that the account name they chose already exists; QuickForm will generate a message to tell them what they did wrong, while preserving the rest of the values they entered.

If you plan to let users change their email addresses once their accounts are created, you'll also need to confirm the addresses before you store them against the appropriate records in the user table. You should be able to reuse the methods provided by the SignUp class for this purpose. You might even consider reusing the signup table to handle this task; some modifications will be required to have the confirm method check to see if a record already exists in the user table, and if so, update it instead of creating a new row. Be *very careful* that you don't create a hole in your security, though. If you're not checking for existing records in the user table, a user could sign up for a new account with details that matched an existing row in the user table. You'll then end up changing the email address of an existing user to that of a new user, which will cause some embarrassing moments at the very least.

How do I protect my site from auto sign ups?

I hope you'll never suffer the misfortune of having someone try to put your site out of action, but when you expose your application to what is, after all, a global network, you need to be prepared for trouble. It's difficult to prevent malicious attacks against your site and still offer genuine users an acceptable service—particularly if a malicious user simply decides to flood your site with requests for pages.

Where user registration systems are concerned, one common method of attack has been to create "robots" (typically Perl or PHP scripts), which act as Web browsers and use the forms you've built for your registration system to swamp your database with false sign ups. Although we've built a registration system that requires email confirmation of the account, the confirmation process can also be built into the "robot," assuming it has access to the account to which the email confirmations are sent. Both Hotmail and Yahoo!, among many others, have been stung by this in the past.

The next level of protection is to introduce a mechanism that sorts the men from the 'bots! Thankfully, the human brain is still vastly more powerful than a computer (at least, the sort of computer likely to be used to attack your site) and is capable of powerful optical character recognition beyond the scope of your average Perl script. Consider Figure 1.3, for example.

Figure 1.3. Humans Still Have the Edge

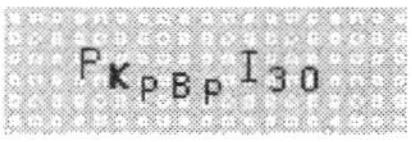

Now, you and I can see that the image contains the characters "PKPBPI30," but a computer program trying to identify those letters will find the challenge a lot more difficult. Of course it's *possible*, but people who have the capability to do it will, I hope, have better things to do with their time.

Here's One I Wrote Earlier

Let's turn to a handy PHP class I've prepared to solve just this problem:

File: **Images/RandomImageText.php (in SPLIB) (excerpt)**

```php
<?php
/**
 * RandomImageText<br />
 * Generate image text which is hard for OCR programs to
 * read but can still be read by humans, for use in registration
 * systems.
 * @package SPLIB
 * @access public
 */
class RandomImageText {
  /**
   * The background image resource
   * @access private
   * @var resource
   */
  var $image;

  /**
   * Image height in pixels
   * @access private
   * @var int
   */
  var $iHeight;

  /**
```

```
 * Image width in pixels
 * @access private
 * @var int
 */
var $iWidth;

/**
 * Font height in pixels
 * @access private
 * @var int
 */
var $fHeight;

/**
 * Font width in pixels
 * @access private
 * @var int
 */
var $fWidth;

/**
 * Tracks the x position in pixels
 * @access private
 * @var  int
 */
var $xPos;

/**
 * An array of font idenfiers
 * @access private
 * @var array
 */
var $fonts;

/**
 * RandomImageText constructor
 * @param string relative or full path to background jpeg
 * @param int font height to use
 * @param int font width to use
 * @access public
 */
function RandomImageText($jpeg, $fHeight = 10, $fWidth = 10)
{
  $this->image = ImageCreateFromJPEG($jpeg);
  $this->iHeight = ImageSY($this->image);
  $this->iWidth = ImageSX($this->image);
```

```
    $this->fHeight = $fHeight;
    $this->fWidth = $fWidth;
    $this->xPos = 0;
    $this->fonts = array(2, 3, 4, 5);
}
```

The class needs to be provided with a JPEG image that will become the background over which we'll scatter the letters. Ideally, you should use an image that has some kind of pattern on it, to make the problem of identifying the letters even more difficult. The $fHeight and $fWidth (font height and width) can be adjusted, but this really only impacts the space that appears around the characters, rather than increasing the size of the characters themselves.

The addText method is where the clever work takes place:

File: **Images/RandomImageText.php (in SPLIB) (excerpt)**

```
/**
 * Add text to the image which is "randomized"
 * @param string text to add
 * @param int red hex value (0-255)
 * @param int green hex value (0-255)
 * @param int blue hex value (0-255)
 * @return boolean true text was added successfully
 * @access public
 */
function addText($text, $r=38, $g=38, $b=38)
{
  $length = $this->fWidth * strlen($text);

  if ($length >= ($this->iWidth - $this->fWidth * 2)) {
    return FALSE;
  }

  $this->xPos = floor(($this->iWidth - $length) / 2);

  $fColor = ImageColorAllocate($this->image, $r, $g, $b);

  srand((float)microtime() * 1000000);
  $fonts = array(2, 3, 4, 5);
  $yStart = floor($this->iHeight / 2) - $this->fHeight;
  $yEnd = $yStart + $this->fHeight;
  $yPos = range($yStart, $yEnd);

  for ($strPos = 0; $strPos < $length; $strPos++) {
    shuffle($fonts);
```

```
      shuffle($yPos);
      ImageString($this->image,
                  $fonts[0],
                  $this->xPos,
                  $yPos[0],
                  substr($text, $strPos, 1),
                  $fColor);
      $this->xPos += $this->fWidth;
    }
    return TRUE;
}
```

Provided with a text string, the class will scatter the letters on the image, using a randomly varying vertical position, and a font chosen at random from a list. Optionally, you can supply this method with red, green, and blue values, which will define the color of the text.

If the string you provide is too big for the image, no text will be displayed; the code generates an error notice, but you'll have to pick this up with your error handler (see Volume I, Chapter 10), as it will be invisible on the image.

The next two methods can be used to clear out any existing fonts registered with the class, and add new fonts. The default PHP fonts are somewhat dull and rather small, so you may want to consider adding your own. Check out PHP's imagestring[6] and imageloadfont[7] functions for further details.

File: **Images/RandomImageText.php (in SPLIB) (excerpt)**

```
/**
 * Empties any fonts currently stored for use
 * @return void
 * @access public
 */
function clearFonts()
{
  return $this->fonts = array();
}

/**
 * Adds a new font for use in text generation
 * @param string relative or full path to font file
 * @return void
 * @access public
```

[6] http://www.php.net/imagestring
[7] http://www.php.net/imageloadfont

```
  */
function addFont($font)
{
  $this->fonts[] = imageloadfont($font);
}
```

The `getHeight` and `getWidth` methods can be useful if you're unsure of the exact dimensions of your background image and want to determine whether the text you want to add will fit on the background before you add it.

File: **Images/RandomImageText.php (in SPLIB) (excerpt)**

```
/**
 * Returns the height of the background image in
 * pixels
 * @return int
 * @access public
 */
function getHeight()
{
  return $this->iHeight;
}

/**
 * Returns the width of the background image in
 * pixels
 * @return int
 * @access public
 */
function getWidth()
{
  return $this->iWidth;
}
```

Finally, the `getImage` method returns the PHP resource identifier for the image.

File: **Images/RandomImageText.php (in SPLIB) (excerpt)**

```
/**
 * Returns the image resource for use with
 * the ImageJpeg() function
 * @return resource
 * @access public
 */
function getImage()
{
  return $this->image;
```

```
    }
}
```

We still have to convert the image to a JPEG with the `imagejpeg` function; I've chosen to return the resource identifier rather than simply displaying the image itself, as I may want to manipulate the image further with other code and classes.

Now that we've prepared the class for adding text to an image, we need to update the `SignUp` class to provide a method that generates the text to appear in the image:

File: **AccessControl/SignUp.php (in SPLIB) (excerpt)**

```php
/**
 * Creates a random string to be used in images
 * @return string
 * @access public
 */
function createRandString()
{
  srand((double)microtime() * 1000000);
  $letters = range ('A','Z');
  $numbers = range(0,9);
  $chars = array_merge($letters, $numbers);
  $randString = '';
  for ($i=0; $i<8; $i++) {
    shuffle($chars);
    $randString .= $chars[0];
  }
  return $randString;
}
```

The trick now is to generate a random string with the above method, then store it in a session variable that's accessible by the code that actually generates the image. First, we need to modify one or two parts of the registration form code from the previous solution.

In the section where we begin to build the form, make the following modifications:

File: **7.php (excerpt)**

```php
// Register a session variable for use in the image
if (!$session->get('randomString'))
  $session->set('randomString', $signUp->createRandString());
```

The above code checks whether the random string has been created and stored in a session variable. If not, it creates one and stores it in a session variable.

Now, we add the form field and an `img` tag containing the image:

File: **7.php (excerpt)**

```
// The image check field for "humanness"
$form->addElement('text', 'imageCheck', 'Image Text:',
                  'class="signupData"');
$form->addRule('imageCheck', 'Please enter text from image',
               'required', false, 'client');

// Server side validation!
// Don't give away random string in JavaScript
$form->addRule('imageCheck',
               'Please confirm the text in the image',
               'regex',
               '/^' . $session->get('randomString') . '$/',
               'server');

// The image check field
$form->addData('
  <tr valign="top">
    <td class="info">
      Enter the text as it<br />appears in the image
    </td>
    <td class="field">
      <img src="8.php" />
    </td>
  </tr>');
```

Note that the validation rule we've applied to this field uses server side validation only, *not* client side. If we *did* use client side validation, a regular expression stating exactly what the image contains would appear in JavaScript, and would be available for a computer program to read.

All that remains is the code that will display the image itself:

File: **8.php**

```
<?php
// Include Session class
require_once 'Session/Session.php';

// Include RandomImageText class
require_once 'Images/RandomImageText.php';

// Instantiate the Session class
$session = new Session;
```

```
// Instantiate RandomImageText giving the background image
$imageText = new RandomImageText('reg_image/reg_image.jpg');

// Add the text from the session
$imageText->addText($session->get('randomString'));

// Send the right mime type
header('Content-type: image/jpeg');

// Display the image
ImageJpeg($imageText->getImage());
?>
```

Note that we passed the random string via a session variable, as opposed to a query string variable, as this, too, would be available for reading by a "robot" script.

Figure 1.4 illustrates the form modified with the new image checking feature.

Figure 1.4. Humans Only, Thank You

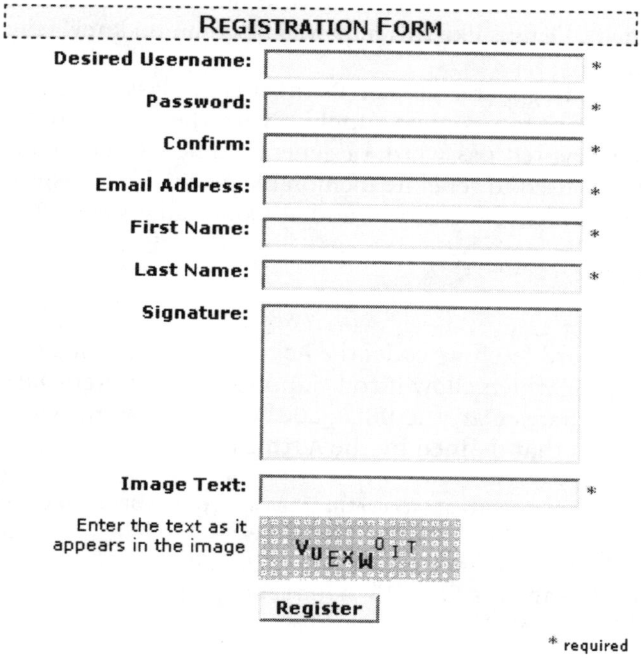

How do I deal with members who forget their passwords?

In the last solution, I was happy to explain just how great human beings are in comparison to computers. Unfortunately, though, we have a tendency to "age out" important information such as the password we need to log into a site. A feature that allows users to retrieve forgotten passwords is an essential time saver. Overlook this, and you can expect to waste a lot of time changing passwords for people who have forgotten them.

If you encrypt the passwords in your database, you'll need a mechanism that generates a new password that, preferably, is easy to remember. If you're storing passwords as-is, without encryption, it's probably acceptable simply to send the password to the user's registered email address. Using an email address that you've already confirmed as valid is more reliable than the "Secret Question" approach. This common tactic asks users simple questions to refresh their memories, such as, "Where were you born?" and "What's your date of birth?" Just ask yourself how many organizations, both on and offline, you've given that information to. Some online applications, such as forums, even make your birthday available for all to see, should you provide it. Details like this may well be common knowledge.

To solve the problem, we'll build a general `AccountMaintenance` class, which will do some of the maintenance work for us, then supply it with the information it needs to either fetch an unencrypted password, or generate a new (memorable) password. The typical approach used to generate memorable passwords is inspired by the Secure Memorable Password Generator found at Codewalkers.com[8].

Password Reminder

Starting with the simple password fetching code, the `AccountMaintenance` class begins with the usual constants, which allow it to be applied to a different table structure if need be. Note, in particular, the USER_LOGIN_VAR constant, which must contain the same value as that defined by the `Auth` class.

File: **AccessControl/AccountMaintenance.php (in SPLIB) (excerpt)**

```php
<?php
/**
 * Constants which define table and column names
```

[8] http://codewalkers.com/seecode/52.html

```php
*/
# Modify this constant to reflect session variable name
// Name to use for login variable used in Auth class
@define('USER_LOGIN_VAR', 'login');
# Modify these constants to match your user login table
// Name of users table
@define('USER_TABLE', 'user');
// Name of user_id column in table
@define('USER_TABLE_ID', 'user_id');
// Name of login column in table
@define('USER_TABLE_LOGIN', 'login');
// Name of password column in table
@define('USER_TABLE_PASSW', 'password');
// Name of email column in table
@define('USER_TABLE_EMAIL', 'email');
// Name of firstname column in table
@define('USER_TABLE_FIRST', 'firstName');
// Name of lastname column in table
@define('USER_TABLE_LAST', 'lastName');
/**
 * AccountMaintenance Class<br />
 * Provides functionality for users to manage their own accounts
 * @access public
 * @package SPLIB
 */
class AccountMaintenance {
  /**
   * Database connection
   * @access private
   * @var object
   */
  var $db;

  /**
   * A list of words to use in generating passwords
   * @access private
   * @var array
   */
  var $words;

  /**
   * AccountMaintenance constructor
   * @param object instance of database connection
   * @access public
   */
  function AccountMaintenance(&$db)
```

```php
{
  $this->db = &$db;
}

/**
 * Given an email address, returns the user details
 * that account. Useful is password is not encrpyted
 * @param string email address
 * @return array user details
 * @access public
 */
function fetchLogin($email)
{
  $email = mysql_escape_string($email);
  $sql = "SELECT
          " . USER_TABLE_LOGIN . ", " . USER_TABLE_PASSW . ",
          " . USER_TABLE_FIRST . ", " . USER_TABLE_LAST . "
        FROM
          " . USER_TABLE . "
        WHERE
          " . USER_TABLE_EMAIL . "='$email'";
  $result = $this->db->query($sql);
  if ($result->size() == 1) {
    return $result->fetch();
  } else {
    return FALSE;
  }
}
```

The `fetchLogin` method looks for a single row that matches the user's email address (note this assumes you have declared a UNIQUE index on the email column so that entries can only appear once. If you use a different table structure, you'll need to modify the query in this method).

Next, we put the simple forgotten password mechanism into action with Quick-Form and `phpmailer`:

File: **9.php (excerpt)**

```php
<?php
// Include MySQL class
require_once 'Database/MySQL.php';

// Include AccountMaintenance class
require_once 'AccessControl/AccountMaintenance.php';
```

```
// Include QuickForm class
require_once 'HTML/QuickForm.php';

// Include phpmailer class
require_once 'ThirdParty/phpmailer/class.phpmailer.php';

$host    = 'localhost'; // Hostname of MySQL server
$dbUser  = 'harryf';    // Username for MySQL
$dbPass  = 'secret';    // Password for user
$dbName  = 'sitepoint'; // Database name

// phpmailer settings
$yourName  = 'Your Name';
$yourEmail = 'you@yourdomain.com';
$subject   = 'Your password';
$msg       = 'Here are your login details. Please change your ' .
             'password.';
```

Here, we've set up the environment as usual, including the necessary classes. We've also defined variables for the `phpmailer` class; these will be the same irrespective of who has forgotten a password.

And now, let's set up `QuickForm`:

File: **9.php (excerpt)**

```
// Instantiate the QuickForm class
$form = new HTML_QuickForm('passwordForm', 'POST');

// Add a header to the form
$form->addHeader('Forgotten Your Password?');

// Add a field for the email address
$form->addElement('text', 'email', 'Enter your email address');
$form->addRule('email', 'Enter your email', 'required', FALSE,
               'client');
$form->addRule('email', 'Enter a valid email address', 'email',
               FALSE, 'client');

// Add a submit button called submit with label "Send"
$form->addElement('submit', 'submit', 'Get Password');
```

If the form has been submitted, we instantiate the `MySQL` and `AccountMaintenance` classes and use the `fetchLogin` method to determine whether there's a matching email address in the user table. If there is, we use `phpmailer` to send the user an email containing the login and password.

```php
// If the form is submitted...
if ($form->validate()) {
  // Instantiate MySQL connection
  $db = &new MySQL($host, $dbUser, $dbPass, $dbName);

  // Instantiate Account Maintenance class
  $aMaint = new AccountMaintenance($db);

  if (!$details =
      $aMaint->fetchLogin($form->getSubmitValue('email'))) {
    echo 'We have no record of your account';
  } else {
    $mail = new phpmailer();
    // Define who the message is from
    $mail->From = $yourEmail;
    $mail->FromName = $yourName;

    // Set the subject of the message
    $mail->Subject = $subject;

    // Build the message
    $mail->Body = $msg . "\n\nLogin: " . $details['login'] .
                  "\nPassword: " . $details['password'];

    // Add the recipient
    $name = $details['firstName'] . ' ' . $details['lastName'];
    $mail->AddAddress($form->getSubmitValue('email'), $name);

    // Send the message
    if(!$mail->Send()) {
      echo 'An email has been sent to ' .
          $form->getSubmitValue('email');
    } else {
      echo 'Problem sending your details. Please contact the ' .
          'site administrators';
    }
  }
} else {
  // If not submitted, display the form
  $form->display();
}
?>
```

New Password

As I mentioned, if you've encrypted the password, you have a different problem to solve. PHP's md5 function provides one-way encryption; once it's scrambled, there's no getting it back! In such cases, if members forget their passwords, you'll have to make new ones for them. You could simply generate a random string of characters, but it's important to remember that if you make your security systems too unfriendly, you'll put legitimate users off.

Here, we'll add to the AccountMaintenance class some further methods that can generate passwords, and subsequently modify the password stored in the database. I've used a list of 1370 words, stored in a text file, to build the memorable passwords. Be aware that if anyone knows the list of words you're using, cracking the new password will be significantly easier, so you should create your own list. First, let's look at the new class methods:

File: **AccessControl/AccountMaintenance.php** (in SPLIB) (excerpt)

```php
/**
 * Given a username / email combination, resets the password
 * for that user and returns the new password.
 * @param string login name
 * @param string email address
 * @return array of user details or FALSE if failed
 * @access public
 */
function resetPassword($login, $email)
{
  $login = mysql_escape_string($login);
  $email = mysql_escape_string($email);
  $sql = "SELECT " . USER_TABLE_ID . ",
          " . USER_TABLE_LOGIN . ", " . USER_TABLE_PASSW . ",
          " . USER_TABLE_FIRST . ", " . USER_TABLE_LAST . "
          FROM
          " . USER_TABLE . "
          WHERE
          " . USER_TABLE_LOGIN . "='$login'
          AND
          " . USER_TABLE_EMAIL . "='$email'";
  $result = $this->db->query($sql);
  if ($result->size() == 1) {
    $row = $result->fetch();
    if ($password = $this->generatePassword()) {
      $sql = "UPDATE " . USER_TABLE . "
              SET
```

```
                   " . USER_TABLE_PASSW . "='" . md5($password) . "'
                   WHERE
                   " . USER_TABLE_ID . "='" . $row[USER_TABLE_ID] .
                   "'";
        $result = $this->dbConn->fetch($sql);
        if (!$result->isError()) {
          $row[USER_TABLE_PASSW] = $password;
          return $row;
        } else {
          return FALSE;
        }
      } else {
        return FALSE;
      }
    } else {
      return FALSE;
    }
  }
}
```

The resetPassword method, when given a combination of a login and an email address, identifies the corresponding row in the user table, and calls the generatePassword method (which we'll discuss in a moment) to create a new password. It then updates the user table with the new password (using md5 to encrypt it), and returns the new password in an array containing the user details. If you're using a different table structure, you'll need to modify this method.

Note that we use both the login and email to identify the row, so it's a little more difficult for other people to reset your members' passwords. Although there's no risk in individuals stealing the new password (unless they have control over a member's email account), it will certainly irritate people if their password was being continually reset. Requiring both the login name and email of the user makes it a little more complex.

Of the next two methods, addWords is used to supply the class with an indexed array of words with which to build memorable passwords, while generatePassword constructs a random password from this list, adding "separators" that could be any number from 0 to 9, or an underscore character. The password itself will contain two words chosen at random from the list, as well as two random separators. The order in which these elements appear in the password is also random. The passwords this system generates look like "7correct9computer" and "48courtclothes," which are relatively easy for users to remember.

File: **AccessControl/AccountMaintenance.php (in SPLIB) (excerpt)**

```php
/**
 * Add a list of words to generate passwords with
 * @param array
 * @return void
 * @access public
 */
function addWords($words)
{
  $this->words = $words;
}


/**
 * Generates a random but memorable password
 * @return string the password
 * @access private
 */
function generatePassword()
{
  srand((double)microtime() * 1000000);
  $seperators = range(0,9);
  $seperators[] = '_';
  $count = count($this->words);
  if ($count == 0) {
    return FALSE;
  }
  $password = array();
  for ($i = 0; $i < 4; $i++) {
    if ($i % 2 == 0) {
      shuffle($this->words);
      $password[$i] = trim($this->words[0]);
    } else {
      shuffle($seperators);
      $password[$i] = $seperators[0];
    }
  }
  shuffle($password);
  return implode('', $password);
}
```

First, we add to the form a new field for the user to enter their login name:

File: **10.php (excerpt)**

```php
// Add a field for the login
$form->addElement('text', 'login', 'Enter your login name');
```

```
$form->addRule('login', 'Enter your login', 'required', FALSE,
               'client');
```

All that's required now is a small modification to the process that occurs upon the form's submission:

File: **10.php (excerpt)**

```
// If the form is submitted...
if ($form->validate()) {

  // Instantiate MySQL connection
  $db = &new MySQL($host, $dbUser, $dbPass, $dbName);

  // Instantiate Account Maintenance class
  $aMaint = new AccountMaintenance($db);

  // Fetch a list of words
  $fp = fopen('./pass_words/pass_words.txt', 'rb');
  $file = fread($fp, filesize('./pass_words/pass_words.txt'));
  fclose($fp);

  // Add the words to the class
  $aMaint->addWords(explode("\n", $file));

  // Reset the password
  if (!$details = $aMaint->resetPassword(
      $form->getSubmitValue('login'),
      $form->getSubmitValue('email'))) {
    echo 'We have no record of your account';
  } else {
    // Instantiate phpmailer class
    $mail = new phpmailer();
    ...
```

This time, we read a file (refer to Volume I, Chapter 4 for details on this process) to obtain a list of words, the file having one word per line. We pass the list of words to the AccountMaintenance class with the addWords method. Whether you choose to use a file, a database or even some cunning code mechanism based upon the pspell_suggest function (see the PHP Manual[9]) is up to you; you simply need to provide a list to add with addWords.

The resetPassword method changes the password behind the scenes and returns an array containing the user details in the same way as the fetchPassword

---

[9] http://www.php.net/pspell-suggest

method; thus, the task of emailing users their new passwords is the same. The code is therefore omitted from the above listing.

How do I let users change their passwords?

You're now able to deal with people who have forgotten their passwords. What about people who want to *change* their passwords?

A good "test of design" for many PHP applications is whether users can change their passwords without needing to log back into the application afterwards. It's important to be considerate to your site's users if you want them to stick around. Changing their passwords should not require users to log back in, provided you construct your application carefully.

Going back to the session-based authentication mechanism you saw earlier in this chapter, you'll remember that the login and password are stored in session variables and rechecked on every new page by the Auth class. The trick is to change the value of the password in both the session variable and the database when users change their passwords.

First things first! Let's build a new login page using QuickForm:

File: **11.php**

```php
<?php
// Include QuickForm class
require_once 'HTML/QuickForm.php';

// If $_GET['from'] comes from the Auth class
if (isset($_GET['from'])) {
  $target = $_GET['from'];
} else {
  // Default URL: usually index.php
  $target = '12.php';
}

// Instantiate the QuickForm class
$form = new HTML_QuickForm('loginForm', 'POST', $target);

// Add a header to the form
$form->addHeader('Please Login');
```

```php
// Add a field for the login name
$form->addElement('text', 'login', 'Username');
$form->addRule('login', 'Enter your login', 'required', FALSE,
               'client');

// Add a field for the password
$form->addElement('password', 'password', 'Password');
$form->addRule('password', 'Enter your password', 'required',
               FALSE, 'client');

// Add a submit button
$form->addElement('submit', 'submit', ' Login ');

$form->display();
?>
```

Note that in this case, we tell QuickForm to direct the submission of the form to another PHP script, rather than handling it locally on the same page.

As we've already been working on an `AccountMaintenance` class, this seems like a reasonable place to add the code that allows users to change their passwords:

File: **AccessControl/AccountMaintenance.php (in SPLIB) (excerpt)**

```php
/**
 * Changes a password both in the database
 * and in the current session variable.
 * Assumes the new password has been
 * validated correctly elsewhere.
 * @param Auth instance of the Auth class
 * @param string old password
 * @param string new password
 * @return boolean TRUE on success
 * @access public
 */
function changePassword(&$auth, $oldPassword, $newPassword)
{
  $oldPassword = mysql_escape_string($oldPassword);
  $newPassword = mysql_escape_string($newPassword);

  // Instantiate the Session class
  $session = new Session();

  // Check the the login and old password match
  $sql = "SELECT *
          FROM " . USER_TABLE . "
          WHERE
```

```
                " . USER_TABLE_LOGIN . " =
                '" . $session->get(USER_LOGIN_VAR) . "'
            AND
                " . USER_TABLE_PASSW . " =
                '" . md5($oldPassword) . "'";
    $result = $this->db->query($sql);
    if ($result->size() != 1) {
      return FALSE;
    }

    // Update the password
    $sql = "UPDATE " . USER_TABLE . "
            SET
                " . USER_TABLE_PASSW . " =
                '" . md5($newPassword) . "'
            WHERE
                " . USER_TABLE_LOGIN . " =
                '" . $session->get(USER_LOGIN_VAR) . "'";
    $result = $this->db->query($sql);
    if (!$result->isError()) {
      // Store the new credentials
      $auth->storeAuth($session->get(USER_LOGIN_VAR),
        $newPassword);
      return TRUE;
    } else {
      return FALSE;
    }
  }
}
```

The changePassword method accepts three parameters: an instance of the Auth class (so it can use the **storeAuth** method it provides), an old password, and a new password.

It first checks that the combination of the old password and the login name (which it retrieves from the session) are correct. It's a good idea to require the old password before changing it to something else; perhaps the user logged in at an Internet café and then left, forgetting to log out, or worse—their session was hijacked. This process at least precludes some potential damage, as it prevents anyone who "takes over" the session being able to change the password and thus assume total control. Instead, they're only logged in as long as the session continues.

It's time to put this into action in the page to which the login form submits...

File: **12.php (excerpt)**

```php
<?php
// Include MySQL class
require_once 'Database/MySQL.php';

// Include Session class
require_once 'Session/Session.php';

// Include Authentication class
require_once 'AccessControl/Auth.php';

// Include AccountMaintenance class
require_once 'AccessControl/AccountMaintenance.php';

// Include QuickForm class
require_once 'HTML/QuickForm.php';

$host   = 'localhost'; // Hostname of MySQL server
$dbUser = 'harryf';    // Username for MySQL
$dbPass = 'secret';    // Password for user
$dbName = 'sitepoint'; // Database name

// Instantiate MySQL connection
$db = &new MySQL($host, $dbUser, $dbPass, $dbName);

// Instantiate the Authentication class
$auth = &new Auth($db, '11.php', 'secret');
```

We include all the classes needed for the code, then instantiate the MySQL and Auth classes. From the moment Auth is instantiated, the provision of an invalid login/password combination will see the visitor returned to the login form.

This time, just for variety, we use a switch statement to control the flow of logic on the page:

File: **12.php (excerpt)**

```php
switch ($_GET['view']) {
  case 'changePassword':
    // Instantiate the QuickForm class
    $form = new HTML_QuickForm('changePass', 'POST',
                               '12.php?view=changePassword');

    // A function for comparing password
    function cmpPass($element, $confirm)
    {
```

```
    global $form;
    $password = $form->getElementValue('newPassword');
    return $password == $confirm;
}

// Register the compare function
$form->registerRule('compare', 'function', 'cmpPass');

// Add a header to the form
$form->addHeader('Change your Password');

// Add a field for the old password
$form->addElement('password', 'oldPassword',
                    'Current Password');
$form->addRule('oldPassword', 'Enter your current password',
                'required', false, 'client');

// Add a field for the new password
$form->addElement('password', 'newPassword', 'New Password');
$form->addRule('password', 'Please provide a password',
                'required', FALSE, 'client');
$form->addRule('password',
                'Password must be at least 6 characters',
                'minlength', 6, 'client');
$form->addRule('password',
                'Password cannot be more than 12 chars',
                'maxlength', 50, 'client');
$form->addRule('password',
                'Password can only contain letters and ' .
                'numbers', 'alphanumeric', NULL, 'client');

// Add a field for the new password
$form->addElement('password', 'confirm', 'Confirm Password');
$form->addRule('confirm', 'Confirm your password',
                'compare', false, 'client');

// Add a submit button
$form->addElement('submit', 'submit', 'Change Password');
```

Here, the usual QuickForm setup code builds a form for changing passwords. Notice again the cmpPass function, which compares the new password and the rules for the newPassword field. We perform most of the validation of the new password within the form, leaving it to the AccountMaintenance class to perform a final check against the old password before making the change.

On validation of the form, we instantiate the `AccountMaintenance` class and tell it to change the password.

File: **12.php (excerpt)**

```
// If the form is submitted...
if ($form->validate()) {

    // Instantiate Account Maintenance class
    $aMaint = new AccountMaintenance($db);

    // Change the password
    if ($aMaint->changePassword(
            $auth,
            $form->getSubmitValue('oldPassword'),
            $form->getSubmitValue('newPassword'))) {
        echo 'Your password has been changed successfully.
            '<br />Click <a href="' .$_SERVER['PHP_SELF'] .
            '">here</a>';
    } else {
        echo 'Error changing your password.<br />' .
            'Click <a href="' . $_SERVER['PHP_SELF'] .
            '">here</a>';
    }

} else {
    // If not submitted, display the form
    $form->display();
}
break;
```

The script finishes with the default behavior of the `switch` statement; a simple menu is displayed, providing users with the option to change their passwords.

File: **12.php (excerpt)**

```
default:
    echo '<b>Options:</b><br />';
    echo '<a href="' . $_SERVER['PHP_SELF'] .
        '?view=changePassword">Change Password</a>';
    break;
}
?>
```

Now that you know how to change passwords, it should be no problem for you to change other account settings, such as the first and last names and the signature, by adding these to the `AccountMaintenance` class. If you want to allow users to change their email address, you'll need to examine the registration procedure used earlier in this chapter, and modify the SignUp class. You should make sure that users confirm a new email address before you allow them to change it.

How do I build a permissions system?

So far, you've already got an authentication system, which provides a global security system for your site. But are all your site's members equal? You probably don't want all of your users to have access to edit and delete articles, for example. To deal with this, you need to add to the security system further complexity that allows you to assign "permissions" to limited groups of members, permitting only these users to perform particular actions.

Rather than assigning specific permissions to particular accounts, which would quickly become a nightmare to administer, the way we'll build a permissions system is to think in terms of **Users**, **Groups** and **Permissions**. Users (login accounts) will be assigned to Groups, which will have names like "Administrators," "Authors," "Managers," and so on. Permissions reflect actions that users will be allowed to perform within the site, and they will also be assigned to Groups. From an administration perspective, managing all this will be easy, as it will be a simple matter to see which Permissions a particular Group has, and which users are assigned to that Group.

To build the relationships I've described requires the construction of many-to-many relationships between tables. This is explained as follows:

❏ A User can belong to many Groups.

❏ A Group may have many Users.

❏ A Permission can be assigned to many Groups.

❏ A Group may have many Permissions.

In practical terms, the way to build many-to-many relationships in MySQL is to use a **lookup table**, which relates to two other tables. The lookup table stores a two column index, each column being the key of one of the two related tables. For example, here's the definition of the user2collection lookup table:

```
CREATE TABLE user2collection (
  user_id INT(11) NOT NULL DEFAULT '0',
  collection_id INT(11) NOT NULL DEFAULT '0',
```

```
  PRIMARY KEY (user_id, collection_id)
)
```

Notice that the primary key for the table uses both columns. In doing so, it makes sure that no combination of `user_id` and `collection_id` can appear more than once.

Note that I use "collection" to refer to "group" in MySQL; the use of "group" would confuse the current versions of the mysqldump utility, which, as you know from Volume I, Chapter 3, is a helpful tool for backing up a database.

Table 1.1 presents sample data from the `user2group` table:

Table 1.1. Sample data from `user2collection`

user_id	collection_id
1	2
2	1
2	2
3	2
4	2

This tells us that User 1 is a member of Group 2, User 2 is a member of Groups 1 and 2, User 3 is a member of Group 2, etc.

With the lookup tables defined (the other being called `collection2permission`), we can now perform queries across the tables to identify the permissions a particular user has been allowed. For example, the following query returns all the permissions for the user with `user_id` 1.

```
SELECT
  p.name as permission
FROM
  user2collection uc, collection2permission cp, permission p
WHERE
  uc.user_id = '1' AND
  uc.collection_id = cp.collection_id AND
  cp.permission_id = p.permission_id
```

Note that I've used aliases for table names, such as `user2collection ug`, to make writing the query easier.

Armed with that knowledge, it's time we put together a class for users. The class will allow us to fetch all the information we need about users and, in particular, to check their permissions.

First, we need to define constants for the table and column names, so that we can use the class against different table structures:

File: **AccessControl/User.php (in SPLIB) (excerpt)**

```php
/**
 * Constants defining table and column names
 */
# Modify this constants to match the session variable names
// Name to use for login variable
@define('USER_LOGIN_VAR', 'login');

# Modify these constants to match your user login table
// Name of users table
@define('USER_TABLE', 'user');
// Name of ID column in usre
@define('USER_TABLE_ID', 'user_id');
// Name of login column in table
@define('USER_TABLE_LOGIN', 'login');
// Name of email column in table
@define('USER_TABLE_EMAIL', 'email');
// Name of firstname column in table
@define('USER_TABLE_FIRST', 'firstName');
// Name of lastname column in table
@define('USER_TABLE_LAST', 'lastName');
// Name of signature column in table
@define('USER_TABLE_SIGN', 'signature');

// Name of Permission table
@define('PERM_TABLE', 'permission');
// Permission table id column
@define('PERM_TABLE_ID', 'permission_id');
// Permission table name column
@define('PERM_TABLE_NAME', 'name');

// Name of Permission table
@define('PERM_TABLE', 'permission');
// Permission table id column
@define('PERM_TABLE_ID', 'permission_id');
// Permission table name column
@define('PERM_TABLE_NAME', 'name');

// Name of User to Collection lookup table
```

```
@define('USER2COLL_TABLE', 'user2collection');
// User to Collection table user_id column
@define('USER2COLL_TABLE_USER_ID', 'user_id');
// User to Collection table collection_id column
@define('USER2COLL_TABLE_COLL_ID', 'collection_id');

// Name of Collection to Permission lookup table
@define('COLL2PERM_TABLE', 'collection2permission');
// Collection to Permission table collection id
@define('COLL2PERM_TABLE_COLL_ID', 'collection_id');
// Collection to Permission table permission id
@define('COLL2PERM_TABLE_PERM_ID', 'permission_id');
```

With the constants defined, we can get down to the meat of the class:

File: **AccessControl/User.php (in SPLIB) (excerpt)**

```
/**
 * User Class<br />
 * Used to store information about users, such as permissions
 * based on the session variable "login"<br />
 * <b>Note:</b> you will need to modify the populate() and
 * checkPermission() methods if your database table structure
 * is different to that used here.
 * @access public
 * @package SPLIB
 */
class User {
  /**
   * Database connection
   * @access private
   * @var   object
   */
  var $db;
  /**
   * The id which identifies this user
   * @access private
   * @var int
   */
  var $userId;
  /**
   * The users email
   * @access private
   * @var string
   */
  var $email;
  /**
```

```
 * First Name
 * @access private
 * @var string
 */
var $firstName;
/**
 * Last Name
 * @access private
 * @var string
 */
var $lastName;
/**
 * Signature
 * @access private
 * @var string
 */
var $signature;
/**
 * Permissions
 * @access private
 * @var array
 */
var $permissions;
/**
 * User constructor
 * @param object instance of database connection
 * @access public
 */
function User(&$db)
{
  $this->db = &$db;
  $this->populate();
}
```

To begin, we've defined some data members as well as the constructor, which takes an instance of the MySQL class. The constructor calls the method, populate:

File: **AccessControl/User.php (in SPLIB) (excerpt)**

```
/**
 * Determines the user's id from the login session variable
 * @return void
 * @access private
 */
function populate()
{
  $session = new Session();
```

```
$sql = "SELECT
        " . USER_TABLE_ID . ", " . USER_TABLE_EMAIL . ",
        " . USER_TABLE_FIRST . ", " . USER_TABLE_LAST . ",
        " . USER_TABLE_SIGN . "
    FROM
        " . USER_TABLE . "
    WHERE
        " . USER_TABLE_LOGIN . " =
        '" . $session->get(USER_LOGIN_VAR) . "'";
$result = $this->db->query($sql);
$row = $result->fetch();
$this->userId = $row[USER_TABLE_ID];
$this->email = $row[USER_TABLE_EMAIL];
$this->firstName = $row[USER_TABLE_FIRST];
$this->lastName = $row[USER_TABLE_LAST];
$this->signature = $row[USER_TABLE_SIGN];
}
```

The populate method pulls this user's record from the database and stores various useful pieces of information in the object's variables, so we can easily get to them when, for example, we want to display that user's name on the page. Most important is gathering the user_id value from the database, for use in checking permissions.

Next, we have some accessor methods that are used simply to fetch the values from the object's variables:

File: **AccessControl/User.php** (in **SPLIB**) (excerpt)

```
/**
 * Returns the user's id
 * @return int
 * @access public
 */
function id()
{
  return $this->userId;
}
/**
 * Returns the users email
 * @return int
 * @access public
 */
function email()
{
  return $this->email;
```

```
}
/**
 * Returns the users first name
 * @return string
 * @access public
 */
function firstName()
{
  return $this->firstName;
}
/**
 * Returns the users last name
 * @return string
 * @access public
 */
function lastName()
{
  return $this->lastName;
}
/**
 * Returns the users signature
 * @return string
 * @access public
 */
function signature()
{
  return $this->signature;
}
```

The checkPermission method determines whether a user has a named permission.
It returns TRUE if it finds the permission named in the local permissions array:

File: **AccessControl/User.php (in SPLIB) (excerpt)**

```
/**
 * Checks to see if the user has the named permission
 * @param string name of a permission
 * @return boolean TRUE is user has permission
 * @access public
 */
function checkPermission($permission)
{
  // If I don't have any permissions, fetch them
  if (!isset($this->permissions)) {
    $this->permissions = array();
    $sql = "SELECT
              p." . PERM_TABLE_NAME . " as permission
```

```
            FROM
              " . USER2COLL_TABLE . " uc,
              " . COLL2PERM_TABLE . " cp,
              " . PERM_TABLE . " p
            WHERE
              uc." . USER2COLL_TABLE_USER_ID . "='" .
                $this->userId . "' AND
              uc." . USER2COLL_TABLE_COLL_ID . "=
                cp." . COLL2PERM_TABLE_COLL_ID . " AND
              cp." . COLL2PERM_TABLE_PERM_ID . "=
                p." . PERM_TABLE_ID;
      $result = $this->db->query($sql);
      while ($row = $result->fetch()) {
        $this->permissions[] = $row['permission'];
      }
    }
    if (in_array($permission, $this->permissions)) {
      return TRUE;
    } else {
      return FALSE;
    }
  }
}
```

We've set it up so that if there are no permissions currently stored in the class's $this->permissions array, checkPermissions fetches all of them. This means that if we need to check permissions more than once on a page, it will only be at the cost of a single query. You may take the alternative view that it's better to use the name of the permission in the query as well, and then count the number of rows returned. This reduces the amount of memory required by PHP, but will generate one query for each permission you check. The SQL statement for this alternative approach (showing the real table and column names, rather than the constants) could be:

```
$sql = 'SELECT
        COUNT(*) AS num_rows
      FROM
        user2collect uc, collection2permission cp, permission p
      WHERE
        uc.user_id = "' . $this->userId . '" AND
        uc.collection_id = cp.collection_id AND
        cp.permission_id = p.permission_id AND
        p.name = "' . $permission . '"';
```

The User class fetches data on a "need to know" basis. That is, it's fairly safe to assume that the basic, available user information will be required shortly after instantiation; hence, the use of the populate method—otherwise, we wouldn't have created the object in the first place. The data pertaining to permissions, however, may *not* be needed every time the User class is instantiated. It's likely that we'll only check permissions on a restricted number of pages, so we can save ourselves a query when the user views public pages, leaving the checkPermission method to be called explicitly as needed. This approach is known as **lazy fetching**, and can be a useful approach to reducing unnecessary queries and performance overhead.

Having seen the class, let's consider a demonstration. This login form script (13.php) is the same as 11.php, but it sends the post data to a different URL. Let's look at a simple example of the permissions in action: first, we'll include and set up the classes as usual, and put the new User class into action:

File: **14.php (excerpt)**

```php
<?php
// Include MySQL class
require_once 'Database/MySQL.php';

// Include Session class
require_once 'Session/Session.php';

// Include Auth class
require_once 'AccessControl/Auth.php';

// Include User class
require_once 'AccessControl/User.php';

$host   = 'localhost'; // Hostname of MySQL server
$dbUser = 'harryf';    // Username for MySQL
$dbPass = 'secret';    // Password for user
$dbName = 'sitepoint'; // Database name

// Instantiate MySQL connection
$db = &new MySQL($host, $dbUser, $dbPass, $dbName);

// Instantiate the Authentication class
$auth = &new Auth($db, '13.php', 'secret');

// Instantiate the User class
$user = &new User($db);
```

Now, we have code that will change the page based on the value of $_GET['view']. Each view has a different permission, which we can then look up with the User object:

File: **14.php (excerpt)**

```php
// Switch on the view GET variable
switch (@$_GET['view']) {
  case 'create':
    // Define permission (a name in permissions table)
    $permission = 'create';
    // Create a message for users with access to this area
    $msg = 'From here you can create new content';
    break;
  case 'edit':
    $permission = 'edit';
    $msg = 'From here you can edit existing content';
    break;
  case 'delete':
    $permission = 'delete';
    $msg = 'From here you can delete existing content';
    break;
  default:
    $permission = 'view';
    $msg = 'From here you can read existing content';
}

// Check the user's permission. If inadequate, change the msg
if (!$user->checkPermission($permission)) {
  $msg = 'You do not have permission to do this';
}
?>
<p><?php echo $msg; ?></p>
<p>
  <a href="<?php echo $_SERVER['PHP_SELF']; ?>">Main</a> |
  <a href="<?php echo $_SERVER['PHP_SELF'];
    ?>?view=create">Create</a> |
  <a href="<?php echo $_SERVER['PHP_SELF'];
    ?>?view=edit">Edit</a> |
  <a href="<?php echo $_SERVER['PHP_SELF'];
    ?>?view=delete">Delete</a>
</p>
```

This is a simple example, of course, but you could use the checkPermission method any way you like—perhaps simply to use if/else statements to decide what a user is allowed to do and see. Another approach would be to use a variable, such as the `$msg` variable we've used here, to store the name of a PHP script for use with an `include` statement.

Otherwise, that's all there is to it. Now, all you need to do is build an administration interface to control Users, Groups and Permissions!

How do I store sessions in MySQL?

As discussed earlier in this chapter, the default behavior of sessions in PHP on the server side is to create a temporary file in which session data is stored. This is usually kept in the temporary directory of the operating system and, as such, presents a security risk to your applications, especially if you are using a shared server. It's a good idea to be aware of the alternative; using a custom session handler provides an alternative data store which is fully under your control.

In this solution, I'll provide you with a custom session handler that will store all session data in MySQL in a manner that will require no modification of any code. The custom handler code is a port of the PostgreSQL Session Handler for PHP[10], written by Jon Parise, and is supplied with the code for this chapter, in the subdirectory `mysql_session_handler`.

To install it, the first thing you need to do is modify the file `mysql_session_handler.php`, changing the lines that identify your database connection, shown here in bold:

File: **mysql_session_handler/mysql_session_handler.php** (excerpt)

```
function mysql_session_open($save_path, $session_name)
{
  global $mysql_session_handle;

  /* See: http://www.php.net/manual/function.mysql-connect.php */
  $host = 'localhost';
  $user = 'harryf';
  $pass = 'secret';
  /* See: http://www.php.net/manual/function.mysql-select-db.php*/
  $dbas = 'sitepoint';

  $mysql_session_handle = mysql_connect($host, $user, $pass);
  mysql_select_db($dbas, $mysql_session_handle);
  return $mysql_session_handle;
}
```

[10] http://www.csh.rit.edu/~jon/projects/pgsql_session_handler/

Once you've done that, the next step is to override some php.ini settings with a .htaccess file[4] containing:

File: **mysql_session_handler/.htaccess**

```
php_value session.save_handler 'user'
php_value session.save_path 'php_sessions'
php_value auto_prepend_file '/path/to/mysql_session_handler.php'
```

The first line tells PHP that rather than using its default session handling mechanism, it will be told how to handle sessions by your own code. The value session.save_path refers to the name of the table where sessions are stored. The last line tells PHP to execute the mysql_session_handler.php file every time any other script is executed.

Finally, you need to create a table called php_sessions with the following structure:

```
CREATE TABLE php_sessions (
  session_id  VARCHAR(40) NOT NULL DEFAULT '',
  last_active INT(11)     NOT NULL DEFAULT '0',
  data        TEXT        NOT NULL,
  PRIMARY KEY (session_id)
)
```

With the .htaccess file placed in your Web root directory, all PHP scripts using sessions will store the session data in MySQL rather than in files.

The data stored by sessions has a format that looks like this:

```
myVar|s:11:"Hello World";ip_address|s:9:"127.0.0.1";
```

Variables themselves are separated by either semicolons or {} in the case of arrays, while within each variable, the name and value is separated by |. The value itself is stored in a serialized form (see the PHP Manual[11] for details).

So the above example corresponds to two variables:

---

[4]The PHP configuration setting auto_prepend_file can only be set in php.ini or by a .htaccess file. If you can't use .htaccess in that way, you'll need to include mysql_session_handler.php in all your scripts, which is best done by adding it to a script which is already included by all others, such as that where you keep central configuration information. The configuration values session.save_handler and session_save_path can both be controlled with the ini_set function (see Appendix A for more details). These will also need to be included in every script.

[11] http://www.php.net/serialize

```
$myVar = "Hello World";
$ip_address = "127.0.0.1";
```

Being able to decode this information with PHP will become important in the next solution.

How do I track who is online?

You may have seen applications such as vBulletin and phpBB, which let visitors see how many users are online (and sometimes, *which* users are online) at a given moment. Now that we have an authentication system, and a custom session handler that stores sessions in MySQL, implementing "Who is Online?" functionality is a breeze (well, almost)!

The first thing we need is (you guessed it!) a class that we can use to read and interpret stored session data from MySQL.

The constructor for the class simply initializes an array. This is used as a "first in first out" (FIFO) queue to which raw session data is added, and from which objects are returned along with properties that correspond to the variables stored in a given session.

File: **Session/SessionAnalyzer.php (in SPLIB) (excerpt)**

```
/**
 * Session Analyzer
 * Examines serialized session data (as it appears on the file
 * system or in a database) and builds objects into which it
 * places the data stored in the session
 * <code>
 * $sa = new SessionAnalyzer();
 * $sa->addSession($some_serialized_session_data);
 * $sessionStore = $sa->fetch();
 * </code>
 * @package SPLIB
 * @access public
 */
class SessionAnalyzer {
  /**
   * A list of sessions, their data held in SessionStore objects
   * @var array
   */
  var $sessions;

  /**
```

```
 * SessionAnalyzer constructor
 * @param object instance of database connection
 * @access public
 */
function SessionAnalyzer()
{
  $this->sessions = array();
}
```

The addSession method is used to put raw session data in the queue. It calls the private parseSession method, which is where the analysis of the raw session data actually occurs. The fetchSessions method allows us to get objects back from the queue, the properties of the object being the variables stored in the raw session data. Note that the objects returned are *not* related to the Session class we worked with earlier in this chapter. They are simply data containers—objects of class SessionStore (below)—and have no methods.

File: **Session/SessionAnalyzer.php (in SPLIB) (excerpt)**

```
/**
 * Gathers the sessions into a local array for analysis
 * @param string raw serialized session data to parse
 * @return void
 * @access public
 */
function addSession($rawData)
{
  $this->sessions[] = $this->parseSession($rawData);
}

/**
 * Iteraters over the SessionStore array
 * @return SessionStore
 * @access public
 */
function fetch()
{
  $session = each($this->sessions);
  if ($session) {
    return $session['value'];
  } else {
    reset($this->sessions);
    return FALSE;
  }
}
```

I'll leave the `parseSession` method to your imagination (or you can look at the code archive), as it has to do some serious string manipulation to interpret the session data correctly.

One word of warning. If you're storing objects of your own classes in sessions, the class file needs to be included before you use `SessionAnalyzer`, or you'll receive PHP errors about undeclared classes.

For your information, here's the `SessionStore` class, which acts as the container for parsed session data:

File: **Session/SessionAnalyzer.php** (in **SPLIB**) (excerpt)

```
/**
 * SessionStore
 * Container class in which to place unserialized session data
 * @package SPLIB
 * @access public
 */
class SessionStore {}
```

Now that we're capable of analyzing sessions, here's a simple script that counts the number of users online. It assumes we're using the MySQL session handler you saw in the previous solution:

File: **15.php**

```php
<?php
// Include MySQL class
require_once 'Database/MySQL.php';

// Include SessionAnalyzer class
require_once 'Session/SessionAnalyzer.php';

$host   = 'localhost'; // Hostname of MySQL server
$dbUser = 'harryf';    // Username for MySQL
$dbPass = 'secret';    // Password for user
$dbName = 'sitepoint'; // Database name

// Instantiate MySQL connection
$db = &new MySQL($host, $dbUser, $dbPass, $dbName);

// Instantiate the SessionAnalyzer class
$sAnalyzer = &new SessionAnalyzer();

$sql = "SELECT data FROM php_sessions";
$result = $db->query($sql);
```

```
while ($row = $result->fetch()) {
    // Add the raw session data
    $sAnalyzer->addSession($row['data']);
}

// Initialize variables for results of session analysis
$guests = 0;
$members = '';

// Loop through the queue of parsed sessions
while ($sessionStore = $sAnalyzer->fetch()) {
  if (isset($sessionStore->login)) {
    $members .= $sessionStore->login . ' ';
  } else {
    $guests++;
  }
}
// Format the output nicely

echo 'There are currently ' . $guests . ' guests online<br />';
echo 'Members online: ' . $members;
?>
```

The display looks like this:

```
There are currently 6 guests online
Members online: HarryF, BillG
```

I confess—I faked the number of users online for the purposes of having something to show you! If my private development PC was getting unknown visitors, I'd be worried.

"Who is Online?" functionality is more than just a nice gimmick. If you plan to add any kind of real time chat system to your site, "Who is Online?" is essential for allowing people to meet up. It also provides a user administration "snap shot" of what's happening on your site, particularly if your authentication system has just sent you an SMS telling you someone is trying to break in.

Further Reading

❑ *The WWW Security FAQ*: http://www.w3.org/Security/Faq/

This is essential reading!

❑ *HTTP Header Reference*: http://www.cs.tut.fi/~jkorpela/http.html

This summary of all HTTP headers is one for the bookmarks...

❑ *Apache HTTP Authentication with PHP*: http://www.sitepoint.com/article/280

This tutorial takes a look at the essentials of HTTP authentication with PHP.

❑ *Session Fixation Vulnerability in Web-based Applications*: http://www.acros.si/papers/session_fixation.pdf

This paper examines a session hijacking strategy where an intruder effectively hijacks the session before it's even started. The PHP `Authentication` class developed in this chapter should prevent this from happening to your site's users.

❑ *Managing Users with PHP Sessions and MySQL*: http://www.sitepoint.com/article/319

This article introduces the principles of user authentication with sessions.

❑ *Write Secure Scripts with PHP 4.2!*: http://www.sitepoint.com/article/758

Here's a tutorial that explains the importance of writing scripts with `register_globals` switched off.

❑ *PHP and the OWASP Top Ten Security Vulnerabilities*: http://www.sklar.com/page/article/owasp-top-ten

This article provides a summary of recent findings from Open Web Application Security Project[19], described in PHP terms. It's required reading!

❑ *Custom Session Handlers in PHP4*: http://www.phpbuilder.com/columns/ying20000602.php3

This handy tutorial does a good job of explaining how to build custom session handlers. Be warned, though, that there have been mixed reports about the final code developed for this tutorial; in some environments it seems to cause various miscellaneous or intermittent errors.

---

[19] http://www.owasp.org/

2

XML

XML, or **Extensible Markup Language**, is becoming an everyday tool for solving a whole range of Web-related issues, from exchanging data between sites with **RSS feeds**[1] or **Web services**, to new approaches for rendering Web pages, such as **Extensible Stylesheet Language Transformations** (XSLT).

What it all boils down to, though, is that XML is simply a set of rules for creating structured documents in plain text. The purpose of XML is to provide a platform- and language-independent technology for exchanging data between systems. In this chapter, we'll examine some examples in which we'll generate and read XML with PHP. In the process, we'll solve some of the common problems you're likely to encounter in modern Web development.

I'll assume you have a basic understanding of XML. If you're new to all this, I'd recommend you read the article, *Introduction to XML*[1], and the others listed at the end of this chapter, to gain the necessary background.

Tip

A Useful Tool

An excellent (and free) tool to help you work with XML is Mozilla's DOM Inspector. It's bundled with the default Mozilla browser distribution, and

---

[1]RSS can stand for RDF Site Summary, Rich Site Summary, or Really Simple Syndication, depending on who you ask.

[1] http://www.sitepoint.com/article/930

can be added to any Gecko-based browser (such as Firebird). A quick tutorial on using the DOM Inspector is available online[2].

SAX, DOM and PHP

First, there's some jargon you need to be clear about. There are two widely used approaches to parsing XML documents: the **Simple API for XML[3] (SAX)** and the **Document Object Model[4] (DOM)**.

Essentially, the SAX approach is to read an XML document from top to bottom and, as it encounters each element, to consult a list that's been provided (by you, the PHP developer) in order to decide what action to take. In a more general sense, SAX looks at an XML document as a sequence of **events**, each event being passed to an **event handler** for action; we'll see how this works shortly.

In contrast, the DOM approach is to read the entire document into memory, and provide an API by which a program (such as a PHP script) can access the elements of the document.

For simple tasks, SAX is the preferred choice. The code involved tends to be simpler, and, as it works with documents one element at a time, it can handle very large documents. PHP's SAX extension is built into PHP by default these days, and is based on James Clark's much respected Expat parser[5]; it provides a solid tool for use in your PHP scripts. Ample details of PHP's SAX functions may be found in the PHP Manual[6].

DOM is better suited to complex tasks, as it provides mechanisms that help you get straight to the parts of an XML document that you need. DOM also makes it possible to *generate* XML, either by making changes to an existing document that you've loaded, or by creating one from scratch. The downside of DOM is that the amount of memory it consumes is directly proportional to the size of the XML document, as it must keep a complete record of the document structure and content in memory while you work on it. Also, PHP's DOM extension has historically been one of its weak points, suffering from memory leaks in older PHP versions (pre-4.2), and is still only partially complete. The PHP Manual[7] contains the ominous warning, "This extension is EXPERIMENTAL." With PHP

---

[2] http://grayrest.com/moz/evangelism/tutorials/dominspectortutorial.shtml
[3] http://www.saxproject.org/
[4] http://www.w3.org/DOM/
[5] http://www.jclark.com/xml/
[6] http://www.php.net/xml
[7] http://www.php.net/domxml

4.3, the DOM extension has undergone substantial improvements, but be warned—it complies only loosely with the official DOM specification and is missing true support for some important XML features, such as **namespaces**[8] and **XML Schema**[9]. With PHP 5, there are plans afoot to rework PHP's XML tools, and they're being discussed in the PHP XML development newsgroup[10]. For now, the DOM extension is usable—but don't expect miracles.

It's also worth being aware that all the XML functionality provided by PHP's extensions could also be implemented using pure PHP. For example, the eZ xml library[11] that comes with eZ publish 3[12] is a more complete implementation of the DOM standard than that provided by the PHP 4.3 extension. PEAR::XML_HTMLSax[13], meanwhile, provides a SAX API for parsing badly formed XML (such as HTML). Search around and you'll find other classes, such as PHP.XPath[14], which is an implementation of the XPath specification[15] in pure PHP.

 Tip

XML and PHP Short Tags

When you're dealing with XML—in particular, when you're constructing XML as PHP strings—it's a good idea to have `short_open_tag` set to `Off` in `php.ini`, or to use a `.htaccess` file with this command:

```
php_flag short_open_tag off
```

Otherwise, PHP will confuse XML processing instructions (e.g. `<?xml … ?>`) with short form PHP script tags (`<? … ?>`), which can result in all sorts of parse errors. Of course, if you do this, you must ensure that all your PHP scripts use full tags (`<?php … ?>`).

We'll begin this chapter by understanding how we can parse documents with SAX and DOM and generate XML with DOM. We'll then look at using XSLT with the Sablotron extension[16], and Web services in XML-RPC and SOAP. Note that a further set of useful XML utilities for PHP can be found at http://phpxmlclasses.sourceforge.net/.

---

[8] http://www.w3.org/TR/REC-xml-names/
[9] http://www.w3.org/XML/Schema
[10] http://news.php.net/group.php?group=php.xml.dev
[11] http://ez.no/developer/ez_publish_3/documentation/development/libraries/ez_xml/
[12] http://ez.no/products/ez_publish_3/
[13] http://pear.php.net/XML_HTMLSax
[14] http://www.carrubbers.org/scripts/php/xpath/
[15] http://www.w3.org/TR/xpath
[16] http://www.php.net/xslt

Installation Issues

PHP's XML-related functionality relies on a number of third party, open source libraries that must be available on your system in order for you to be able to use the PHP XML extension.

The XML extension, which implements SAX, is distributed with PHP by default, and to use it, all you should need to do is make sure the required third party libraries are available (see below).

The DOM XML extension has undergone many changes of late, and I can only recommend using it if you're working with PHP 4.3 or later. Do not expect the examples in this chapter to work 100% correctly on older versions. Support among Web hosts is limited for the time being, as few are sufficiently up to date to have installed the latest version of PHP on their servers and *also* to have provided the DOM extension. However, if you do some research, you might find someone who has it. This situation will likely have improved by the time you read this, as hosting companies strive to catch up with the latest in PHP. Using DOM on your own installations requires you explicitly to tell PHP to use the extension in `php.ini` for Windows-based systems, or at compile time on Unix-based systems.

The XSLT extension is, sadly, rarely installed by most shared Web hosting companies; this is a shame, as there are a number of noteworthy PHP projects, such as Popoon[18] and Krysalis[19], which rely on it. Setting it up requires you explicitly to tell PHP to use it in `php.ini` on Windows-based systems, or at compiled time on a Unix-based system.

If you're using a Unix-based system, such as Linux, setting up the XML extensions will require compilation of the relevant third party libraries. In some cases, such as Expat, they may already be compiled and available in your distribution. Be sure to consult the PHP manual to find the relevant pages on XML[20], DOM XML[21] and XSLT[22], which provide detailed instructions for setting them up on Unix-based systems.

To set up the XML extensions on Windows, you'll need to perform the following steps:

---

[18] http://www.bitflux.ch/developer/cms/popoon.html
[19] http://www.interakt.ro/products/Krysalis/
[20] http://www.php.net/xml
[21] http://www.php.net/domxml
[22] http://www.php.net/xslt

1. In the directory on your system in which PHP is installed, you should find a subdirectory called `dlls`. These files need to be available in your system's PATH environment variable, and are required for you to use PHP's XML related functionality. The best approach is to modify your system's PATH environment variable (from Control Panel > System > Advanced > Environment Variables), and add the full path to this directory. Once you've done this, if your Web service is installed as a Windows service, you'll need to restart your system for it to be able to find the DLL files. The alternative approach is to copy all the files in the `dlls` directory to your `system32` directory (e.g. `c:\windows\system32`). This approach can be a little messy when it comes to upgrading PHP, though.

2. Access your `php.ini` file and ensure that the `extension_dir` is set to point to the `extensions` subdirectory of your PHP installation. Alternatively, copy the `php_domxml.dll` and `php_xslt.dll` files from that directory to the location to which the `extension_dir` points.

3. Modify the line containing `;extension=php_domxml.dll` and `;extension=php_xslt.dll` under the `[Windows Extensions]` section. Remove the semicolons to uncomment those lines.

4. Save the changes to `php.ini`, then restart your Web server.

About DOM

The first thing to realize is that the DOM XML extension is used a little differently than most of the PHP functions, as it's object oriented and bears a close resemblance to the in-built PHP `dir` class you saw in Volume I, Chapter 4—albeit with much more complexity.

What this means in practice is that, of the functions provided by this extension, the ones that will actually be available to you will depend on the part of the XML document with which you're working.

As the DOM extension still has experimental status as of PHP 4.3, the documentation[23] in the PHP manual is minimal. So, be warned—you won't find many examples of how to use it in the manual right now. There are also some cases in which the documentation is inaccurate, as it hasn't caught up with the latest state of the extension, so you'll need to stay on your toes when you're working with DOM.

---

[23] http://www.php.net/domxml

The point that's important to grasp, which the documentation doesn't make too clear, is that the DOM extension is a collection of classes, much like classes you might write yourself in PHP.

When you look at the documentation, you'll find the "functions" in the extension listed in the form `DomNode->child_nodes`. In this example, `DomNode` is a class defined by the extension, and `child_nodes` is a method of this class. The classes available with the DOM extension form a family; that is, they have a class inheritance structure, as shown by the UML class diagram in Figure 2.1.

The `DomNode` class is **abstract**; that is, you never instantiate it directly; rather, you'll always use a class that inherits from it. The methods available in `DomNode` will also be available from those subclasses, in addition to any methods defined by the subclass. So, if you have a `DomElement` object, you can call its `get_attribute` method, as well as the `has_attributes` method it inherits from `DomNode`.

When you first open an XML document for parsing with the DOM extension, you'll always begin with a `DomDocument` object. This has "factory" methods, such as `get_elements_by_tagname`, which can be used to fetch instances of other classes defined by the DOM extension, including `DomElement`.

That should give you a conceptual grasp of how the DOM extension works; the examples in this chapter will put it into practice.

Figure 2.1. Rough Sketch of the PHP DOM Extension

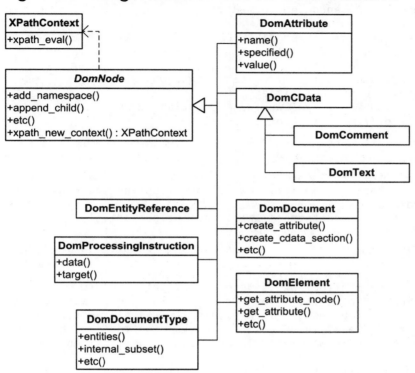

How do I parse an RSS feed with PHP and SAX?

RSS is a mechanism for publishing information about a site's content, and is most commonly used to broadcast latest news or fresh article headlines. It allows you to place on your site an XML document that other sites can use to display a summary of your content. Here, I'll assume you know roughly what RSS is (see the section called "Further Reading" at the end of this chapter if your knowledge of the topic is shaky), and jump straight into the challenge of parsing the SitePoint RSS feed[24]. Here's an example of the SitePoint feed:

---

[24] http://www.sitepoint.com/rss.php

File: **sitepointrss.php (excerpt)**

```
<?xml version="1.0" encoding="utf-8"?>
<rdf:RDF
 xmlns:rdf="http://www.w3.org/1999/02/22-rdf-syntax-ns#"
 xmlns="http://purl.org/rss/1.0/">

  <channel rdf:about="http://www.sitepoint.com/rss.php">
    <title>SitePoint.com</title>
    <description>Master the Web!</description>
    <link>http://www.sitepoint.com/</link>

    <items>
      <rdf:Seq>
        <rdf:li
          rdf:resource="http://www.sitepoint.com/article/1040" />
        <rdf:li
          rdf:resource="http://www.sitepoint.com/article/1037" />
      </rdf:Seq>
    </items>
  </channel>

  <item rdf:about="http://www.sitepoint.com/article/1040">
    <title>Link Popularity - The 'Other' Business Benefits</title>
    <description>You thought link popularity was all about your
      Google PageRank? Think again! Ken explains the real benefits
      to be gained from a well-planned link strategy - and how to
      create one!</description>
    <link>http://www.sitepoint.com/article/1040</link>
  </item>
  <item rdf:about="http://www.sitepoint.com/article/1037">
    <title>Using The Tabular Data Control in Internet
      Explorer</title>
    <description>The Tabular Data Control is an ActiveX control
      that's built into Internet Explorer. Premshree explains
      what it does, and how to manipulate it in JavaScript.
      </description>
    <link>http://www.sitepoint.com/article/1037</link>
  </item>
</rdf:RDF>
```

I've reduced the number of items to save space, but the two `item` tags containing the tags `title`, `description` and `link` are what we're interested in. We want to extract the contents of each `item` and turn it into an HTML table.

The XML extension[25], which implements SAX, is usually the ideal choice in cases in which you wish to process an unknown number of tags that have a pre-dictable structure. What takes a little getting used to is the way it uses **callback functions** to deal with the elements it encounters in the XML document. If you've ever written any JavaScript, you probably already use callback functions when you specify a JavaScript function to handle the response to an event, such as the user clicking a link. Because of this, callback functions are often called **event handlers**.

Since this is a tricky concept to master, we'll start with a more familiar approach. PHP's `xml_parse_into_struct` function lets us avoid using callback functions by placing the elements of an XML document into an array.

To begin with, we load the entire document into a string (Volume I, Chapter 4 for more details on file-related functions). Here, I've used the `file` function so you can concentrate on the XML-related code, but be aware that it's often a better idea to use `fsockopen` so that you can deal with unusual error scenarios, such as the site being down or the document having been moved. I provided an example of this in Volume I, Chapter 4.

File: **1.php (excerpt)**

```php
<?php
// Fetch the entire document
$rssDoc = file('http://www.sitepoint.com/rss.php');
$rssDoc = implode('', $rssDoc);
```

Next, I use the `xml_parser_create` function to fire up the SAX parser and tell it to use UTF-8 character encoding, which the first line of the RSS feed indicates is required. Other supported encodings include ISO-8859-1 (the default) and US-ASCII.

File: **1.php (excerpt)**

```php
// Start the xml parser tell it the character encoding
$sax = xml_parser_create('UTF-8');
```

The `xml_parser_set_option` function is used to instruct the parser *not* to convert all element and attribute names to uppercase, which is the default behavior. Note that this line is included mainly for the sake of example. When we parse XML documents provided by third parties like this, it's often a *good* idea to have all tags converted to upper case. If one site owner writes the RSS feed in lower case, another in upper case, and a third with a mixture of upper and lower case, you'll

[25] http://www.php.net/xml

have a hard time dealing with each unless you've converted them all to upper case.

File: **1.php (excerpt)**

```php
// Perserve the orginal case of the XML document
xml_parser_set_option($sax, XML_OPTION_CASE_FOLDING, false);
```

Next, `xml_parse_into_struct` reads the XML document stored in `$rssDoc` and stores it in `$rssData` as an array:

File: **1.php (excerpt)**

```php
// Read the XML document and drop it into the array $rssData
xml_parse_into_struct($sax, $rssDoc, $rssData);
```

Note that by loading the entire document into an array at once, we lose the inherent benefit of SAX—its ability to deal with an XML document one element at a time. In this case, the document is fairly small, so it's not a problem, but before we're done, we'll see how to take full advantage of SAX.

The `xml_parser_free` function clears up the memory used by the parser. Though the script will be cleared up when it terminates, it's a good idea to do this immediately in large applications where a lot of code will be executed and available memory may be at a premium.

File: **1.php (excerpt)**

```php
// Free up the memory used by the parser
xml_parser_free($sax);
```

Finally, with the document stored in an array, we can use a `foreach` loop to display the elements we're after:

File: **1.php (excerpt)**

```php
// Start displaying a table
echo "<table width=\"400\" border=\"1\">\n";

// Loop through the array
foreach ($rssData as $element) {

  // If this element contains a value
  if (isset($element['value'])) {

    // Watch for particular tags and display the correct HTML
    switch ($element['tag']) {
      case 'title':
```

```
        echo "<tr>\n<td><b>" . $element['value'] . "</b><br />";
        break;
    case 'description':
        echo $element['value'] . '<br />';
        break;
    case 'link':
        echo "<a href=\"" . $element['value'] . "\">" .
            $element['value'] . "</a></td>\n</tr>\n";
        break;
    }
  }
}
echo "</table>\n";
?>
```

Viewing this script with a browser, we see SitePoint's RSS displayed in a simple table, as shown in Figure 2.2.

Figure 2.2. XML as an Array

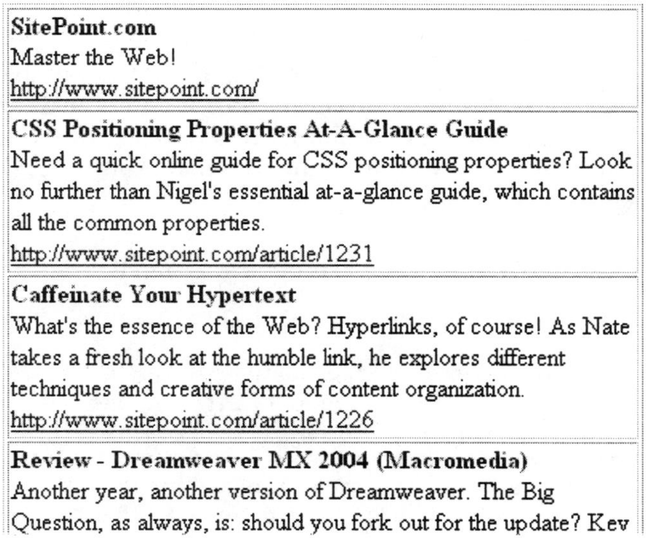

SitePoint.com
Master the Web!
http://www.sitepoint.com/

CSS Positioning Properties At-A-Glance Guide
Need a quick online guide for CSS positioning properties? Look no further than Nigel's essential at-a-glance guide, which contains all the common properties.
http://www.sitepoint.com/article/1231

Caffeinate Your Hypertext
What's the essence of the Web? Hyperlinks, of course! As Nate takes a fresh look at the humble link, he explores different techniques and creative forms of content organization.
http://www.sitepoint.com/article/1226

Review - Dreamweaver MX 2004 (Macromedia)
Another year, another version of Dreamweaver. The Big Question, as always, is: should you fork out for the update? Kev

Although it's possible to handle XML documents in this manner competently, this example definitely rates as a hack. Notice the switch statement, which is geared to expect the elements in the RSS feed to appear in a particular order, such as:

```
<item rdf:about="http://www.sitepoint.com/article/1037">
  <title>Using The Tabular Data Control in Internet
    Explorer</title>
  <description>The Tabular Data Control is an ActiveX control
    that's built into Internet Explorer. Premshree explains
    what it does, and how to manipulate it in JavaScript.
    </description>
  <link>http://www.sitepoint.com/article/1037</link>
</item>
```

If, for whatever reason, the order of the title, description, and link tags was to change, our neat table would become a disaster.

In general, it's a lot easier to use the method of callback functions, which allows your code to *respond* to tags as they appear, instead of proactively seeking them out in an array as we've just seen.

When parsing a document with SAX, the common strategy that's used when you only need certain parts of the document, is to devise a filter that will catch the elements you're looking for. Let me walk you through an example that demonstrates this.

The following are variables we'll need to access globally. The $newItem variable will be used like a switch; the code will turn it "on" every time it enters an item element and switch it "off" when it leaves. By consulting this variable, the code will know when it should take action, and will catch the contents of the title , description, and link tags.

File: **2.php (excerpt)**

```php
<?php
// Variables which will need to be accessed "globally"

$newItem     = FALSE; // A "marker" for when we're inside an item
$element     = ''; // Stores the name of the current element
$title       = ''; // Holds the contents of a title element
$description = ''; // Holds the contents of a description element
$link        = ''; // Holds the contents of a link element
$table       = "<table width=\"400\">\n"; // Stores HTML table
```

With those variables in place, we proceed to define our callback functions.

The open function will respond to opening tags found by the parser. The arguments $sax, $element, and $attributes are passed by the parser itself, when it calls this function. They contain a reference to the parser, the name of the element (the tag), and an array of the tag's attributes, respectively.

This function first checks to see whether the parser is inside an item element. If so, it stores the element's name (which will be either TITLE, DESCRIPTION, or LINK) in the global $element variable. If it's not inside an item element, but has just encountered an opening item tag, it switches on the $newItem marker.

File: **2.php (excerpt)**

```php
// Responds to opening tags
function open($sax, $element, $attributes)
{

  // If we're inside an <item /> tag
  if ($GLOBALS['newItem'] == true) {

    // ...store the name of the element
    $GLOBALS['element'] = $element;

  // If it's a new <item /> tag
  } else if ($element == 'ITEM') {

    // Switch on the newItem marker
    $GLOBALS['newItem'] = TRUE;
  }
}
```

Note that I've used the $GLOBALS array to access the variables I declared outside the function. Also, the tag names that appear in the $element argument will be in uppercase letters (e.g. ITEM), as we allow the parser to perform its default conversion to uppercase, discussed previously.

The data function collects the contents of the title, description, and link tags, storing them in global variables until the close function is called to deal with them.

File: **2.php (excerpt)**

```php
// Responds to the character data inside an element
function data($sax, $data)
{
  // If we're inside an <item /> tag...
  if ($GLOBALS['newItem'] == true) {

    // ... store the data for the elements in this list...
    switch ($GLOBALS['element']) {
```

```
        case 'TITLE':
          $GLOBALS['title'] .= $data;
          break;
        case 'DESCRIPTION':
          $GLOBALS['description'] .= $data;
          break;
        case 'LINK':
          $GLOBALS['link'] .= $data;
          break;
      }
    }
}
```

The close function, which is called whenever the parser encounters a closing tag, builds the HTML for the table. It looks for the closing item tag, gathers all the data from the $title, $description, and $link global variables, and uses them to add another row to the table.

File: **2.php (excerpt)**

```
// Responds to closing tags
function close($sax, $element)
{
  // If it's the closing tag of an <item> element...
  if ($element == 'ITEM') {

    // ... add the contents of <title> etc. to the table
    $GLOBALS['table'] .= "<tr>\n<td><a href=\"" .
      $GLOBALS['link'] . "\">" . $GLOBALS['title'] .
      "</a><br />\n" . $GLOBALS['description'] .
      "</td>\n</tr>";

    // Rest the contents variables
    $GLOBALS['title'] = '';
    $GLOBALS['description'] = '';
    $GLOBALS['link'] = '';

    // Switch off the newItem marker
    $GLOBALS['newItem'] = FALSE;
  }
}
```

Once this is done, it resets the $title, $description, and $link variables to prepare them for new data, and switches off the $newItem marker.

With all the callback functions in place, we start up the parser as before, and use the `xml_set_element_handler` and `xml_set_character_data_handler` functions to **register** the callback functions. In other words, we tell the parser to call **open** when it encounters an opening tag, **close** for a closing tag, and **data** for character data.

File: **2.php (excerpt)**

```php
// Create the XML parser
$sax = xml_parser_create('UTF-8');

// Register the open and close callback functions
xml_set_element_handler($sax, 'open', 'close');

// Register the character data callback function
xml_set_character_data_handler($sax, 'data');
```

Note that other `xml_set…` functions exist for handling things like XML processing instructions and external entity references, but in the vast majority of cases the two functions provided here are all you'll need.

Now, we'll fetch the SitePoint RSS feed from the Website and loop through the file in chunks, parsing each chunk as we go. This means the parser will begin work before it's finished receiving the complete document! This is great for performance, and means the complete XML document never has to be stored in PHP's memory.

File: **2.php (excerpt)**

```php
// Open a connection to SitePoint
$fp = fopen('http://www.sitepoint.com/rss.php', 'r');

// Loop until the end of the file
while (!feof($fp)) {
  // Fetch a chunk of data
  $data = fgets($fp);

  // Parse it
  xml_parse($sax, $data);
}

// Now free up the parser
xml_parser_free($sax);

// Finish off the table
$table .= "</table>\n";
?>
```

As before, we then free up the parser and finish off building the table. Finally, we'll add a splash of HTML with which to display the table:

File: **2.php (excerpt)**

```
<!DOCTYPE html PUBLIC "-//W3C//DTD XHTML 1.0 Transitional//EN"
  "http://www.w3.org/1999/xhtml">
<html xmlns="http://www.w3.org/1999/xhtml">
<head>
<title> SitePoint News </title>
<meta http-equiv="Content-Type"
  content="text/html; charset=iso-8859-1" />
<style type="text/css">
table {
  background-color: silver;
}
td {
  background-color: white;
  font-family: verdana;
  font-size: 11px;
}
a {
  font-weight: bold;
}
</style>
</head>
<body>
<?php echo $table; ?>
</body>
</html>
```

Figure 2.3 shows the SitePoint feed displayed in glorious HTML on my local Web server.

Figure 2.3. PHP and SAX Present: The SitePoint RSS Feed

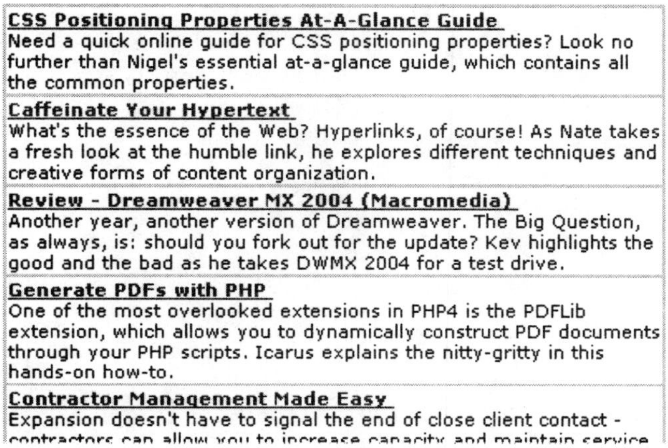

CSS Positioning Properties At-A-Glance Guide
Need a quick online guide for CSS positioning properties? Look no further than Nigel's essential at-a-glance guide, which contains all the common properties.

Caffeinate Your Hypertext
What's the essence of the Web? Hyperlinks, of course! As Nate takes a fresh look at the humble link, he explores different techniques and creative forms of content organization.

Review - Dreamweaver MX 2004 (Macromedia)
Another year, another version of Dreamweaver. The Big Question, as always, is: should you fork out for the update? Kev highlights the good and the bad as he takes DWMX 2004 for a test drive.

Generate PDFs with PHP
One of the most overlooked extensions in PHP4 is the PDFLib extension, which allows you to dynamically construct PDF documents through your PHP scripts. Icarus explains the nitty-gritty in this hands-on how-to.

Contractor Management Made Easy
Expansion doesn't have to signal the end of close client contact - contractors can allow you to increase capacity and maintain service

Now, there are a few things I don't like about the code so far. First of all, it relies on global variables, which in any other than very small PHP applications is a recipe for disaster. Later, I may forget what I've done here, and write other code that uses the same variable names, which will perhaps cause the RSS feed parsing to scramble. This solution is also tied to a particular HTML table layout; if I want a different layout later, I'll have to modify the gritty parts of this code. And, of course it's not a class! No, I'm not happy...

I think you know what I'm hinting at: a `SaxRssParser` class. It's very simple to use, as it has only three public methods to worry about. We'll look at it in detail so you understand how it was built.

First, we define all the member variables of the class, which, as you can see, correspond to the global variables we used in the previous procedural example. Note that this time, we don't have a variable in which to store an HTML table. Instead, we have the variable `$items`, which will be used to store a data structure that can be later used to generate an HTML table, if that is the desired outcome.

File: **XML/SaxRssParser.php (in SPLIB) (excerpt)**

```php
<?php
/**
 * SaxRssParser Class
 * Parses an RSS feed with SAX
 * @access public
 * @package SPLIB
 */
```

```php
class SaxRssParser {
  /**
   * Instance of the PHP SAX XML parser
   * @access private
   * @var resource
   */
  var $sax;

  /**
   * The marker for item tags
   * @access private
   * @var boolean
   */
  var $newItem;

  /**
   * Stores the name of the current element either
   * title, description or link
   * @access private
   * @var string
   */
  var $element;

  /**
   * Stores the contents of <title />
   * @access private
   * @var  string
   */
  var $title;

  /**
   * Stores the contents of <description />
   * @access private
   * @var  string
   */
  var $description;

  /**
   * Stores the contents of <link />
   * @access private
   * @var  string
   */
  var $link;

  /**
   * An array of items stored as stdClass objects
```

```
 * @access private
 * @var   array
 */
var $items;
```

In the constructor, we set the variables to their starting values, then create the parser and store it in its member variable. The next function called is xml_set_object, which allows us to specify an object reference where the parser can find the callback functions it will need. We've used the object's self-referencing variable, $this, to tell the parser that the methods it needs are inside this very object. The open, close, and data callbacks are registered as before, but using the member variable where the SAX parser is stored.

File: **XML/SaxRssParser.php (in SPLIB) (excerpt)**

```
/**
 * SaxRssParser constructor
 * @access public
 */
function SaxRssParser()
{
  $this->newItem = false;
  $this->element = '';
  $this->title = '';
  $this->description = '';
  $this->link = '';
  $this->items = array();
  $this->sax = xml_parser_create();
  xml_set_object($this->sax, $this);
  xml_set_element_handler($this->sax, 'open', 'close');
  xml_set_character_data_handler($this->sax, 'data');
}
```

The parse method is what we'll use in client code to parse chunks of an XML document. I discussed the trigger_error function used here in Volume I, Chapter 10.

File: **XML/SaxRssParser.php (in SPLIB) (excerpt)**

```
/**
 * Parses a chunk of XML document
 * @param string a chunk of XML
 * @return boolean
 * @access public
 */
function parse($data)
{
```

```
    if (!xml_parse($this->sax, $data)) {
      $error = xml_error_string(xml_get_error_code($this->sax));
      $line = xml_get_current_line_number($this->sax);
      trigger_error('XML error ' . $error . ' at line ' .$line);
      return FALSE;
    } else {
      return TRUE;
    }
  }
```

The `destroy` method allows us to clear up the memory used by the parser.

File: **XML/SaxRssParser.php (in SPLIB) (excerpt)**

```
/**
 * Destroys the parser
 * @return void
 * @access public
 */
function destroy()
{
  xml_parser_free($this->sax);
}
```

The `fetch` method is used to iterate over the contents of the member array, `$items`. In brief, successive calls to the `fetch` method will return the items retrieved from the RSS feed. See Chapter 7 for more about iterators.

File: **XML/SaxRssParser.php (in SPLIB) (excerpt)**

```
/**
 * Iterator for RSS Items, returning prepared items as
 * stdClasses
 * Returns an instance of stdClass containing the parameters
 * title, description and link or false if at end of collection
 * @return mixed
 * @access public
 */
function fetch()
{
  $item = each($this->items);
  if ($item) {
    return $item['value'];
  } else {
    reset($this->items);
    return FALSE;
  }
}
```

Last come the handler functions, which are more or less the same as you've seen before, now repurposed as methods:

File: **XML/SaxRssParser.php (in SPLIB) (excerpt)**

```php
/**
 * Handles opening tags
 * @param resource instance of PHP SAX XML
 * @param string element name
 * @param array element attributes
 * @return void
 * @access private
 */
function open($sax, $element, $attributes)
{
  if ($this->newItem) {
    $this->element = $element;
  } else if ($element == 'ITEM') {
    $this->newItem = TRUE;
  }
}

/**
 * Handles character data
 * @param resource instance of PHP SAX XML
 * @param string element name
 * @return void
 * @access private
 */
function data($sax, $data)
{
  if ($this->newItem) {
    switch ($this->element) {
      case 'TITLE':
        $this->title .= $data;
        break;
      case 'DESCRIPTION':
        $this->description .= $data;
        break;
      case 'LINK':
        $this->link .= $data;
        break;
    }
  }
}

/**
```

```
 * Handles closing tags
 * @param resource instance of PHP SAX XML
 * @param string element name
 * @return void
 * @access private
 */
function close($sax, $element)
{
  if ($element == 'ITEM') {
    $item = new stdClass;
    $item->title = $this->title;
    $item->link = $this->link;
    $item->description = $this->description;
    $this->items[] = $item;

    $this->title = '';
    $this->description = '';
    $this->link = '';
    $this->newItem = false;
  }
 }
}
```

The `close` method has a bit of a twist. Instead of dropping a chunk of HTML code into a global variable, it creates a new object to represent each item as it is processed. The built-in class `stdClass` is used to create an object with no properties or methods; then, the `title`, `link`, and `description` properties are added.[2] The objects are then dropped into an array for later retrieval with the `fetch` method.

With the class in place, let's use it:

File: **3.php**

```
<?php
// Include the SaxRssParser
require_once 'XML/SaxRssParser.php';

// Instantiate it
$parser = new SaxRssParser();

// Open a connection to SitePoint
```

---

[2]This is something of a cheat in strictly object oriented circles, where adding properties to an object on the fly is considered somewhat uncouth. Ideally, you would write a separate, `RSSItem` class with the necessary properties, which you would use here. For this example, however, I have elected to take advantage of PHP's flexibility, saving you from reading yet another class definition!

```php
$fp = fopen('http://www.sitepoint.com/rss.php', 'r');

// Loop until the end of the file
while (!feof($fp)) {
  // Fetch a chunk of data
  $data = fgets($fp);

  // Parse the date with the SaxRssParser object
  $parser->parse($data);
}

// Start building a table
$table = "<table width=\"400\">\n"; // Stores HTML table

// Loop through the items
while ($item = $parser->fetch()) {
  $table .= "<tr>\n<td>";
  $table .= "<a href=\"" . $item->link . "\">" . $item->title .
          "</a><br />\n";
  $table .= $item->description . "\n";
  $table .= "</td>\n</tr>\n";
}

// Finish off the table
$table .= "</table>\n";
?>
```

In the above code, we still read through the SitePoint feed in chunks, parsing each one as we go. Once the process is finished, we can use the `fetch` method to loop, and again build the table. As you saw, `fetch` returns an object containing the item data in three properties, which can be accessed as demonstrated here.

Thanks to the class, this code is much simpler. All the dirty work of juggling XML elements has been delegated to the class; we're also able to render whatever HTML we like, without having to modify the class again.

One thing to be aware of as you use the `SaxRssParser` class is that you can use the `xml_set_object` function as many times as you like with a single instance of the parser. This means you could pass to the class other objects that would act as filters for different elements—something you'll likely need to do for more complex XML documents. Alternatively, you might consider PEAR::XML_SaxFilters[26], which is based on Luis Argerich's Sax Filters[27] class library, and provides a framework for filtering an XML document.

How do I parse an RSS feed with PHP and DOM?

Now that you've seen how to parse an RSS feed using the SAX processor, how about using the DOM to perform the same task? Although you may be happy to stick with SAX, being able to compare the two will help you understand which represents the better choice for different problems. As with SAX, let's start by using PHP's DOM XML extension in a procedural fashion.

First, let's switch off error notices so we can perform a check on the elements of the document later (more on that in a moment).

File: **4.php (excerpt)**

```php
<?php
// Switch off error notices
error_reporting(E_ALL ^ E_NOTICE);
```

Next, we create a `DOMDocument` object by fetching the SitePoint RSS feed, using the `domxml_open_file` function. Two alternative functions are available: `domxml_open_mem`, which can be used to read an XML document stored in a PHP variable, and `domxml_new_doc`, which can be used to create a blank XML document that you can add content to.

File: **4.php (excerpt)**

```php
// Instantiate an instance of DOM from file
$dom = domxml_open_file('http://www.sitepoint.com/rss.php');
```

On the next line, we use the `DOMDocument` API to fetch the root element (the outermost tag) of the document with the `document_element` method. Note that `document_element` returns an instance of `DOMElement`.

File: **4.php (excerpt)**

```php
// Get the root RDF element
$rdf = $dom->document_element();
```

---

[26] http://pear.php.net/XML_SaxFilters
[27] http://phpxmlclasses.sourceforge.net/show_doc.php?class=class_sax_filters.html

Now that we've got the root node of the document, we can begin to fetch what we need from it, using `get_elements_by_tagname` to return an array of `DomElement` objects representing the `item` tags within the document.

File: **4.php (excerpt)**

```php
// Fetch all the <item> elements from the document
$items = $rdf->get_elements_by_tagname('item');
```

We first use the `child_nodes` method to loop through the items we've collected, and again to find the `title`, `description` and `link` elements for each item.

File: **4.php (excerpt)**

```php
// Start displaying a table
echo "<table width=\"450\" border=\"1\">\n";

// Loop through each item
foreach ($items as $item) {

  // Get the children of each item
  $itemNodes = $item->child_nodes();

  // Loop through the children
  foreach ($itemNodes as $itemNode) {

    // Get the contents of each child
    $itemContents = $itemNode->child_nodes();
```

Finally, we fetch the children of each `item`'s child, then check the `tagname` property of each to see whether it's one we're interested in. If we find a child we want, we loop again through its respective children, using the `node_type` method, to find the `XML_TEXT_NODE` that contains the text we're interested in.

File: **4.php (excerpt)**

```php
    // Deal with the specific elements we want
    switch (strtoupper($itemNode->tagname)) {

    case 'TITLE':
      // Loop through the contents to find the text node
      foreach ($itemContents as $itemContent) {
        // If it's a text node, display the HTML
        if ($itemContent->node_type() == XML_TEXT_NODE) {
          echo "<tr>\n<td><b>" . $itemContent->content .
            "</b><br />\n";
        }
      }
```

```
      break;

    case 'DESCRIPTION':
      foreach ($itemContents as $itemContent) {
        if ($itemContent->node_type() == XML_TEXT_NODE) {
          echo $itemContent->content . "<br />\n";
        }
      }
      break;

    case 'LINK':
      foreach ($itemContents as $itemContent) {
        if ($itemContent->node_type() == XML_TEXT_NODE) {
          echo "<a href=\"" . $itemContent->content . "\">" .
              $itemContent->content . "</a><br />\n";
        }
      }
      break;

    }
  }
}
echo "</table>\n";
?>
```

This again displays a simple table containing the RSS data from SitePoint's feed.

Notice that, unlike the SAX example, there was no need to make use of variables to keep track of our current location in the XML document. DOM objects keep track of where they are in the overall structure of the document; as a result, there are methods like `parent_node` and `child_nodes`, which can be used to locate the element(s) you need.

Using a procedural approach, it's fairly easy to get what we want from an XML document. However, as you can see above, it requires loops within loops within loops, which, aside from creating ugly looking code, will prove difficult to maintain in future should we wish to make use of other elements in the document, or change the HTML we're building.

A more common approach with DOM is to use functions that call each other, which makes it easier to break the problem into manageable steps.

This time, we'll build a data structure for storing the information we gather from the RSS feed, then we'll loop through the data structure and wrap it in HTML. The `$rssItem` variable will be used as temporary storage for the contents of an item tag; we initialize it with an empty stdClass object. As we finish processing each item, we'll move that item's data into the $rssItems array.

File: **5.php (excerpt)**

```php
<?php
// Set up global variables
$rssItem  = new stdClass; // Temporary variable stores contents of
                          // <item>
$rssItems = array();      // Stores a list of <item> objects
```

The rdf function is the first function we'll call, passing it an instance of the DOM Document class from which it will get the root element. It then calls the items function, passing it the root element. This triggers further function calls like dominoes, which will extract all the data we want when they're finished.

File: **5.php (excerpt)**

```php
// Get the root RDF element
function rdf($dom)
{
  $rdf = $dom->document_element();

  // Call Items() to fetch all <item> tags
  items($rdf);
}
```

Next up, the items function fetches all the item tags from the document using the DOM get_elements_by_tagname method, which returns an array of the named elements. Then, we call the item function to process the individual item tags.

File: **5.php (excerpt)**

```php
// Gets all the <item> tags
function items($rdf)
{
  // Fetch all the <item /> elements from the document
  $items = $rdf->get_elements_by_tagname('item');
  item($items);
}
```

Inside the item function, we loop through the array of items. For each item, we call the itemNode function, passing it an array containing all the child nodes of that item tag. As we'll see shortly, this stores the contents of the item as properties of the $rssItem object. We then add the $rssItem object to the array $rssItems, and reset $rssItem to an empty stdClass.

File: **5.php (excerpt)**

```php
// Populates $rssItems with single <item>s
function item($items)
{
  global $rssItem, $rssItems;
  // Loop through each item
  foreach ($items as $item) {
    // Get the children of each item
    $itemNodes = $item->child_nodes();
    itemNode($itemNodes);
    $rssItems[] = $rssItem;
    $rssItem = new stdClass;
  }
}
```

The `itemNode` function loops through all the child nodes of an `item`, fetching the children of each in turn. It then calls the `itemContent` function, which finds the text nodes that contain the data we're interested in.

File: **5.php (excerpt)**

```php
// Fetches the contents within at <item />
function itemNode($itemNodes)
{
    // Loop through the children
    foreach ( $itemNodes as $itemNode ) {
        // Get the contents of each child
        $itemContents=$itemNode->child_nodes();
        itemContent($itemNode,$itemContents);
    }
}
```

`itemContent` searches for the text nodes and, upon finding them, calls the `storeData` function:

File: **5.php (excerpt)**

```php
// Collects the text nodes from within the content
function itemContent($itemNode, $itemContents)
{
  foreach ($itemContents as $itemContent) {
    // If it's a text node, display the HTML
    if ($itemContent->node_type() == XML_TEXT_NODE) {
      $itemData = $itemContent->content;
      storeData($itemNode, $itemData);
    }
```

```
    }
}
```

The `storeData` function is where the `$rssItem` variable is populated with the contents of the named text node:

File: **5.php (excerpt)**

```php
// Stores the text node in the current $rssItem global variable
function storeData($itemNode, $itemData)
{
  global $rssItem;
  // Deal with the specific elements we want
  switch (strtoupper($itemNode->tagname)) {
    case 'TITLE':
      $rssItem->title = $itemData;
      break;
    case 'DESCRIPTION':
      $rssItem->description = $itemData;
      break;
    case 'LINK':
      $rssItem->link = $itemData;
      break;
  }
}
```

What we've done here is break the previous example into more manageable pieces, and store the results as an array of objects, instead of directly generating HTML. Here's a script that makes use of these functions:

File: **5.php (excerpt)**

```php
// Fetch the entire document
$rssDoc = file('http://www.sitepoint.com/rss.php');
$rssDoc = implode('', $rssDoc);

// Instantiate an instance of DOM from file
$dom = domxml_open_mem($rssDoc);

// Call the Rdf function to start parsing
rdf($dom);

// Build a table out of the $rssItems array
$table = "<table width=\"450\">\n";
foreach ($rssItems as $rssItem) {
  $table .= "<tr>\n<td><a href=\"" . $rssItem->link . "\">" .
            $rssItem->title . "</a><br />\n";
```

```
    $table .= $rssItem->description . "</td>\n</tr>\n";
}
$table .= "</table>\n";

echo $table;
?>
```

Now that we've separated the HTML from the data we're interested in, we can display the data using whatever HTML we like.

Of course, I'm still not satisfied! We're using a collection of functions and global variables that could easily cause trouble on a more complex site. Let's move the lot into a class, DomRssParser, which more or less represents the same code with a simple API that makes it easy to use. Let's begin with the constructor:

File: **XML/DomRssParser.php (in SPLIB) (excerpt)**

```
/**
 * DomRssParser constructor
 * @access public
 * @param string the RSS document
 */
function DomRssParser($rssDoc)
{
  $dom = domxml_open_mem($rssDoc);
  $this->rssItem = new stdClass;
  $this->rssItems = array();
  $this->Rdf($dom);
}
```

The constructor takes the RSS document as a string (so it's still your job to fetch the document in the first place).

The only other code that differs significantly from the previous example is the fetch method, which iterates over the parsed item elements of the RSS feed:

File: **XML/DomRssParser.php (in SPLIB) (excerpt)**

```
/**
 * Iterator for RSS Items, returning prepared items as
 * stdClasses
 * Returns an instance of stdClass containing the parameters
 * title, description and link or false if at end of collection
 * @return mixed
 * @access public
 */
function fetch()
```

```
{
    $item = each($this->rssItems);
    if ($item) {
      return $item['value'];
    } else {
      reset($this->rssItems);
      return FALSE;
    }
  }
```

Using the class is very simple:

File: **6.php (excerpt)**

```php
<?php
// Include the DomRssParser class
require_once 'XML/DomRssParser.php';

// Fetch the entire document
$rssDoc = file('http://www.sitepoint.com/rss.php');
$rssDoc = implode('', $rssDoc);

// Instantiate the parser
$parser = new DomRssParser($rssDoc);

// Build a table out of the $rssItems array
$table = "<table width=\"450\">\n";

// Loop through the items building the HTML
while ($item = $parser->fetch()) {
  $table .= "<tr>\n<td><a href=\"" . $item->link . "\">" .
            $item->title . "</a><br />\n";
  $table .= $item->description . "</td>\n</tr>\n";
}

// Finish the table
$table .= "</table>\n";
?>
```

Now, all we need to do is drop the table into a simple HTML page:

File: **6.php (excerpt)**

```
<!DOCTYPE html PUBLIC "-//W3C//DTD XHTML 1.0 Transitional//EN"
  "http://www.w3.org/TR/xhtml1/DTD/xhtml1-transitional.dtd">
<html xmlns="http://www.w3.org/1999/xhtml">
<head>
<title> SitePoint News </title>
```

```
<meta http-equiv="Content-Type"
  content="text/html; charset=iso-8859-1" />
<style type="text/css">
table {
  background-color: silver;
}
td {
  background-color: white;
  font-family: verdana;
  font-size: 11px;
}
a {
  font-weight: bold;
}
</style>
</head>
<body>
<?php echo $table; ?>
</body>
</html>
```

The result is a page that looks exactly the same as the one we built with the SaxRssParser class. See for yourself in Figure 2.4!

Figure 2.4. Sponsored by DOM

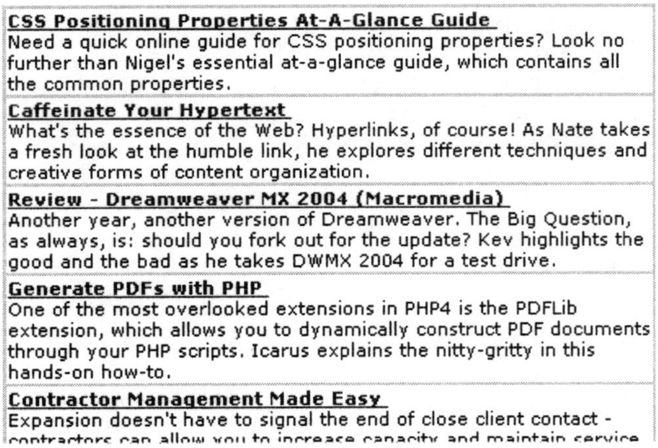

This demonstrates that SAX and DOM can be used to achieve the same end result. As a loose comparison, the SaxRssParser class turned out to require more member variables, which were used as temporary stores for content from the document, but it only needed three methods (open, close, and data) to handle the XML. The DomRssParser class, meanwhile, uses more methods to sort through the XML structure (the alternative being deeply nested control structures). This is typical of DOM code.

Well, the theory seems fine, but what about its practical application? Which solution is better from the perspective of actually using the classes? If you compare examples three and six, you'll notice the code is more or less the same; you could replace one with the other, without having to alter the code radically. The SaxParser code requires the client code to fetch the document in chunks using a loop, so there's a little more work to do there, but the functionality could easily be encapsulated in a subclass. This approach guarantees that even if we're dealing with a massive feed, PHP won't run out of memory.

How do I generate an RSS document with PHP and DOM?

XML documents can easily be generated in much the same way as HTML documents; it's simply a matter of writing strings:

File: **7.php**

```php
<?php
$date = date('h:ia l jS M Y');
$xml=<<<EOD
<?xml version="1.0"?>
<example>
<date>$date</date>
</example>
EOD;
echo $xml;
?>
```

Viewed in an XML-aware browser like Internet Explorer or Mozilla, this code displays a pleasantly rendered XML document, as shown in Figure 2.5.

Figure 2.5. XML Time

```
- <example>
    <date>06:44pm Friday 1st Aug 2003</date>
  </example>
```

But some applications of XML can make this simple, top-to-bottom approach to writing documents impractical.

For example, you might need to add elements or set attributes near the top of a document after you generate all the tags that follow. Additionally, writing XML requires you to replace correctly special characters such as &, <, and >, as well as non-English characters such as Ü, with the appropriate character entities. Attempting to achieve these feats simply by manipulating PHP strings is a fast track to hair loss.

The DOM XML extension allows you to add, remove, and modify elements throughout a document in any order, and will take care of all the character escaping for you. For example, constructing an RSS feed, most of which is rendered straight from database content that's likely to contain more than a few special characters, will be a lot easier if you use the DOM rather than render the XML yourself.

The following example shows the above XML document built using the DOM:

File: **8.php**

```php
<?php
// Instantiate new XML document
$dom = domxml_new_doc('1.0');

// Create the root <example> element
$example = $dom->create_element('example');

// Create the date element
$date = $dom->create_element('date');

// Create a text node to place the date in
$dateText = $dom->create_text_node(date('h:ia l jS M Y'));

// Append the date text node to the <date> element
$date->append_child($dateText);

// Append the <date> element to the <example> element
$example->append_child($date);

// Append the root element to the document
$dom->append_child($example);

// Send the XML MIME type
header('Content-Type: text/xml');
```

```
// Display the XML
echo $dom->dump_mem();
?>
```

The node creation methods available with the DOM XML extension are all accessible via the DOMDocument class, which is why the above code contains statements like this:

```
// Create a text node to place the date in
$dateText = $dom->create_text_node(date('h:ia l jS M Y'));

// Append the date text node to the <date> element
$date->append_child($dateText);
```

Notice that the $dom variable is used to create the $dateText node. Yet, to actually add the text, the append_child method is called via the $date variable, which is an instance of DOMElement.

With PHP 4.3, the following methods are available to create XML nodes:

DomDocument->create_attribute
create new attribute

DomDocument->create_cdata_section
create new character data (cdata) node

DomDocument->create_comment
create new comment node

DomDocument->create_element_ns
create new element node with an associated namespace

DomDocument->create_element
create new element node

DomDocument->create_entity_reference
create new entity reference

DomDocument->create_processing_instruction
create new processing instruction node

DomDocument->create_text_node
create new text node

Further details on these and all other DOM XML methods may be found in the PHP Manual[28].

RSS Generated

DOM makes a very good choice for generating your own RSS feed, as it deals with XML character entities so well. Using the DOM features, I've built a class called `RssGenerator` which complies to the RSS 1.0 specification[29], although it does not implement the entire spec. Here, we'll concentrate on the public methods for this class, then see how we can use it to create a feed. The complete code is provided in the `RssGenerator.php` class code; it should help as useful reference material for the generation of other XML documents.

The constructor sets up the `DOMDocument` object, then calls a private method to create the root node for the document:

File: **XML/RssGenerator.php (in SPLIB) (excerpt)**

```
/**
 * RssGenerator constructor
 * @access public
 */
function RssGenerator()
{
  $this->dom = domxml_new_doc('1.0');
  $this->initialize();
}
```

As it doesn't require any parameters, instantiating the `RssGenerator` can be achieved simply, as follows:

```
$rssGen = new RssGenerator;
```

The next public method adds the RSS channel information. We provide it with the name of our site, its URL, a description of the site, and another URL containing more information about the site:

File: **XML/RssGenerator.php (in SPLIB) (excerpt)**

```
/**
 * Add the basic channel information
 * @param string title of the channel e.g. "SitePoint"
 * @param string mail URL of channel
```

---

[28] http://www.php.net/domxml
[29] http://purl.org/rss/1.0/

```
 *                         e.g. "http://www.sitepoint.com/"
 * @param string description of channel
 * @param string about URL
 *                         e.g. "http://www.sitepoint.com/about/"
 * @return void
 * @access public
 */
function addChannel($title, $link, $desc, $aboutUrl)
{
  $this->channel->set_attribute('rdf:about', $aboutUrl);

  $titleNode = $this->dom->create_element('title');
  $titleNodeText = $this->dom->create_text_node($title);
  $titleNode->append_child($titleNodeText);
  $this->channel->append_child($titleNode);

  $linkNode = $this->dom->create_element('link');
  $linkNodeText = $this->dom->create_text_node($link);
  $linkNode->append_child($linkNodeText);
  $this->channel->append_child($linkNode);

  $descNode = $this->dom->create_element('description');
  $descNodeText = $this->dom->create_text_node($desc);
  $descNode->append_child($descNodeText);
  $this->channel->append_child($descNode);
}
```

The addImage method provides a means to inform those who use our feed where they can find the site's logo. We provide the source URL of the image, some alternative text to display instead of the image, and a link to which people who click on the image will be sent.

File: **XML/RssGenerator.php (in SPLIB) (excerpt)**

```
/**
 * Adds the channel logo description to the feed
 * @param string src URL of the image
 * @param string alternative text to display for image
 * @param string link for image e.g. http://www.sitepoint.com/
 * @return void
 * @access public
 */
function addImage($src, $alt, $link)
{
  $this->addChannelImage($src);

  $this->image = $this->dom->create_element('image');
```

```
    $this->image->set_attribute('rdf:about', $src);

    $titleNode = $this->dom->create_element('title');
    $titleNodeText = $this->dom->create_text_node($alt);
    $titleNode->append_child($titleNodeText);
    $this->image->append_child($titleNode);

    $urlNode = $this->dom->create_element('url');
    $urlNodeText = $this->dom->create_text_node($src);
    $urlNode->append_child($urlNodeText);
    $this->image->append_child($urlNode);

    $linkNode = $this->dom->create_element('link');
    $linkNodeText = $this->dom->create_text_node($link);
    $linkNode->append_child($linkNodeText);
    $this->image->append_child($linkNode);
}
```

The addSearch method allows us to describe the site's search functionality.

File: **XML/RssGenerator.php (in SPLIB) (excerpt)**

```
/**
 * Adds the description of the site search URL
 * @param string title of search e.g. "Search"
 * @param string description of search e.g. "Search SitePoint..."
 * @param string search URL
 * @param string GET variable for search e.g. "q" for "?q="
 * @return void
 * @access public
 */
function addSearch($title, $desc, $url, $var)
{
    $this->addChannelTextInput($url);
    $this->textinput = $this->dom->create_element('textinput');
    $this->textinput->set_attribute('rdf:about', $url);

    $titleNode = $this->dom->create_element('title');
    $titleNodeText = $this->dom->create_text_node($title);
    $titleNode->append_child($titleNodeText);
    $this->textinput->append_child($titleNode);

    $descNode = $this->dom->create_element('description');
    $descNodeText = $this->dom->create_text_node($desc);
    $descNode->append_child($descNodeText);
    $this->textinput->append_child($descNode);
```

```
$nameNode = $this->dom->create_element('name');
$nameNodeText = $this->dom->create_text_node($var);
$nameNode->append_child($nameNodeText);
$this->textinput->append_child($nameNode);

$linkNode = $this->dom->create_element('link');
$linkNodeText = $this->dom->create_text_node($url);
$linkNode->append_child($linkNodeText);
$this->textinput->append_child($linkNode);
}
```

SitePoint, for example, has a search available on its site. To search SitePoint for all PHP-related articles, we could use a URL like this:

http://www.sitepoint.com/search/search.php?q=PHP

The GET variable, q, contains the string that will be used as the search. The addSearch method lets us broadcast this sort of information so that RSS aggregation services can make available a search of the site.

When we call this method, we must supply the title of the search (perhaps it's as simple as "Search SitePoint"), a description ("Search the complete library of SitePoint books, articles, and newsletters"), the URL of the search ("http://www.sitepoint.com/search/search.php"), and the GET variable that contains the search text ("q").

The addItem method adds the items advertised in our feed to the body of the document. We supply the title, link, and description of the item, and it will be appended to the document. We'd typically use this method while looping through the results of a database query.

File: **XML/RssGenerator.php (in SPLIB) (excerpt)**

```
/**
 * Adds an RSS item to the document
 * @param string title of item
 * @param string link for item
 * @param string description of item
 * @return void
 * @access public
 */
function addItem($title, $link, $desc)
{
  $this->addChannelItem($link);
  $itemNode = $this->dom->create_element('item');
  $itemNode->set_attribute('rdf:about', $link);
```

```
$titleNode = $this->dom->create_element('title');
$titleNodeText = $this->dom->create_text_node($title);
$titleNode->append_child($titleNodeText);
$itemNode->append_child($titleNode);
$linkNode = $this->dom->create_element('link');
$linkNodeText = $this->dom->create_text_node($link);
$linkNode->append_child($linkNodeText);
$itemNode->append_child($linkNode);
$descNode = $this->dom->create_element('description');
$descNodeText = $this->dom->create_text_node($desc);
$descNode->append_child($descNodeText);
$itemNode->append_child($descNode);
$this->items[] = $itemNode;
}
```

The `toString` method returns the RSS feed document when we're finished adding to it.

File: **XML/RssGenerator.php (in SPLIB) (excerpt)**

```
/**
 * Returns the RSS document as a string
 * @return string XML document
 * @access public
 */
function toString()
{
  $this->finalize();
  return $this->dom->dump_mem(TRUE);
}
```

Note that DOMDocument's dump_mem method will return a neatly formatted version if it's provided a Boolean TRUE as we've done here; otherwise, it leaves out white space between the elements, which makes it difficult for us lowly humans to read.

Let's see how the `RssGenerator` class could be used. First, we'll create an array of arrays that simulates a database query result of two rows.

File: **9.php (excerpt)**

```
<?php
// Include the RssGenerator class
require_once 'XML/RssGenerator.php';

// Some sample data representing a database query
$articles = array(
  array(
```

```
    'title' => 'Verify a User\'s Email Address Using PHP',
    'link' => 'http://www.sitepoint.com/article/1051',
    'description' => 'So you published a registration page on your
        site... and all you get is fake email addresses? Joe shows
        how to use PHP\'s checkdnsrr function to ensure the mail
        domain exists, and those addresses are valid.'
  ),
  array(
    'title' => 'Using Regular Expressions in PHP',
    'link' => 'http://www.sitepoint.com/article/974',
    'description' => 'Are you getting stuck on PHP\'s regular
        expressions? Look no further than James\' down-and-dirty
        how-to, which tells you all the basics you need to know,
        and shows how to put them to good use!'
  )
);
```

The following variables, which describe the feed as a whole, are something we'd probably store in a configuration file:

File: **9.php (excerpt)**

```
// Define variables to be used in building the feed
$title       = 'SitePoint';
$link        = 'http://www.sitepoint.com/';
$desc        = 'Empowering Web Developers since 1997';
$about       = 'http://www.sitepoint.com/about/';
$logo        = 'http://www.sitepoint.com/images/sitepoint-logo.gif';
$searchTitle = 'Search';
$searchDesc  = 'Search SitePoint...';
$searchUrl   = 'http://www.sitepoint.com/search/search.php';
$searchVar   = 'q';
```

After instantiating it, we add the channel, image, and search information with the respective RssGenerator methods and the variables we've just defined.

File: **9.php (excerpt)**

```
// Instantiate the RssGenerator
$rssGen = new RssGenerator();

// Add the channel information
$rssGen->addChannel($title, $link, $desc, $about);

// Add the image description
$rssGen->addImage($logo, $title, $link);

// Add the search description
```

```
$rssGen->addSearch($searchTitle, $searchDesc, $searchUrl,
  $searchVar);
```

Next, we loop through the array of articles, using the `addItem` method to add each to the feed.

File: **9.php (excerpt)**

```
// Loop through the articles...
foreach ($articles as $article) {

  // Add the <item> for each article
  $rssGen->addItem($article['title'], $article['link'],
                   $article['description']);
}
```

Finally, we simply send the correct HTTP `Content-Type` header and display the document:

File: **9.php (excerpt)**

```
// Send the XML Mime type
header('Content-type: text/xml');

// Display the document
echo $rssGen->toString();
?>
```

Here's the `channel` element created by the class. It refers to **resources** (the channel items, the search facility, and the logo image) that are defined later in the document.

File: **generatedRss.xml (excerpt)**

```
<?xml version="1.0"?>
<rdf:RDF xmlns:rdf="http://www.w3.org/1999/02/22-rdf-syntax-ns#"
  xmlns="http://purl.org/rss/1.0/">
  <channel rdf:about="http://www.sitepoint.com/about/">
    <title>SitePoint</title>
    <link>http://www.sitepoint.com/</link>
    <description>Empowering Web Developers since 1997
    </description>
    <image rdf:resource=
    "http://www.sitepoint.com/images/sitepoint-logo.gif"/>
    <textinput
    rdf:resource="http://www.sitepoint.com/search/search.php"/>
    <items>
      <rdf:seq>
```

```
        <rdf:li resource="http://www.sitepoint.com/article/1051"/>
        <rdf:li resource="http://www.sitepoint.com/article/974"/>
      </rdf:seq>
    </items>
  </channel>
```

Note that many of the elements here are created by private methods that are called by the public methods we use. For example, when we add the image description, the method defines an `image` resource in the body of the document, and refers to it with the `image` tag in the `channel` above.

The `image` resource looks like this:

File: **generatedRss.xml (excerpt)**

```
  <image
rdf:about="http://www.sitepoint.com/images/sitepoint-logo.gif">
    <title>SitePoint</title>
    <url>http://www.sitepoint.com/images/sitepoint-logo.gif</url>
    <link>http://www.sitepoint.com/</link>
  </image>
```

You should be able to see how this corresponds to the `addImage` method provided by the `RssGenerator` class.

Here are the two items added to the body of the document:

File: **generatedRss.xml (excerpt)**

```
<item rdf:about="http://www.sitepoint.com/article/1051">
    <title>Verify a User's Email Address Using PHP</title>
    <link>http://www.sitepoint.com/article/1051</link>
    <description>So you published a registration page on your
      site... and all you get is fake email addresses? Joe
      shows how to use PHP's checkdnsrr function to ensure the
      mail domain exists, and those addresses are valid.
    </description>
</item>
<item rdf:about="http://www.sitepoint.com/article/974">
    <title>Using Regular Expressions in PHP</title>
    <link>http://www.sitepoint.com/article/974</link>
    <description>Are you getting stuck on PHP's regular
      expressions? Look no further than James' down-and-dirty
      how-to, which tells you all the basics you need to know,
      and shows how to put them to good use!</description>
</item>
```

Finally, the `textinput` element contains the information we told it via the `addSearch` method about how to search SitePoint:

File: **generatedRss.xml**

```
<textinput
    rdf:about="http://www.sitepoint.com/search/search.php">
    <title>Search</title>
    <description>Search SitePoint...</description>
    <name>q</name>
    <link>http://www.sitepoint.com/search/search.php</link>
  </textinput>
</rdf:RDF>
```

If you build your own RSS feed, there is available a number of validation services that allow you to check that your feed is defined correctly. These include:

W3C RDF Validation Service[30]
> This service is kept up to date with the latest W3 RDF specification, so it may complain about older RSS specs having depreciated syntax.

FEED Validator[31]
> This validator gives you an "It works" message if all is fine; if not, it provides a little information about the problem.

The UserLand RSS Validator[32]
> The Userland aggregator provides a "yes" or "no" check to see if your feed is correctly formatted.

Once your feed is validated, you may want to consider registering it with RSS aggregators, such as Syndic8[33] and UserLand[34]. These aggregator services keep watch on your site's feeds.

RSS can be a great way to reach exactly the audience you're looking for.

---

[30] http://www.w3.org/RDF/Validator/
[31] http://feedvalidator.org/
[32] http://aggregator.userland.com/validator/
[33] http://syndic8.com/
[34] http://aggregator.userland.com/register/

How do I perform XPath queries with PHP?

XPath is a syntax for accessing nodes within an XML document that's not unlike most file naming systems. From an XPath expression, PHP's DOM extension can perform an **XPath query**, a powerful mechanism for accessing elements within an XML document. In this solution, I'll assume you have some knowledge of XPath; if you don't, see the section called "Further Reading" at the end of this chapter for more information.

Let's say you have this XML document:

File: **articles.xml (excerpt)**

```
<?xml version="1.0" encoding="iso-8859-1"?>
<sitepoint xmlns:spt="http://www.sitepoint.com/">
  <spt:article>
    <spt:article_id>1</spt:article_id>
    <spt:title>Give me back my MySQL Command Line!</spt:title>
    <spt:body><p>One of the essential skills you must acquire to
      become proficient in the development of PHP/MySQL driven
      websites is a good understanding of Structured Query
      Language (SQL). In Chapter 2 of my article series, Build
      your own Database Driven Website using
      <a href="http://www.php.net/">PHP</a> and
      <a href="http://www.mysql.com/">MySQL</a>, I focus on getting
      beginners comfortable with typing SQL queries on the MySQL
      command line.</p>
    </spt:body>
    <spt:author>KevinY</spt:author>
    <spt:published>1013554800</spt:published>
    <spt:public>1</spt:public>
  </spt:article>
  <spt:article>
    ...
  </spt:article>
  ...
```

The document is not unlike a database query result set. Using XPath, we have a means to get to the data without multiple loops:

File: **10.php**

```php
<?php
// Get the contents of the XML document
$articles = file('articles.xml');
$articles = implode('', $articles);

// Instantiate a DOM Document from the file
$dom = domxml_open_mem($articles);

// Fetch new XPathContext object
$ctx = $dom->xpath_new_context();

// Register the SitePoint namespace
$ctx->xpath_register_ns("spt", "http://www.sitepoint.com/");

// Fetch the titles with an XPath statement into an XPath object
$titles = &$ctx->xpath_eval("//spt:title/text()");

// Display the data structure
echo '<pre>';
print_r($titles);
echo '</pre>';
?>
```

First, we fetch the XML document and create a new instance of DOMDocument, as usual. Next, we use xpath_new_context to create a new XpathContextObject; this initializes the XPath functionality to perform queries from the root of the document. We then have to register the namespace defined by the document, using the xpath_register_ns method. If we don't, the XpathContext object will fail to recognize the prefix, and errors will result.

Using the xpath_eval method, we can execute an XPath expression to fetch an XPathObject containing the data we need. Note that we've used the & operator to pass the nodes by reference so that, should we need to, we can manipulate them with the standard DOM methods and have those changes reflected in the stored document structure.

The XPath statement in this example is //spt:title/text(), which should get us the text inside every spt:title element in the document. Again, the detailed syntax of this expression is beyond the scope of this book, and resources are provided in the section called "Further Reading".

So that the format of the returned data is clear, we'll simply print the array as-is, using print_r. Here are the results:

```
XPathObject Object
(
    [type] => 1
    [nodeset] => Array
        (
            [0] => domtext Object
                (
                    [type] => 3
                    [name] => #text
                    [content] => Give me back my MySQL Command Lin
                    [0] => 5
                    [1] => 18318008
                )

            [1] => domtext Object
                (
                    [type] => 3
                    [name] => #text
                    [content] => Build your own Database Driven We
                    [0] => 6
                    [1] => 18297520
                )
```

Notice that the data we want is contained within a property of the XpathObject called nodeset. Displaying a nicely-formatted list of article titles would be a simple matter of performing a foreach loop on this property.

But what if you wanted not only the titles of the articles, but the author names as well? Assuming every article has a spt:title and spt:author tag, you could simply perform two XPath queries—one to fetch the titles, and one to fetch the authors. But when you're querying a complex XML document, such searches can be time-consuming. It could be more efficient to find the articles *first*, then fetch the title and author of each. Here's how:

File: **11.php (excerpt)**

```
// Fetch the articles with an XPath statement into an XPath object
$articles = &$ctx->xpath_eval("//spt:article");

echo '<b>Current Articles</b><br />';

// Loop through the articles
foreach ($articles->nodeset as $article) {

  // Fetch the title with the $article object as the context node
  $title = &$ctx->xpath_eval("spt:title/text()", $article);
```

```
    // Fetch the author with the $article object as the context node
    $author = &$ctx->xpath_eval("spt:author/text()", $article);

    // Display the content
    echo '- ' . $title->nodeset[0]->content . ' (' .
        $author->nodeset[0]->content . ')<br />';
}
```

Notice the three separate XPath statements here. The first, as before, searches from the root element. This time, it fetches all the `spt:article` nodes in the document. The script then loops through this node set, using each `spt:article` as the **context** for two additional queries: one fetching the text of the `spt:title`, the other, the text of the `spt:author`. As these queries only search a small piece of the XML document (a single article), they're very quick and efficient when compared with the relatively laborious whole-document search for articles.

The result is a list of the articles, their titles, and their authors, as shown in Figure 2.6.

Figure 2.6. Success with XPath

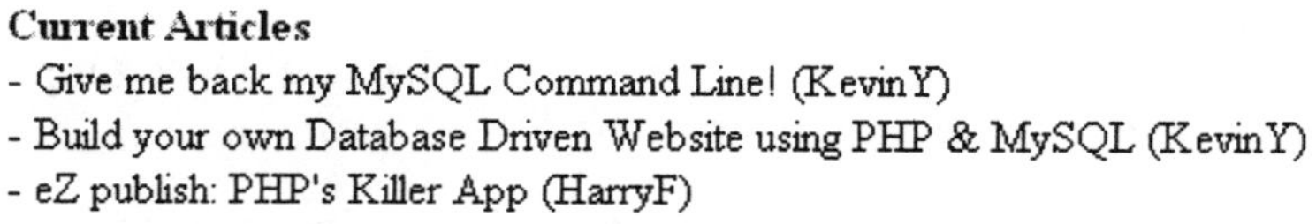

Current Articles
- Give me back my MySQL Command Line! (KevinY)
- Build your own Database Driven Website using PHP & MySQL (KevinY)
- eZ publish: PHP's Killer App (HarryF)

As you can see, XPath provides for fetching nodes from an XML document a more nimble mechanism than the bulky DOM API, thanks in large part to its ability to perform queries from any location in the document.

In addition to sets of elements and tag contents, XPath can also fetch attribute values. For example, this script fetches the `href` attribute of every `a` tag in the document:

File: **12.php**

```
<?php
// Get the contents of the XML document
$articles = file('articles.xml');
$articles = implode('', $articles);

// Instantiate a DOM Document from the file
$dom = domxml_open_mem($articles);
```

```
// Fetch new XPathContext object
$ctx = $dom->xpath_new_context();

// Register the SitePoint namespace
$ctx->xpath_register_ns("spt", "http://www.sitepoint.com/");

// Fetch all link targets
$links = &$ctx->xpath_eval("//a/@href");

// Display the links
echo '<b>Document contains the following links</b><br />';
foreach ($links->nodeset as $link) {
  echo '- ' . $link->value . '<br />';
}
?>
```

A Note on Default Namespaces

The XPath 1.0 specification[35] does not provide a mechanism to single out tags in the **default namespace** specified by the root element. PHP offers a workaround, however.

Consider this very simple RSS feed:

```
<?xml version="1.0"?>
<rdf:RDF
 xmlns:rdf="http://www.w3.org/1999/02/22-rdf-syntax-ns#"
 xmlns="http://purl.org/rss/1.0/">
</rdf:RDF>
```

Here, the default namespace is `http://purl.org/rss/1.0/`. If I wanted to perform an XPath query for elements in that default namespace (i.e. tags with no `rdf:` prefix), I'd need to declare a "dummy" prefix for this namespace. Here's how to do it in the case of an RSS feed:

```
// Register the dummy namespace
$ctx->xpath_register_ns("prl", "http://purl.org/rss/1.0/");

// Fetch the titles using that dummy namespace
$titles = &$ctx->xpath_eval("//prl:item/prl:title/text()");
```

[35] http://www.w3.org/TR/1999/REC-xpath-19991116

With this trick, you could use XPath to implement a much simpler version of the DOM RSS feed parser we saw earlier in this chapter.

Dynamic Content with XPath

Now that you have a basic grasp of how XPath can be used in PHP, it's time to do something interesting with it. Let's take the `articles.xml` document we've already used with XPath, and build it a database-like interface that displays a list of articles in brief and a single article in detail, depending on the link the visitor clicks. Before we can get started, we need a couple of classes that represent the articles list, and an individual article, respectively. These classes fetch data from the `articles.xml` document.

First, let's look at the class representing a list of articles. The constructor performs an XPath query to fetch all the `spt:article` elements *as well as* their children:

```
//spt:article/descendant-or-self::*
```

This allows us to use the `spt:article` to identify each new "row" in `articles.xml`, and at the same time provides the child nodes, giving us access to the content within them. With this content, we can build a data structure that we can begin to use immediately. Each "row" is placed in a new instance of the `Article` class (which I'll be looking at in detail in Chapter 3), then the object is placed inside the `$articles` member variable of the `ArticlesXML` class. If you compare this example with the work we did earlier to parse the RSS feed with DOM, immediately it becomes clear how much easier XPath makes the extraction of data from an XML document.

File: **ExampleApps/ArticlesXML.php (in SPLIB) (excerpt)**

```php
<?php
/**
 * Articles XML class
 * Fetches data from articles.xml
 * @access public
 * @package SPLIB
 */
class ArticlesXML {
    /**
     * An array of Article objects
     * @access private
     * @var   array
     */
    var $articles;
```

```
/**
 * ArticlesXML constructor
 * @param string the articles.xml document
 * @access public
 */
function ArticlesXML($articlesDoc)
{
  $dom   = domxml_open_mem($articlesDoc);
  $xpath = $dom->xpath_init();
  $ctx   = $dom->xpath_new_context();
  $ctx->xpath_register_ns("spt", "http://www.sitepoint.com/");

  $articles =
    &$ctx->xpath_eval("//spt:article/descendant-or-self::*");

  foreach ($articles->nodeset as $node) {
    switch ($node->tagname) {
      case 'article':
        if (isset($article)) {
          $this->articles[] = new Article($article);
        }
        $article = array();
        break;
      case 'body':
        $article['body'] = $dom->dump_node($node);
        break;
      default:
        $article[$node->tagname] = $node->get_content();
        break;
    }
  }
  if (isset($article)) {
    $this->articles[] = new Article($article);
  }
}
```

In the `foreach` loop above we used the tagname property of the `$node` object to implement some switching logic. If the node is an article corresponding to a `spt:article` tag, we first check to see if the variable $article exists (which it won't on the first iteration). If it does exist, we pass it to a new instance of the class `Article`, which is basically just a data store that provides some methods for formatting the data, the constructed object being stored in the articles property. Once any construction has been dealt with, the `'article'` section of the `switch` re-initializes $article as an empty array.

The `spt:body` is handled as a special case in the `switch`. Because the content of the `spt:body` will be a mix of text and XHTML, and because we want to preserve the XHTML, we need to use the `dump_node` method of PHP's `DomDocument` class, which converts a given node into an XML string. Strictly speaking, this method is not part of the W3C DOM specification, but, as this example demonstrates, life would be much more difficult without it.

The final section of the `switch` treats all the remaining child nodes of `spt:article` as equals. It stores their contents in the `$article` array, to be placed in an `Article` object the next time a `spt:article` tag is encountered.

After the `switch`, we add the final article (if any were found) into the array, as it will not be caught by the start of another `spt:article` tag.

Let's continue with the rest of the `ArticlesXML` class. The `fetch` method is used to fetch single articles from the internal array:

File: **ExampleApps/ArticlesXML.php (in SPLIB) (excerpt)**

```
/**
 * Returns an single ArticleXML object, iterating of the
 * collection of articles
 * @return object
 * @access public
 */
function fetch()
{
  $article = each($this->articles);
  if ($article) {
    return $article['value'];
  } else {
    reset($this->articles);
    return FALSE;
  }
}
```

The `getArticleByID` method allows us to fetch a single article by specifying its unique ID, which was given by the `spt:article_id` child of each `spt:article` element in the XML input.

File: **ExampleApps/ArticlesXML.php (in SPLIB) (excerpt)**

```
/**
 * Returns an Article object by its article_id value
 * @param int ID of article
 * @return object
```

```
 * @access public
 */
function getArticleById($id)
{
  foreach ($this->articles as $article) {
    if ($article->id() == $id) {
      return $article;
    }
  }
  return FALSE;
}
}
```

Now that we've defined `ArticlesXML`, here's how it can be used:

File: **13.php (excerpt)**

```php
<?php
// Include classes for accessing data from articles.xml
require_once 'ExampleApps/ArticlesXML.php';
require_once 'ExampleApps/Article.php';

// Get the contents of articles.xml
$articlesDoc = file('articles.xml');
$articlesDoc = implode('', $articlesDoc);

// Instantiate the Articles class
$articles = new ArticlesXML($articlesDoc);

// Begin constructing a table
$table = "<table>\n";

// If visitor is viewing a single article...
if (isset($_GET['id'])) {

  // Get the article by its id
  if ($article = $articles->getArticleById($_GET['id'])) {

    // Build the body of the table
    $table .= "<tr>\n<td class=\"title\">" . $article->title() .
              "</td>\n</tr>\n";
    $table .= "<tr>\n<td class=\"author\">by " .
              $article->author() . "</td>\n</tr>\n";
    $table .= "<tr>\n<td>" . $article->body() . "</td>\n</tr>\n";
  }
```

The `if` statement uses the `$_GET['id']` variable to decide whether the visitor is looking at a single article or should see the full list of articles.

The following code builds a table for the list of articles. Again, by separating the data structure we extracted from the XML document from the HTML that's used to display the data, we can build whatever output we like, while keeping the class itself reusable.

File: **13.php (excerpt)**

```php
// Build a list of articles
} else {
  $table .= "<tr>\n<th>Title</th><th>Author</th>\n</tr>\n";

  // Loop through the articles and build into table body
  while ($article = $articles->fetch()) {
    $table .= "<tr>\n";
    $table .= "<td><a href=\"" . $_SERVER['PHP_SELF'] .
              "?id=" . $article->id() . "\">" .
              $article->title() . "</a></td>";
    $table .= "<td>" . $article->author() . "</td>";
    $table .= "</tr>\n";
  }
}

// Finish the table
$table .= "</table>\n";
?>
```

Finally, we need some HTML with which to display the table:

File: **13.php (excerpt)**

```html
<!DOCTYPE html PUBLIC "-//W3C//DTD XHTML 1.0 Strict//EN"
  "http://www.w3.org/TR/xhtml1/DTD/xhtml1-strict.dtd">
<html xmlns="http://www.w3.org/1999/xhtml">
<head>
<title> SitePoint Articles </title>
<meta http-equiv="Content-Type"
  content="text/html; charset=iso-8859-1" />
<style type="text/css">
h1 {
    font-family: verdana;
    font-size: 15px;
    font-weight: bold;
    color: navy;
}
```

```
table {
    background-color: silver;
    width: 450px;
}
th {
    background-color: #f2f3f5;
    font-family: verdana;
    font-size: 11px;
    font-weight: bold;
    text-align: left;
}
td {
    background-color: white;
    font-family: verdana;
    font-size: 11px;
}
a {
    font-weight: bold;
}
.title {
    font-size: 14px;
    font-weight: bold;
}
.author {
    font-weight: italic;
    text-align: right;
}
</style>
</head>
<body>
<h1>Latest Articles</h1>
<?php echo $table; ?>
</body>
</html>
```

Now, when we view the articles as a list, we see a display like Figure 2.7.

Figure 2.7. Latest Articles Powered by XPath

Latest Articles

Title	Author
Give me back my MySQL Command Line!	KevinY
Build your own Database Driven Website using PHP & MySQL	KevinY

Each article has a link that, when clicked on, displays only a single article, as shown in Figure 2.8.

Figure 2.8. Give Me Back my XPath Command Line!

Latest Articles

Give me back my MySQL Command Line!

by KevinY

One of the essential skills you must acquire to become proficient in the development of PHP/MySQL driven websites is a good understanding of Structured Query Language (SQL). In Chapter 2 of my article series, Build your own Database Driven Website using **PHP** & **MySQL**, I focus on getting beginners comfortable with typing SQL queries on the MySQL command line.

A common problem faced by people getting started with MySQL is that most Web hosts these days don't provide shell access to the server, nor do they allow remote connections to their MySQL servers. The net result is that the MySQL command line is not available to users of most Web hosts. To learn SQL, developers are often forced to install a MySQL server on their own computer just to have a command line to play with.

In this article, I'll provide a convenient alternative -- a Web-based MySQL command line! Written in PHP, this script will let you type SQL queries into a text field and view the results or, in the case of error, any error messages generated.

We'll look at each component of the script separately, and I'll provide the complete code at the end of the article, so focus on the code segment at hand, and we'll see how it all fits together at the end.

In other words, we can use XPath to "mine" an XML document in pretty much the same way we use SQL to "mine" a database.

Tip

XQuery Lite

If you need more power for accessing XML than XPath provides, you might consider XQuery Lite[36].

[36] http://phpxmlclasses.sourceforge.net/class_xquery_lite.html

XPath can be an extremely powerful tool. For example, XPath makes it possible to base a dynamic, hierarchical menu system (such as that as covered in Volume I, Chapter 9) on an XML configuration file, rather than a database table.

How do I transform XML with PHP?

Another offshoot of the XML specification is **Extensible Stylesheet Language Transformations**[37] (XSLT), a standard that lets you transform XML documents. "…Into what?" you ask. Well, transforming one XML document type into another—such as XHTML—is the most common application, but with XSLT you can output just about any text-based file format you can think of.

XSLT can be useful for solving all sorts of problems. You can generate PHP code on the fly from an XML configuration file. You can generate documents in different formations—HTML and Wireless Markup Language (WML), for instance—from a single XML source. The possibilities are endless!

In this solution, I'll assume that you have some experience with XSLT, so I'll concentrate on the PHP code. If your knowledge of XSLT is lacking, the section called "Further Reading" has reference suggestions.

Using the XSLT extension[38] is similar in some ways to using PHP's SAX XML functionality. Let's look at an example based on the `articles.xml` document we saw in the last solution. First, we have an XSL document:

File: **articles.xsl** (excerpt)

```
<?xml version="1.0" encoding="iso-8859-1"?>
<xsl:stylesheet version="1.0"
 xmlns:xsl="http://www.w3.org/1999/XSL/Transform"
 xmlns:spt="http://www.sitepoint.com/"
 exclude-result-prefixes="spt">
```

In declaring the root element of the stylesheet, we've specified the SitePoint namespace used in `articles.xml`, and used the `exclude-result-prefixes` attribute to specify that the namespace prefix should not be added to the transformed elements.

Next, we use a template to match each `article` element that has a `public` element containing the value 1, and display it. The articles are placed into HTML table

[37] http://www.w3.org/TR/xslt
[38] http://www.php.net/xslt

rows. A second template catches all other (i.e. unpublished) articles and suppresses them.

Note that implementing within the stylesheet the logic that controls which articles are and aren't displayed is probably a bad idea, though it creates a more interesting example here. In fact, this is better handled by PHP in a uniform security/permissions system that's easy to maintain and administer. We've used the XPath **predicate**[3] in the template's condition to demonstrate an interesting capability of stylesheets, rather than to encourage you to take this approach.

File: **articles.xsl (excerpt)**

```
<xsl:output method="html" indent="yes" encoding="iso-8859-1" />
<!-- Strip whitespace from original -->
<xsl:strip-space elements="*" />
<!-- Match each published article -->
<xsl:template priority="1" match="spt:article[spt:public='1']">
  <tr>
    <td class="title">
      <xsl:value-of select="spt:title" />
    </td>
    <td class="author">
      <xsl:value-of select="spt:author" />
    </td>
  </tr>
  <tr>
    <td colspan="2">
      <xsl:value-of select="spt:body"/>
    </td>
  </tr>
</xsl:template>
<!-- Match and hide unpublished articles -->
<xsl:template match="spt:article"/>
</xsl:stylesheet>
```

OK, let's use PHP to perform the transformation. First, we define the full path to the XML and XSL documents:

File: **14.php (excerpt)**

```
<?php
// Define paths to XML and XSL documents (MODIFY THIS!)
$xml = '/full/path/to/XML/articles.xml';
$xsl = '/full/path/to/XML/articles.xsl';
```

---

[3]A predicate is a portion of an XPath expression between square brackets that filters the nodes according to a given condition. In this example, the predicate filters out non-public articles.

Note that on Windows systems, the path to these documents needs to be preceded by `file://`. For example:

File: **14.php (excerpt)**

```php
$xml = 'file://c:/htdocs/sitepoint/XML/articles.xml';
$xsl = 'file://c:/htdocs/sitepoint/XML/articles.xsl';
```

Next, we instantiate the XSLT processor with the `xslt_create` function:

File: **14.php (excerpt)**

```php
// Instantiate the XSLT processor
$xp = xslt_create();
```

The `xslt_process` function transforms the XML to HTML according to the template(s) in the stylesheet. Should anything go wrong, we use the `xslt_errno` and `xslt_error` functions to access information about what happened.

File: **14.php (excerpt)**

```php
// Perform the XSL Transformation
$result = xslt_process($xp, $xml, $xsl) or
  // If there's a problem, display the error
  "<tr>\n<td>Error (" . xslt_errno($xp) .
  ") performing XSLT:" . xslt_error($xp) . "</td>\n</tr>\n";

// Embed the result in an HTML table
$table = "<table>\n";
$table .= $result;
$table .= "</table>\n";
```

That's it! The XML document is now transformed into HTML, which we can embed into a table and display as part of a page constructed by PHP. The output will look like that shown in Figure 2.9.

Figure 2.9. Looks Like Normal HTML to Me...

Latest Articles

Give me back my MySQL Command Line!	KevinY
One of the essential skills you must acquire to become proficient in the development of PHP/MySQL driven websites is a good understanding of Structured Query Language (SQL). In Chapter 2 of my article series, Build your own Database Driven Website using PHP & MySQL, I focus on getting beginners comfortable with typing SQL queries on the MySQL command line.A common problem faced by people getting started with MySQL is that most Web hosts these days don't provide shell access to the server, nor do they allow remote connections to their MySQL servers. The net result is that the MySQL command line is not available to users of most Web hosts. To learn SQL, developers are often forced to install a MySQL server on their own computer just to have a command line to play with.In this article, I'll provide a convenient alternative -- a Web-based MySQL command line! Written in PHP, this script will let you type SQL queries into a text field and view the results or, in the case of error, any error messages generated.We'll look at each component of the script separately, and I'll provide the complete code at the end of the article, so focus on the code segment at hand, and we'll see how it all fits together at the end.	
Build your own Database Driven Website using PHP & MySQL	KevinY
On the Web today, content is king. Once you've mastered HTML and learned a few neat tricks in JavaScript and Dynamic HTML, you can probably build a pretty impressive-looking Web site design. But then comes the time to fill that fancy page layout with some real information. Any site that successfully attracts repeat visitors has to have fresh and constantly-updated content. In the world of traditional site building, that means HTML files -- and lots of 'em.The problem is that, more often than not, the people who provide the content for a site are not the same people who handle its design. Oftentimes,	

XML to SQL

Another task we could complete with XSLT is to convert the XML document into an SQL query, which can then be used to place the data into the database. I'll take this opportunity to demonstrate how to pass PHP variables to the XSLT processor.

Here's our stylesheet:

File: **article2sql.xsl**

```
<?xml version="1.0" encoding="iso-8859-1"?>
<!-- Note the: exclude-result-prefixes ... -->
<xsl:stylesheet version="1.0"
 xmlns:xsl="http://www.w3.org/1999/XSL/Transform"
 xmlns:spt="http://www.sitepoint.com/"
 exclude-result-prefixes="spt">

  <xsl:param name="tableName" />
```

```
<xsl:variable name="squote">'</xsl:variable>

<xsl:output method="text" indent="yes" encoding="iso-8859-1" />
<!-- Strip whitespace from original -->
<xsl:strip-space elements="*" />

<xsl:template match="spt:article">
INSERT
  INTO
    <xsl:value-of select="$tableName"/>
  SET
    article_id='<xsl:value-of select="spt:article_id"/>',
    title=
'<xsl:value-of select="translate(spt:title,$squote,'')" />',
    author=
'<xsl:value-of select="translate(spt:author,$squote,'')" />',
    body=
'<xsl:value-of select="translate(spt:body,$squote,'')" />',
    published='<xsl:value-of select="spt:published"/>',
    public='<xsl:value-of select="spt:public"/>';
  </xsl:template>
</xsl:stylesheet>
```

The stylesheet is geared to convert the document into an SQL query. Note that we've set the output method to text. For this example, we've used a crude method for solving the problem of single quotes inside the SQL statement—we've simply removed them all with the XPath **translate** function. In a practical situation, you'd need to write your own escaping template, which you would call as needed with a **xsl:call-template** tag. However, as this is a book on PHP, not XSLT, we'll stick to this simple solution.

It's worth noting the XSL parameter we've defined:

```
<xsl:param name="tableName" />
```

This parameter needs to hold the name of the table for the resulting SQL query in order to work as intended. As we'll see in a moment, it will be populated by a PHP variable.

Next, we'll look at the code that makes the transformation. This time, we'll use XSLT's error handling functionality to implement my own custom function for reacting to errors.

```php
<?php
// Define paths to XML and XSL documents (MODIFY THIS!)
$xml = '/full/path/to/sitepoint/XML/articles.xml';
$xsl = '/full/path/to/sitepoint/XML/article2sql.xsl';

// Define the XSLT error handler
function xslt_error_handler($xp, $errNo, $level, $fields)
{
  $errMsg = 'Error #' . $errNo . ', Level ' . $level .
            ', Fields:<br />';
  if (is_array($fields)) {
    foreach ($fields as $key => $value) {
      $errMsg .= $key .' => '.$value.'<br />';
    }
  } else {
    $errMsg .= $fields.'<br />';
  }
  trigger_error($errMsg);
}

// Instantiate the XSLT processor
$xp = xslt_create();

// Set the error handler
xslt_set_error_handler($xp, 'xslt_error_handler');

// An array of params to pass to the processor
$params = array('tableName' => 'articles');

// Perform the transform using the PHP variables
$result = xslt_process($xp, $xml, $xsl, null, null, $params);

// Display the result
echo "<pre>" . $result . "</pre>";
?>
```

Notice the $params array, where we define the variable tableName. This is passed to the XSLT processor, then used in the transformation to render the SQL. Figure 2.10 shows the output of this script, which simply displays the generated SQL code.

Figure 2.10. Back to SQL

```
INSERT
    INTO
      articles
    SET
      article_id='1',
      title='Give me back my MySQL Command Line!',
      author='KevinY',
      body='One of the essential skills you must acc
      published='1013554800'
      public='1';

INSERT
    INTO
      articles
    SET
      article_id='2',
      title='Build your own Database Driven Website
      author='KevinY',
      body='On the Web today, content is king. Once
      published='1033423200'
      public='1';
```

How do I build an XML-RPC service with PHP?

XML Remote Procedure Calling[39] (XML-RPC) is an XML standard that's commonly used for exchanging data between Web servers on the Internet. It allows you to store your data on one server, while displaying it in a Web page on a completely separate server. This would allow you to make that data available to other Webmasters, for example. Think of it as a generalized variant of an RSS feed, and you're not far off.

XML-RPC is a complete messaging protocol, where all the requests and responses are XML documents. The standard falls under the umbrella buzzword **Web services**, and is the forerunner to Simple Object Access Protocol[40] (SOAP), the current "king" of Web services. Here, I'll assume you have a grasp of what Web services are about, if not the actual syntax of XML-RPC. If you're not sure, you'll find recommended material in the section called "Further Reading" at the end of this chapter, including an article that focuses purely on XML-RPC.

---

[39] http://www.xmlrpc.com/
[40] http://www.w3.org/TR/SOAP/

Why would we bother with XML-RPC if SOAP's around? The answer is a combination of preference and practicality. XML-RPC is a lightweight protocol for data exchange, which is very easy to understand and well-supported in many languages. It's great for intranet applications and data exchange on the Internet where you'll be collaborating with a small group of like-minded developers. SOAP has a much more complicated specification and, as a result, is much more difficult to support correctly and reliably. Today, few, if any, of the SOAP implementations, including commercial offerings from the likes of Microsoft and IBM, fully support all facets of SOAP to 100% perfection. Part of the problem is its reliance on XML Schema[41], which most XML toolkits are still struggling to catch up with. Having said that, SOAP has the advantage that it comes with supporting technologies such as Web Services Description Language[42] (WSDL). These make it possible to build SOAP Web services that can be consumed by the many, rather than the few. If you're planning something "big," such as the delivery of commercial Web services, SOAP is probably the right choice for you.

To implement an XML-RPC based Web service for your site, it's generally a good idea to take advantage of one of the many PHP XML-RPC libraries available. There's even an XML-RPC extension to PHP, although it's not easy to find a hosting company that's enlightened enough to have installed it. Here, we'll be taking advantage of Simon Willison's Incutio XML-RPC library[43], currently at version 1.6. It provides arguably the best basis, from the point of view of code design, for building your own XML-RPC clients and servers. The code is well documented and numerous examples are provided to make its usage clear. Simon is currently working on a separate `HttpClient` class, which should significantly improve the functionality of the XML-RPC client in the near future.

The Server

In this example, we'll build an XML-RPC server that provides the contents of the MySQL `articles` table we used in Volume I, Chapter 3.

First of all, we need a class to fetch data from the `articles` table and turn it into XML-RPC responses.

The `ArticleServer` class extends the `IXR_Server` class provided by the Incutio library, which means that the methods in `IXR_Server` are also available in the `ArticleServer` class. We can pass the `ArticleServer` an instance of the `MySQL`

---

[41] http://www.w3.org/XML/Schema
[42] http://www.w3.org/TR/wsdl
[43] http://scripts.incutio.com/xmlrpc/

class so we can use it to fetch data. Within the constructor, we also define the XML-RPC methods available from the server and point them at local methods defined in the class. When an XML-RPC client calls an XML-RPC method, the processing will be handled by a method inside the `ArticleServer` class.

File: **ExampleApps/XMLRPCArticleServer.php** (in **SPLIB**) (excerpt)

```php
<?php
require_once 'ThirdParty/xmlrpc/IXR_Library.inc.php';

/**
 * XML-RPC Article Server class
 * Builds an XML-RPC server for the articles database using
 * Simon Wilsons XML-RPC implementation
 * http://scripts.incutio.com/xmlrpc/
 * @access public
 * @package SPLIB
 */
class XMLRPCArticleServer extends IXR_Server {
  /**
   * Database access object
   * @access private
   * @var   object
   */
  var $db;

  /**
   * XMLRPCArticleServer constructor
   * @param object instance of database access class
   * @access public
   */
  function XMLRPCArticleServer(&$db)
  {
    $this->db = &$db;
    // Define the XML-RPC methods
    $this->IXR_Server(array(
      'articles.getArticles' => 'this:getArticles',
      'articles.getArticleById' => 'this:getArticleById'
    ));
  }
```

The `getArticles` method is used to fetch a list of articles and return them as an array, which the `IXR_Server` class will automatically wrap in an XML-RPC response document. Notice that when we check for errors, we use the `IXR_Error` class to build an error object that's returned to the XML-RPC client. We're free to choose our own error code, but it's a good idea to avoid those defined in the

XML-RPC Fault Codes RFC[44], which are implemented by many popular XML-RPC libraries, in a variety of programming languages.

File: **ExampleApps/XMLRPCArticleServer.php** (in **SPLIB**) (excerpt)

```
/**
 * Returns an array of articles
 * @return array
 * @access public
 */
function getArticles()
{
  $sql = "SELECT article_id, title, author
          FROM articles
          WHERE public = '1'
          ORDER BY title";

  $result = $this->db->query($sql);

  if ($result->isError()) {
    return new IXR_Error(-2, 'Problem fetching data');
  }

  while ($row = $result->fetch()) {
    $articles[] = $row;
  }
  return $articles;
}
```

The getArticleById method is used to display a single article, including its body. It accepts a single parameter, $articleID, which corresponds to the article_id column in the database. Notice that we've been careful to check that $articleID is a number (if not, we return an error code) and we've also been sure to apply addslashes to the $articleID to prevent any potential SQL injection attacks (see Volume I, Chapter 3).

File: **ExampleApps/XMLRPCArticleServer.php** (in **SPLIB**) (excerpt)

```
/**
 * Return a single article
 * @param int article_id
 * @return array
 * @access public
 */
function getArticleById($articleID)
```

---

[44] http://xmlrpc-epi.sourceforge.net/specs/rfc.fault_codes.php

```
{
  if (!is_numeric($articleID)) {
    return new IXR_Error(-1, 'Expecting numeric article ID');
  }

  $articleID = addslashes($articleID);

  $sql = "SELECT title, author, body
          FROM articles
          WHERE article_id = '" . $articleID . "'
          AND public = '1'";
  $result = $this->db->query($sql);

  if ($result->isError()) {
    return new IXR_Error(-2, 'Problem fetching data');
  }

  return $row = $result->fetch();
  }
}
```

That's the ArticleServer class finished. Now all we need to do is instantiate it with an example:

File: **ExampleApps/XMLRPCArticleServer.php (in SPLIB) (excerpt)**

```php
<?php
// Include the MySQL class
require_once 'Database/MySQL.php';

// Include the XMLRPCArticleServer
require_once 'ExampleApps/XMLRPCArticleServer.php';

// Define variables for MySQL class
$host   = 'localhost';  // Hostname of MySQL server
$dbUser = 'harryf';     // Username for MySQL
$dbPass = 'secret';     // Password for user
$dbName = 'sitepoint';  // Database name

// Instantiate MySQL class
$mysql = &new MySQL($host, $dbUser, $dbPass, $dbName);

// Instantiate ArticleServer class
$server = new XMLRPCArticleServer($mysql);
?>
```

That's it. The `ArticleServer` is ready to begin accepting requests from XML-RPC clients.

The script executes on your Web server in exactly the same way as would any PHP script used to deliver (X)HTML to a client Web browser. That is, when an XML-RPC request is received as an HTTP POST request, the script is executed, examining the incoming request and returning the appropriate response in the same way a script might respond to a form. The only difference between serving XML-RPC and displaying a normal Web page is that the client will not be a Web browser; perhaps it's another Web server using an XML-RPC client to fetch data from your site. This will be clearer once you've seen a client script access the above server, which is exactly what we're going to do next.

The Client

The "client side" is where we'll render the HTML to display the articles. Remember, the client could be placed on a Web server on the far side of the world, although in this example you'll start by running them from the same Web server. Of course, someone else using the XML-RPC server may not want to render exactly the same HTML we create, so it's important that we provide a client class that accesses the service without restricting it to any particular output design.

The constructor takes a URL that represents the location of the XML-RPC server, as well as an optional `$debug` variable, which, if set to `TRUE`, will turn on the display of the Incutio library debugging messages (these are useful for understanding what's happening between client and server should things go wrong). The constructor uses the URL to instantiate an instance of `IXR_Client` provided by the Incutio library, and stores it in the local data member `$client`.

File: **ExampleApps/XMLRPCArticleClient.php (in SPLIB) (excerpt)**

```php
<?php
/**
 * XMLRPCArticleClient class
 * Builds an XML-RPC client for the XMLRPC Articles service
 * Uses Simon Wilson's XML-RPC implementation
 * http://scripts.incutio.com/xmlrpc/
 * @see XMLRPCArticleServer
 * @access public
 */
class XMLRPCArticleClient {
  /**
   * Instance of IXR_Client class
   * @access private
```

```
  * @var IXR_Client
  */
 var $client;

 /**
  * ArticleClient constructor
  * @param string URL of server
  * @param boolean true switches on debugging
  * @access public
  */
 function XMLRPCArticleClient($url, $debug = false)
 {
   $this->client = new IXR_Client($url);
   $this->client->debug = $debug;
 }
```

The `getArticles` method corresponds to the method of the same name on the server; it uses the data member `$client` to perform an XML-RPC request via the query method. The XML-RPC method in this case is `articles.getArticles`, which we saw when we registered the methods on the server in the previous section.

File: **ExampleApps/XMLRPCArticleClient.php (in SPLIB) (excerpt)**

```
/**
 * Returns an array of articles
 * @return array
 * @access public
 */
function getArticles()
{
  if (!$this->client->query('articles.getArticles')) {
    trigger_error($this->client->getErrorCode() .
      ' : ' . $this->client->getErrorMessage());
    return FALSE;
  }
  return $this->client->getResponse();
}
```

If anything goes wrong, the method triggers an error using the information provided by the `IXR_Client` `getErrorCode` and `getErrorMessage` methods. Otherwise, it returns the response it received from the XML-RPC server, using the `IXR_Client` `getResponse` method; this returns a PHP variable data structure that's ready for use; the XML parsing has been handled behind the scenes by the Incutio library.

The `getArticleById` method is similar to the `getArticles` method, but accepts a parameter, `$articleID`, which it uses in making the XML-RPC request using the `IXR_Client` query method. The response it returns is the article, identified by the ID.

File: **ExampleApps/XMLRPCArticleClient.php** (in SPLIB) (excerpt)

```
/**
 * Returns a single article
 * @param int article id
 * @return array
 * @access public
 */
function getArticleById($articleID)
{
  if (!$this->client->query('articles.getArticleById',
      $articleID)) {
    trigger_error($this->client->getErrorCode() .
      ' : ' . $this->client->getErrorMessage());
    return FALSE;
  }
  return $this->client->getResponse();
}
}
?>
```

Now, let's put the client class into action and use the service. First, we define the URL of the server (which you should modify to match the location on your own server), then instantiate the `XMLRPCArticleClient` class using the URL:

File: **17.php** (excerpt)

```
<?php
// Include the client class
require_once 'ExampleApps/XMLRPCArticleClient.php';

// Define the URL of the server (MODIFY THIS!!)
$server = 'http://localhost/XML/16.php';

// Instantiate the ArticleClient class
$articleClient = new XMLRPCArticleClient($server);
```

A simple `if-else` statement displays either a single article, if an article ID was provided by the visitor (when they clicked on a link), or a list of available articles:

```php
// Start building a table
$table = "<table>\n";

// If we're viewing a single article
if (isset($_GET['id'])) {

  // Get the article from the client class
  if ($article = $articleClient->getArticle($_GET['id'])) {

    // Build the table
    $table .= "<tr>\n<td class=\"title\">" . $article['title'] .
              "</td>\n</tr>\n";
    $table .= "<tr>\n<td class=\"author\">by " .
              $article['author'] . "</td>\n</tr>\n";
    $table .= "<tr>\n<td>" . $article['body'] . "</td>\n</tr>\n";
  } else {
    $table .= "<tr>\n" .
              "<td>Service unavailable at this time</td>\n" .
              "</tr>";
  }
} else {

  // Get an array of articles
  if ($articles = $articleClient->getArticles()) {

    // Loop through each article building the table
    foreach ($articles as $article) {
      $table .= "<tr>\n";
      $table .= "<td><a href=\"" . $_SERVER['PHP_SELF'] .
                "?id=" . $article['article_id'] . "\">" .
                $article['title'] . "</a></td>";
      $table .= "<td>" . $article['author'] . "</td>";
      $table .= "</tr>\n";
    }
  } else {
    $table .= "<tr>\n" .
              "<td>Service unavailable at this time</td>\n" .
              "</tr>";
  }
}

// Finish the table
$table .= "</table>\n";
?>
```

The table we've constructed can be dropped into a simple HTML page, and displays the same interactive list of articles as we saw in "How do I perform XPath queries with PHP?".

How do I consume SOAP Web services with PHP?

In the previous solution, you learned to build and use XML-RPC Web services with PHP. Most of the publicly-available Web services out there, however, use the newer **Simple Object Access Protocol**[45] (SOAP), not XML-RPC. In this solution, I'll show you how to consume SOAP Web services with your PHP scripts.

Client-Server or Consume-Deploy?

The Web services terminology describes the use of a client to access a Web service as **consuming** the Web service, while the act of providing a Web service is typically referred to as **deploying**. This is a marked change from the terms client and server, the exact definitions of which are blurred by Web services. For instance, your site may act as a server to visitors using their Web browsers, while simultaneously acting as a client to a Web service on a remote site.

There's really nothing new here. PHP scripts, for example, often act as clients to database servers, while at the same acting as a server to visitors browsing your site. If the act of consuming a Web service is hard to grasp, just think of it as being the same as connecting to MySQL and fetching some data.

As I mentioned in the last chapter, SOAP has a supporting technology called **Web Services Description Language**[46] (WSDL), which is one of the main reasons SOAP has an edge over XML-RPC. WSDL is a specification that allows an XML-based messaging protocol like SOAP to be described in a manner that relates directly to the object oriented paradigm. In practical terms, all this means is that you can generate a client to a Web service on the fly if necessary, simply by reading the associated WSDL document.

CapeScience[47] is one of a number of sites that provide free Web services today. They have also put together a great set of resources for Web service developers,

---

[45] http://www.w3.org/TR/SOAP/
[46] http://www.w3.org/TR/wsdl
[47] http://www.capescience.com/

including a free-to-download WSDL editor[48], which can help you visualize what a WSDL document is telling you.

It's beyond the scope of this book to provide an in-depth analysis of how SOAP and WSDL work, but if you'll take my word that you really don't need to know much about these technologies to take advantage of them, I'll use the CapeScience GlobalWeather service[49] to show you how easy it is.

The WSDL description of this service can be found at http://live.capescience.com/wsdl/GlobalWeather.wsdl (a nicely-formatted, simplified version is also available on the site). To cut a long story short, what you should be most interested in is the contents of the `portType` tag—namely the `operation` names, as these will correspond to the method names you'll use to consume the service.

Looking at the GlobalWeather service, in particular the `portType` element named `StationInfo`, this is what we see:

```
<portType name="StationInfo">
  <operation name="getStation">
    <input message="tns:getStation"/>
    <output message="tns:getStationResponse"/>
  </operation>
  <operation name="isValidCode">
    <input message="tns:isValidCode"/>
    <output message="tns:isValidCodeResponse"/>
  </operation>
  <operation name="listCountries">
    <input message="tns:listCountries"/>
    <output message="tns:listCountriesResponse"/>
  </operation>
  <operation name="searchByCode">
    <input message="tns:searchByCode"/>
    <output message="tns:searchByCodeResponse"/>
  </operation>
  <operation name="searchByCountry">
    <input message="tns:searchByCountry"/>
    <output message="tns:searchByCountryResponse"/>
  </operation>
  <operation name="searchByName">
    <input message="tns:searchByName"/>
    <output message="tns:searchByNameResponse"/>
```

[48] http://www.capescience.com/downloads/index.shtml
[49] http://www.capescience.com/webservices/globalweather/

```
  </operation>
  <operation name="searchByRegion">
    <input message="tns:searchByRegion"/>
    <output message="tns:searchByRegionResponse"/>
  </operation>
</portType>
```

Enough theory! It's time to put my money where my mouth is, and show you how easy it is to create SOAP clients with the help of WSDL (as well as PEAR::SOAP and Shane Caraveo, its maintainer). Using the latest version of PEAR::SOAP (version 0.75 at time of writing), we can generate a proxy class from the above WSDL description like this:

File: **18.php**

```php
<?php
// Include the PEAR::SOAP client class
require_once 'SOAP/Client.php';

// Instantiate the SOAP_WSDL class using the online document
$wsdl = new SOAP_WSDL(
  'http://live.capescience.com/wsdl/GlobalWeather.wsdl');

// Get the proxy class for the service
$proxy = $wsdl->generateProxyCode('', 'StationInfo');

// Display the code
echo '<pre>';
echo htmlspecialchars($proxy);
echo '</pre>';
?>
```

What this will display is an outline of a PHP class generated as a result of reading the WSDL document. Here's that outline in a more familiar format:

```php
class StationInfo extends SOAP_Client {
  function StationInfo()
  {
    $this->SOAP_Client(
      "http://live.capescience.com:80/ccx/GlobalWeather", 0);
  }
  function getStation($code)
  {
    // Code here
  }
  function isValidCode($code)
  {
```

```
    // Code here
  }
  function listCountries()
  {
    // Code here
  }
  function searchByCode($code)
  {
    // Code here
  }
  function searchByCountry($country)
  {
    // Code here
  }
  function searchByName($name)
  {
    // Code here
  }
  function searchByRegion($region)
  {
    // Code here
  }
}
```

I've replaced the code inside each method with a comment to make it easier for us to see the big picture. Notice that the method names correspond to the names of the operation elements in the WSDL code we saw above. To use this generated class, we need only run the generated code using PHP's eval function, then instantiate the StationInfo class as usual.

Of course, using eval is too much like hard work, given that PEAR::SOAP provides a getProxy method that does it for you:

File: **19.php (excerpt)**

```php
<?php
// Include the PEAR::SOAP client class
require_once 'SOAP/Client.php';

// Include the Session class
require_once 'Session/Session.php';

// Instantiate the Session class
$session = new Session();

// Instantiate the SOAP_WSDL class using the online document
```

```
$wsdl = new SOAP_WSDL(
  'http://live.capescience.com/wsdl/GlobalWeather.wsdl');

// Get the proxy class for the service
$stationInfo = $wsdl->getProxy();
```

This time, what we get back in the `$stationInfo` variable is an object we can use immediately. Note also that we've made the **Session** class available. One trick when dealing with Web services is to store fetched data that you can reuse in a local cache; this avoids the performance delay involved in fetching the data from the remote site for each page request.

File: **19.php (excerpt)**

```
// If the Countries session variable exists, use it
if ($session->get('Countries')) {
  // Get the data from the local session variable
  $countries = $session->get('Countries');
} else {
  // Otherwise get a list of countries from the service
  $countries = $stationInfo->listCountries();
  $session->set('Countries', $countries);
}
```

Here, we attempt to use a session variable to get the list of countries, if it has been created. Otherwise, we call the `listCountries` SOAP method available from the GlobalWeather service. What this means is that we only have to fetch the data from the remote site once; I don't think there are likely to be any new countries appearing while the session is active, so I can justify caching this data, as it is, essentially, static.

Next, we build an HTML `select` drop-down menu which we'll display in a page shortly:

File: **19.php (excerpt)**

```
// A select box to choose a country
$select = "<select name=\"country\">\n";
foreach ($countries as $country) {
  if ( $country == 'switzerland' ) {
    $select .= "<option selected>" . $country . "</option>\n";
  } else {
    $select .= "<option>" . $country . "</option>\n";
  }
}
$select .= "</select>";
```

Now, we check to see if a user has submitted the GET variable **country**, and, if he or she has, we begin building a table while calling the GlobalWeather service's **searchByCountry** SOAP method.

File: **19.php (excerpt)**

```php
// Initialize a variable to store a table
$table = '';

// If a country search has been performed...
if (isset($_GET['country']) &&
    in_array($_GET['country'], $countries)) {

  // Start building the table
  $table = "<table>\n";
  $table .= "<tr>\n<th>Airports in " . $_GET['country'] .
            "</th>\n</tr>\n";

  // Use the services searchByCountry() method
  $country = $stationInfo->searchByCountry($_GET['country']);

  // Display the airports in the country as table rows
  foreach ($country as $airport) {
    $table .= "<tr>\n<td>" . $airport->string . "</td>\n</tr>\n";
  }
  $table .= "</table>";
}
?>
```

Finally, we just need some HTML in which to display everything:

File: **19.php (excerpt)**

```html
<!DOCTYPE html PUBLIC "-//W3C//DTD XHTML 1.0 Transitional//EN"
  "http://www.w3.org/TR/xhtml1/DTD/xhtml1-transitional.dtd">
<html xmlns="http://www.w3.org/1999/xhtml">
<head>
<title> Global Weather Service </title>
<meta http-equiv="Content-Type"
  content="text/html; charset=iso-8859-1" />
</head>
<!-- CSS code omitted here for brevity -->
<body>
<form method="GET" action="<?php echo $_SERVER['PHP_SELF']; ?>">
<table>
<tr>
<td><b>Pick a Country:</b></td>
```

```
<td><?php echo $select; ?></td>
<td><input type="submit" value=" Search " /></td>
</tr>
</table>
</form>
<?php echo ( $table );?>
</body>
</html>
```

The script begins by displaying a list of countries inside a `select` menu in a form. On the form's submission, a search is performed to find all the airports in that country. Be warned that if you use this script, countries that have a lot of airports, such as the United States, will probably cause the script to time out as it takes too long to fetch all the data. In this case, I've primed it to search for airports in Switzerland, as there are only eleven (see Figure 2.11).

Figure 2.11. Airports in Switzerland

Pick a Country: switzerland   Search

Airports in switzerland

LSGG (GVA) - Geneve-Cointrin, Switzerland @ 46.25'N 6.133'E 420m

LSZR - Saint Gallen-Altenrhein, Switzerland @ 47.485'N 9.562'E 398m

LSGL - Lausanne, Switzerland @ 46.55'N 6.617'E 616m

LSGS - Sion, Switzerland @ 46.217'N 7.333'E 482m

LSMP - Payerne, Switzerland @ 46.817'N 6.95'E 490m

LSZA - Lugano, Switzerland @ 46'N 8.967'E 273m

LSZG - Grenchen, Switzerland @ 47.181'N 7.416'E 430m

LSZB (BRN) - Bern / Belp, Switzerland @ 46.917'N 7.5'E 505m

LSGN - Neuchatel, Switzerland @ 47'N 6.95'E 485m

LSZH (ZRH) - Zurich-Kloten, Switzerland @ 47.483'N 8.533'E 436m

LSGC - Les Eplatures, Switzerland @ 47.084'N 6.794'E 1027m

Note that the approach we used to cache data in a session variable could be improved upon with PEAR::Cache_Lite[51], which we'll see in Chapter 5.

---

[51] http://pear.php.net/Cache_Lite

How do I build a SOAP server with PHP?

Now that you know how to build an XML-RPC service and consume a Web service with the help of its WSDL document, it's time to look at building a SOAP server using PEAR::SOAP. Again, I'll have to skip the details of the SOAP protocol itself and its supporting technology, WSDL, as these subjects potentially could be a complete book in themselves (see the section called "Further Reading" at the end of this chapter). However, you should be able to accomplish a lot without having a detailed understanding of SOAP and WSDL; when you construct SOAP clients and servers, the implementation you use (in this case, PEAR::SOAP[52]) should handle these issues for you, and allow you to concentrate on getting the PHP code correct.

> **NuSOAP**
>
> An alternative to PEAR::SOAP is NuSOAP[53], which, in fact, uses the project PEAR::SOAP as a basis for its code. In comparison, NuSOAP is a lightweight library that's easy for those who have trouble with PEAR to install, and is ideally suited to quickly building clients and servers based on procedural code.
>
> When constructing Web services, you can make it easier for those who will use the service by providing a downloadable PHP client based on NuSOAP. NuSOAP also has the `getProxy` method, which can be used with WSDL documents to generate a class from a service on the fly, but its WSDL support is not as complete as PEAR::SOAP at the time of this writing.

Here, we'll build the Article Server that you saw in "How do I build an XML-RPC service with PHP?", but this time we'll use SOAP instead of XML-RPC. Again, we'll use a class to build the server; when dealing with Web services, it usually proves a lot easier to write classes rather than procedural code, as the following example should help make clear.

To begin, we need to make available the PEAR::SOAP server class and the `MySQL` class we created in Volume I, Chapter 3. First, as usual, we defined some instance variables:

File: **ExampleApps/SOAPArticleServer.php** (in **SPLIB**) (excerpt)

```
require_once 'SOAP/Server.php';
/**
```

---

[52] http://pear.php.net/package/SOAP
[53] http://dietrich.ganx4.com/nusoap/index.php

```
 * SOAP Article Server class<br/>
 * Builds a SOAP server for the articles database using
 * PEAR::SOAP<br/>
 * @access public
 * @package SPLIB
 */
class SOAPArticleServer {
  /**
   * Database access object
   * @access private
   * @var object
   */
  var $db;

  /**
   * Instance of PEAR::SOAP Server
   * @access private
   * @var object
   */
  var $soapServer;

  /**
   * SOAP dispatch map maps SOAP methods to class methods
   * defined here
   * @access private
   * @var array
   */
  var $__dispatch_map;

  /**
   * Type definition is used to define the variable types accepted
   * and returned from the server. The type map is used to
   * generate WSDL
   * @access private
   * @var array
   */
  var $__typedef;
```

The SOAPArticleServer constructor requires an instance of the MySQL class, as with the XMLRPCArticleServer. The difference this time is that, rather than the SOAPArticleServer extending another class, it will create its own instance of the PEAR::SOAP server class (i.e. it *composes* the SOAP_Server class rather than extending it—see Volume I, Chapter 2 for further discussion). The class will be capable of automatically "starting" the SOAP server itself, which makes it easier to use. However, if necessary, that behavior can be disabled by passing FALSE to the constructor as a second argument. After doing this, you'd need to call the **start** method yourself.

File: **ExampleApps/SOAPArticleServer.php (in SPLIB) (excerpt)**

```
/**
 * SOAPArticleServer constructor<br/>
 * @param object instance of database access class
 * @param boolean auto start server
 * @access public
 */
function SOAPArticleServer(&$db, $autostart = true)
{
  $this->db = &$db;
  $this->defineServer();
  if ($autostart) {
    $this->start();
  }
}
```

Now, have a look at the defineServer method, which was called by the constructor:

File: **ExampleApps/SOAPArticleServer.php (in SPLIB) (excerpt)**

```
/**
 * Sets up the dispatch map and type definition for WSDL
 * generation
 * @return void
 * @access private
 */
function defineServer()
{
  $this->__dispatch_map['getArticles'] = array(
    'in'  => array(),
    'out' => array('result' => '{urn:sitepoint}Articles')
  );
  $this->__dispatch_map['getArticleById'] = array(
    'in' => array('article_id' => 'int'),
    'out' => array('result' => '{urn:sitepoint}ArticleFull')
  );
  $this->__typedef['Articles'] = array(
    array('article' => '{urn:sitepoint}ArticleShort')
  );
  $this->__typedef['ArticleShort'] = array(
    'article_id' => 'int',
    'title' => 'string',
```

```
      'author' => 'string'
   );
   $this->__typedef['ArticleFull'] = array(
      'title' => 'string',
      'author' => 'string',
      'body' => 'string'
   );
}
```

What's happening here is a little more difficult to explain. First, we've defined the **dispatch map**, which contains a list of the SOAP method calls that can be made to this server. For each method, we need to define the input (arguments the method accepts) and the output (the value returned from the method). For a primitive type (such as a string or integer value) that's used as input or output, this can be defined simply by naming the variable type. You can see we've specified that the `article_id` argument of `getArticleById` must be of type `int` (an integer).

The output types in this example are a little more tricky and really require some understanding of WSDL to be grasped completely. Simply put, because the results of the two methods are complex types—an array of articles and a full article, respectively—we need to use a pointer to the full type definition. The definition for the full article type, for example, is provided by this code:

```
   $this->__typedef['ArticleFull'] = array(
      'title' => 'string',
      'author' => 'string',
      'body' => 'string'
   );
```

Here, you see the name of the complex type, `ArticleFull`, and a definition of the primitive types of which it is composed. A complex type definition can also contain additional complex types. Careful scrutiny of the code will reveal that we've done this to describe the array of articles returned by `getArticles`.

All this information enables the PEAR::SOAP server to generate a WSDL document that describes the server, allowing clients to benefit from the ease of use that WSDL affords. It's worth examining the examples provided with PEAR::SOAP for further help with setting up the dispatch map and type definitions. If you run into trouble, the best place to get help is the PHP SOAP Mailing list[54].

---

[54] http://www.php.net/mailing-lists.php

The getArticles method is almost exactly the same as the one we saw for the XMLRPCArticleServer class, except that if there's an error, we return an instance of SOAP_Fault, which will send a SOAP fault message to the client that called this server method.

File: **ExampleApps/SOAPArticleServer.php (in SPLIB) (excerpt)**

```php
/**
 * Returns an array of articles
 * @return array of objects
 * @access public
 */
function getArticles()
{
  $sql = "SELECT article_id, title, author
          FROM articles
          WHERE public = '1'
          ORDER BY title";
  $result = $this->db->query($sql);

  if ($result->isError()) {
    return new SOAP_Fault('Problem fetching data', 'Server');
  }

  $articles = array();
  while ($row = $result->fetch()) {
    $articles[] = $row;
  }
  return $articles;
}
```

The getArticleById method is also the same as what we've seen before, except that it uses SOAP_Fault to return errors.

File: **ExampleApps/SOAPArticleServer.php (in SPLIB) (excerpt)**

```php
/**
 * Return a single article
 * @param int article_id
 * @return object
 * @access public
 */
function getArticleById($articleID)
{
  if (!is_numeric($articleID)) {
    return new SOAP_Fault('Expecting numeric article ID',
      'Client');
```

```
    }
    $articleID = addslashes($articleID);

    $sql = "SELECT title, author, body
            FROM articles
            WHERE article_id = '$articleID'";
    $result = $this->db->query($sql);

    if ($result->isError()) {
      return new SOAP_Fault('Problem fetching data', 'Server');
    }
    return $row = $result->fetch();
  }
?>
```

The start method creates and invokes a SOAP_Server object. First, it uses the addObjectMap method to pass it a copy of the SOAPArticleServer object with the $this variable. The addObjectMap method registers the available methods in the SOAPArticleServer with the SOAP_Server object, examining the $__dispatch_map and $__typedef variables to see how the server should behave. Along with the object, addObjectMap requires a URL—an XML namespace. In this example, we've elected to pass http://www.sitepoint.com/ as that URL. Namespaces are used in SOAP to allow different SOAP methods of the same name to coexist. SOAP clients are required to identify the namespace and a method when making a request. For example, a SOAP server run by SitePoint might allow clients to retrieve the ten most popular articles published and the ten most popular posts on the forums. In both cases, the SOAP methods might be called topTen but to distinguish between the two, one might be assigned to the namespace http://www.sitepoint.com/#articles, the other to http://www.site-point.com/#forum. For simple Web services, however, you shouldn't need to worry about this—you can simply use a single, convenient URL, such as the URL of your site.

File: **ExampleApps/SOAPArticleServer.php (in SPLIB) (excerpt)**

```
/**
 * Starts the server, telling it to listen for incoming
 * requests.<br/>
 * Called automatically is auto start argument not passed as
 * false to constructor
 * @return void
 * @access public
 */
function start()
{
```

```
$this->soapServer = new SOAP_Server();
$this->soapServer->addObjectMap($this,
    'http://www.sitepoint.com/');
```

Next, we look to see what the type is of the incoming request. Incoming SOAP requests will use the HTTP POST method. In this case, we switch on the PEAR::SOAP Server using its `service` method and tell it to read the variable `$GLOBALS['HTTP_RAW_POST_DATA']`, which is where it will find the incoming SOAP request.

File: **ExampleApps/SOAPArticleServer.php (in SPLIB) (excerpt)**

```
if (isset($_SERVER['REQUEST_METHOD']) &&
    $_SERVER['REQUEST_METHOD'] == 'POST') {
  $this->soapServer->service($GLOBALS['HTTP_RAW_POST_DATA']);
```

If the page was *not* requested using the HTTP POST method, we'd instantiate the PEAR::SOAP_Disco class, which deals with the generation of WSDL documents.

As a result, if you simply point your browser at the server URL (which generates a GET request), you'll see an HTML document telling you where to find the WSDL description. In practice, the WSDL description can be viewed if you add `?wsdl` to the end of the server URL.

File: **ExampleApps/SOAPArticleServer.php (in SPLIB) (excerpt)**

```
} else {
  require_once 'SOAP/Disco.php';
  $disco = new SOAP_DISCO_Server($this->soapServer,
    'SitePoint');
  $disco->_service_desc = "SitePoint Article Server";
  if (isset($_SERVER['QUERY_STRING']) &&
      strcasecmp($_SERVER['QUERY_STRING'], 'wsdl') == 0) {
    header("Content-type: text/xml");
    echo $disco->getWSDL();
  } else {
    echo 'This is the SitePoint SOAP Server. Click
          <a href="?wsdl">here</a> for WSDL';
  }
  exit;
  }
 }
}
?>
```

As you can see, the `SOAPArticleServer` class does most of the work involved in providing this Web service. All we need now is a script that will connect to the database and create the server:

File: **20.php**

```php
<?php
// Include the MySQL class
require_once 'Database/MySQL.php';

// Include the SOAP Article Server
require_once 'ExampleApps/SOAPArticleserver.php';

// Define variables for MySQL class
$host   = 'localhost'; // Hostname of MySQL server
$dbUser = 'harryf';    // Username for MySQL
$dbPass = 'secret';    // Password for user
$dbName = 'sitepoint'; // Database name

// Instantiate MySQL class
$db = &new MySQL($host, $dbUser, $dbPass, $dbName);

// Instantiate ArticleServer class
$server = new SOAPArticleServer($db);
?>
```

Now, a server is not much good without a client to access it. As with XML-RPC, SOAP is a platform- and language-independent protocol, so you could build a client in any language (ideally, though, the language would have a SOAP library of some sort so you won't have to reinvent the wheel). In "How do I consume SOAP Web services with PHP?", you learned how to build a SOAP client in PHP automatically from a Web service's WSDL description. Here's how that would work for this Web service:

File: **21.php**

```php
<?php
// Include PEAR::SOAP Client class
require_once 'SOAP/Client.php';

// Instantiate the SOAP_WSDL class
$wsdl = new SOAP_WSDL('http://localhost/XML/20.php?wsdl');

// Instantiate the ArticleClient class
$articleClient = $wsdl->getProxy();
```

With the proxy object dynamically generated from the WSDL, we're ready to use the Web service:

File: **21.php**

```php
// If we're viewing a single article
if (isset($_GET['id'])) {
  // Call the getArticle() SOAP method
  $article = $articleClient->getArticle($_GET['id']);

  // Handle any errors
  if (PEAR::isError($article)) {
    $fault = $article->getFault();
    trigger_error('Fault: ' . $fault->faultcode . ' ' .
      $fault->faultstring);
    $table .= "<tr>\n" .
              "<td>Service unavailable at this time</td>\n" .
              "</tr>\n";
  } else {
    // Build the table
    $table .= "<tr>\n<td class=\"title\">" . $article->title .
              "</td>\n</tr>\n";
    $table .= "<tr>\n<td class=\"author\">by " .
              $article->author . "</td>\n</tr>\n";
    $table .= "<tr>\n<td>" . $article->body . "</td>\n</tr>\n";
  }...
```

If you're interested in the rest of the code of this script, you'll find it in the code archive for this chapter.

Security and Authentication in Web Services

One point you should be aware of when dealing with Web services is that you may well need to consider the security implications. Do you want all users (and their dogs) fetching content from your site and displaying it on theirs? You probably want some kind of authentication mechanism so that only permitted sites can fetch your content. If the content that's being sent is confidential, or you're using an authentication system and you're worried about a user "sniffing" login credentials, you'll need to make sure that the conversation is encrypted.

Solving these problems is best handled using the mechanisms that are already available with HTTP, namely SSL to encrypt conversations, and HTTP authentication (which you saw in Chapter 1) to "wrap up" a Web service in an environment that requires authentication.

Further Reading

❏ *Introduction to XML*: http://www.sitepoint.com/article/930

This article contains everything you need to know about the basics of XML.

❏ *XML Namespaces Explained*: http://www.sitepoint.com/article/932

An explanation of what XML namespaces are and why they are important is provided in this tutorial.

❏ *PHP and XML: Parsing RSS 1.0*: http://www.sitepoint.com/article/560

This tutorial looks at what RSS is and how it can be parsed with PHP.

❏ *XPath Basics*: http://www.devshed.com/Server_Side/XML/XPath/

This article explains what XPath is about and provides an introduction to using it.

❏ *XPath Tutorial*: http://www.zvon.org/xxl/XPathTutorial/General/examples.html

This is an in-depth tutorial that provides plenty of examples and will bring your XPath knowledge right up to speed.

❏ *Get XSL To Do Your Dirty Work*: http://www.sitepoint.com/article/595

Kevin Yank introduces XSL and shows how it can be used to transform XML into HTML in this handy guide.

❏ *Transform your PHP with XSLT*: http://www.sitepoint.com/article/602

Kevin goes on to provide examples of how to use PHP and XSLT to perform the transformation in this follow-up piece.

❏ *Web Services Demystified*: http://www.sitepoint.com/article/692

This article delivers an introduction to the technologies and terminologies behind Web services.

❏ *Build your own Web Service with PHP and XML-RPC*: http://www.sitepoint.com/article/827

This tutorial puts XML-RPC into context with Web services and provides some simple examples in PHP.

❏ *A Busy Developer's Guide to SOAP 1.1*: http://www.soapware.org/bdg

This article provides a quick tour of SOAP, which should prove familiar to those who are comfortable with the XML-RPC specification.

❏ *A Busy Developers Guide to WSDL 1.1*:
http://radio.weblogs.com/0101679/stories/2002/02/15/aBusyDevelopersGuideToWsdl11.html

Sam Ruby (the brains behind PHP's Java extension) gives a quick run down of WSDL in this tutorial.

❏ *Building XML Web Services with PHP and NuSOAP*:
http://www.devarticles.com/art/1/414

Consuming and building Web services with the NuSOAP PHP class is the focus of this article.

3

Alternative Content Types

As you're probably aware, (X)HTML is not the only format in which you can display content on the Internet. Aside from `.gif`, `.jpeg` and `.png` there are a number of other alternative content types which have proven themselves useful on the Web, including Adobe's PDF format and Macromedia's Flash, as well as alternative XML formats such as SVG (Scalable Vector Graphics), WML (wireless markup language), and XUL (Mozilla's XML User interface Language). Each has its own arena, through which it can enhance your Website and provide visitors with an alternative experience.

The subject of this chapter is using PHP to render such formats, perhaps as an alternative or in addition to your existing (X)HTML based content. What this chapter should also emphasize is that using classes and **layering** in your applications can help you add new functionality to your site while taking advantage of existing code.

How do I render PDF documents with PHP?

Adobe's PDF format has established itself as the *de facto* standard content type for displaying documents in a predictable form online. Not all users like to read long articles on a computer monitor, and PDF provides content in a form that's easily printed.

PHP has two extensions (PDFlib[1] and ClibPDF[2]) that make it possible to render PDF documents, but, unfortunately, both are commercial and require the payment of some kind of license fee if you're using them in a commercial application. This means that many hosts don't support them and, as a spoilt PHP coder who always wants something for nothing, I'm not going to use them, either.

Instead, I'm going to work with R&OS PDF Class[3], a PDF rendering class written purely in PHP. R&OS PDF is one of two respected PDF generating libraries written in pure PHP, the other being FPDF[4]. The drawback to using either is that it takes a long time to render the PDF and you may find better maturity and features in one of the extensions. Yet, both pure PHP libraries are still very capable of rendering an attractive "printable version" of your content, and with a little cunning, such as caching the rendered PDF file, the performance impact can be negated.

PDF To Go...

The R&OS PDF library is a truly outstanding piece of open source code. It's a true credit to the author, Wayne Munro, that he's been so generous as to allow others to use it for free. The version used here is 0.9 and, although it's not yet a full release, it's very stable and really only lacks a few "nice to have" features such as PDF bookmarks. Otherwise, it provides a powerful and fairly friendly interface for creating PDF documents, including the ability to add images, links, shapes, and much more, not to mention encryption, which requires the reader to provide a password in order to view the document. R&OS PDF has everything you need to render PDF "on the fly" with PHP.

The documentation provided with the library is very thorough (and in PDF format, naturally). Here, we'll concentrate on an example that's specifically geared to rendering examples; the comments on R&OS PDF's classes will be minimal (you could write a lot about this class), but detailed enough to get you started and referring to the documentation for further help.

Be warned that building a PDF document with this class takes some patience, as you'll need to position some parts of the page (usually, the content you want

---

[1] http://www.php.net/pdf
[2] http://www.php.net/cpdf
[3] http://www.ros.co.nz/pdf/
[4] http://www.fpdf.org/

displayed on every page) based on x and y coordinates. The work is greatly simplified by the `Cezpdf` class, which provides a simpler interface to the base `Cpdf` class, and handles things like text positioning—so that a new paragraph will always appear correctly after the last, for example. As mentioned previously, being written purely in PHP, R&OS PDF takes a little time to render large documents; you'll probably want to consider some kind of caching.

At the end of this section, I've provided a strategy that may help you plan your documents; overall, it's definitely worth the effort.

The first thing you'll need to do once you download the R&OS PDF library is edit the file `class.ezpdf.php` and comment out line three. Here's how the line should look:

File: **ThirdParty/rospdf/class.ezpdf.php** (in **SPLIB**) (excerpt)

```php
// include_once('class.pdf.php');
```

This allows you to place both classes in a subdirectory from which you can access them without having to add them to your `include_path`; it also means you have to include both classes specifically:

File: **1.php** (excerpt)

```php
<?php
error_reporting(E_ALL ^ E_NOTICE);

// Include the R&OS PDF Classes
require_once 'ThirdParty/rospdf/class.pdf.php';
require_once 'ThirdParty/rospdf/class.ezpdf.php';
```

Also notice the call to `error_reporting`, which is necessary because the R&OS PDF library produces a lot of notices if you don't suppress them (see Volume I, Chapter 10 for more on suppressing errors).

Now, let's see an example. I've created two text files, `intro.txt` and `body.txt` from Kevin Yank's first *Build your own Database Driven Website using PHP & MySQL* article[5]. I've made sure these are pure text (i.e. they contain no HTML formatting), so that we can concentrate on getting the PDF document to look right before we have to deal with HTML (we'll tackle that problem later in this chapter).

---

[5] http://www.sitepoint.com/article/228

```php
// Some information about the article
$title      = 'Build your own Database Driven Website using ' .
              'PHP & MySQL';
$author     = 'Kevin Kank';
$producer   = 'SitePoint';
$articleUrl = 'http://www.sitepoint.com/article/228';
$date       = 'October 1st 2001';

// Get the intro from a text file
$intro = file('intro.txt');
$intro = implode('', $intro);

// Get the body from a text file
$body  = file('body.txt');
$body  = implode('', $body);
```

This code sets up the environment in a way that will simulate a single database record later.

Now, we start up the PDF generation class. It uses an A4 page size by default.

```php
// Start the PDF document (A4 size x:595.28 y:841.89)
$pdf = &new Cezpdf();
```

Next, let's add the document information, which is available in Acrobat Reader from the File, Document Properties, Summary menu item:

```php
// Add document information (File > Document Properties > Summary)
$pdf->addInfo('Title', $title);
$pdf->addInfo('Author', $author);
$pdf->addInfo('Producer', $producer);
$pdf->addInfo('CreationDate', $date);
```

Next, we set the page margins relative to the outer edges of the page:

```php
// Set the page margins
$pdf->ezSetMargins(40, 40, 155.28, 90);
```

The class makes all measurements in **points**; a single point is 1/72 of an inch. This information is important when we're working out the coordinates to place elements on the page.

The Origin is at the Bottom Left

The position x = 0, y = 0 is at the bottom left side of the page. Make sure you remember that—it can be confusing, as we read from top to bottom.

Next, we create an object and store it in a variable, $headfoot. Objects created by the openObject method are used to create elements that will repeat throughout the document. On calling the openObject method, the class stops adding content to the main document, and adds content to the object instead. Here, we've created an object that will display the SitePoint logo at the top right of the page, as well as a horizontal line at the top and bottom of each page. The class will continue to add to the object until we call the closeObject method, at which point it returns to work on the main document.

File: **1.php (excerpt)**

```
// Set up header and footer as a recurring object
$headfoot = $pdf->openObject(); // Create object
$pdf->saveState(); // Save document state
$pdf->addJpegFromFile('sitepoint_logo.jpg', 430, 813, 70, 20);
$pdf->setStrokeColor(0, 0.2, 0.4); // set line color
$pdf->setLineStyle(2, 'round'); // set line style
$pdf->line(155.28, 811.89, 505.28, 811.89); // Add top line
$pdf->line(155.28, 30, 505.28, 30); // Add bottom line
$pdf->restoreState(); // Restore document state
$pdf->closeObject(); // Close the object
```

Note that I've used the saveState method to allow me to make temporary changes to colors, fonts and so on. When I'm done, the restoreState method lets me return to the original style values automatically.

Next I'll create another object which is a link which will appear on the bottom right of every even page, showing where the original HTML version can be found. Once created, I'll add both objects to the document with the addObject method.

File: **1.php (excerpt)**

```
// Set up bottom link object
$bottomUrl = $pdf->openObject(); // Create object
$pdf->saveState(); // Save document state
$pdf->selectFont('rospdf/fonts/Helvetica.afm'); // Select font
$pdf->addText(155.28, 24, 6, 'Found at: ' . $articleUrl);
$pdf->restoreState(); // Restore document state
$pdf->closeObject(); // Close the object

// Add the $headfoot object to every page (all,odd or even)
```

```
$pdf->addObject($headfoot, 'all'); // Add to 'all' pages

// Add the bottom URL to even pages
$pdf->addObject($bottomUrl, 'even'); // Add to 'even' pages
```

The following block of code builds a title page:

File: **1.php (excerpt)**

```
// Add the title page
$pdf->selectFont('rospdf/fonts/Helvetica-Bold.afm');
$pdf->ezSetY(650); // Set current Y position
$pdf->saveState(); // Save document state
$pdf->setColor(1, 0.4, 0); // Change the text color
$pdf->ezText($title, 20, array('justification' => 'center'));
$pdf->restoreState(); // Restore state (color returns to black)
$pdf->ezSetDy(-50); // Move down 50
$pdf->ezText('by ' . $author, 15,
  array('justification' => 'center')); // Author
$pdf->ezSetDy(-50); // Move down 50
$pdf->ezText("<c:alink:" . $articleUrl . ">" . $articleUrl .
            "</c:alink>", 11,
            array('justification' => 'centre'));
$pdf->ezSetDy(-50); // Move down 50
$pdf->ezText($date, 13, array('justification' => 'center'));
$pdf->ezSetDy(-50); // Move down 50
$pdf->selectFont('rospdf/fonts/Helvetica.afm'); // Change font
$pdf->ezText($intro, 10, array('justification' => 'full'));
$pdf->ezNewPage(); // New page
```

Notice that where we add the link, we use a special markup to wrap the text. This is a syntax provided by the R&OS PDF library to allow us to use special callback functions within the class. The c:alink tag is handled by an in-built method, called alink, that adds external links to text. You can define more tags like this by extending the Cezpdf class with another class and defining methods that correspond to tag names.

Also worthy of note is the use of the ezSetY and ezSetDy methods. The ezSetY method sets an absolute Y position (remember, 0 is at the bottom of the page) at which to begin placing content. The ezSetDy method moves the cursor vertically, relative to its last position (usually you provide a negative number to move the cursor down).

Where do I get .afm fonts?

About.com has a list of sources for free `.afm` fonts:

http://desktoppub.about.com/cs/postscriptfonts/

Finally, we start up the page number (after adding the title page) and add the body text:

File: **1.php (excerpt)**

```php
// Start the rest of the document
$pdf->ezStartPageNumbers(505, 24, 6); // Page numbering
$pdf->selectFont('rospdf/fonts/Helvetica.afm'); // Change font
$pdf->ezText($body, 10, array('justification' => 'full')); // Body

// Display the document
$pdf->ezStream();
?>
```

The library respects the new line character, so basic formatting is preserved. The `ezStream` method sends the finished PDF document straight to the Web browser, taking care to send the right HTTP headers. The alternative is the `output` method, which returns the document as a string that can be saved as a file.

Programming Tip

If your scripts automatically send HTTP headers that tell the browser not to cache pages, this causes problems when Internet Explorer renders PDF documents on the fly with R&OS PDF. Internet Explorer has a strange way of caching downloaded files, which involves making two requests for a file.

There are two solutions. You can avoid rendering PDF straight to the browser, instead using the `output` method to store it as a file that you can link to with HTML. Alternatively, make sure you don't send any headers that instruct the browser not to cache; rather, send a `Last-Modified` header set to the present time. See Chapter 5 for full details.

Figure 3.1 shows what the page generated by this example will look like in Acrobat Reader.

Figure 3.1. PDF on the Fly

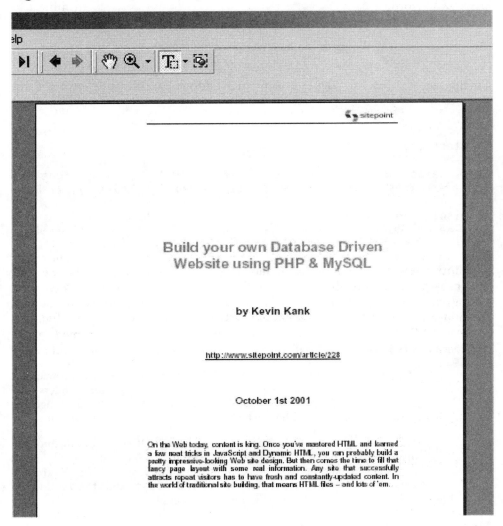

PDF Strategy

To summarize the code above into a more general strategy for creating documents with R&OS PDF,

1. Begin by defining the document margins; take note of the corresponding X and Y coordinates defining the edges of the margins, bearing in mind the paper size you're using.

2. Create objects for any elements that will repeat throughout the document. Headers and footers will generally appear outside the margins you've defined.

3. If you plan to have a title page, it's likely you won't want the headers and footers to appear there. Make sure you build the title page next, and make allowances to start page numbering, for example, afterwards.

4. Add the page numbering first, then start building the body of the document.

How do I convert HTML to PDF?

Before we can jump into rendering PDF straight from the content in our database, there's a problem we have to overcome. The content we've stored contains HTML markup that we can't simply "drop" into a PDF document. At the same time, the HTML is there for a good reason; it provides useful formatting for the content, positioning text and images correctly, adding links, and so on. We don't want to lose this formatting information, so we can't just strip it out; rather, we need to use it somehow to lay out the PDF document. For the solution, we turn toPEAR::XML_HTMLSax[7]. This is a SAX-like parser for "badly formed" XML documents, which will allow us to strip the HTML out of the content and at the same time take advantage of the formatting information it contains. The version used here was 2.0.2.

Parsing HTML with SAX?!?

HTML does not obey the rules of XML; by XML standards, most HTML code is badly formed. The basic specification allows for tags that are not closed and attributes that have no values. Worse still, Web browsers allow us to get away with murder, such as violating the tag nesting and case sensitivity rules (e.g. `<I><b>Text</I></B>`). Attempt to parse HTML with a normal XML parser, and it will pass you back error messages in disgust. In other words, the native SAX XML extension that comes with PHP won't do.[1]

---

[7] http://pear.php.net/XML_HTMLSax
[1]The good news is that newer incarnations of DOM will be able to parse HTML, but right now that's neither stable, nor widely available on common Web hosts.

But if a Web browser can understand HTML, why shouldn't you be able to parse it with PHP? You can! PEAR::XML_HTMLSax will let you get away with having a badly formed HTML document. As a parser, the `XML_HTMLSax` class guarantees to parse anything you give it without a word of complaint. The downside of this is that there are no warnings should something be seriously wrong with the HTML code. This places a greater burden on you to make sure the document is valid before you parse it.

Make sure you read the SAX related solutions in Chapter 2 for a general understanding of the principles behind SAX.

To see `XML_HTMLSax` in action, let's begin with a chunk of HTML stored in our database:

```
<p>If you've ever trawled the PHP listings over at Hotscripts in
search of a content management system to save you from writing
your own, you've probably run into
<a href="http://developer.ez.no/">eZ publish</a>, a PHP-based CMS
application, and thought <i><b>"Wow!"</i></b> Jubilant, you tried
to install it... to no avail. Desperately, you tried reading the
code, only to discover it made no sense whatsoever. Finally, you
skulked away to a quiet corner to lick your wounds, resorting to
PHP Nuke instead.

<p>This series is all about eZ publish and why it deserves the
title of "PHP's killer app." We'll start from the ground up:
first, we'll install eZ publish in your development environment.
```

You'll notice this exhibits two of the classic HTML problems; the `p` tags are not closed and we have some incorrectly nested tags here:

```
<i><b>"Wow!"</i></b>
```

Here's a simple example of how to parse it with `XML_HTMLSax`. First, as always, we need a class to act as the handler for `XML_HTMLSax`:

File: **XML/ParseHTML.php (in SPLIB) (excerpt)**

```
/**
 * ParseHTML class demonostrates simple parsing of HTML using
 * PEAR::XML_HTMLSax
 * <br />Defines handlers for responding to HTML elements<br />
 * Requires PEAR::XML_HTMLSax
 * @package SPLIB
 * @access public
 */
```

```
class ParseHTML {
  /**
   * Stores the parser
   * @var XML_HTMLSax instance of PEAR::XML_HTMLSax
   * @access private
   */
  var $parser;
  /**
   * ParseHTML Constructor sets up the parser
   * @access public
   */
  function ParseHTML()
  {
    $this->parser = &new XML_HTMLSax();
    $this->parser->set_object($this);
    $this->parser->set_element_handler('open', 'close');
    $this->parser->set_data_handler('data');
  }
```

In the constructor for ParseHTML, we set up XML_HTMLSax, telling it that we're
using the current object instance, $this, as the handler object, and the methods
open, close, and data to act as "listeners" for open and closing tags and the data
between them.

Next, we'll define the handler methods themselves, as well as the method parse,
which simply calls the XML_HTMLSax method of the same name:

File: **XML/ParseHTML.php (in SPLIB)** (excerpt)

```
  /**
   * Opening tag event "listener"
   * @param XML_HTMLSax the parser
   * @param string HTML tag name
   * @param array of tag attributes
   * @return void
   * @access private
   */
  function open($parser, $tag, $attr)
  {
    echo '<hr />Opening Tag: ' . $tag . '<br />';
    if (count($attr) > 0) {
      echo '...has attributes: <pre>';
      print_r($attr);
      echo '</pre>';
    }
  }
```

```php
/**
 * Closing tag event "listener"
 * @param XML_HTMLSax the parser
 * @param string HTML tag name
 * @return void
 * @access private
 */
function close($parser, $tag)
{
    echo 'Closing Tag: ' . $tag . '<br />';
}
/**
 * Character data event "listener"
 * @param XML_HTMLSax the parser
 * @param string character data
 * @return void
 * @access private
 */
function data($parser, $data)
{
    echo 'Character data: ' . $data . '<br />';
}
/**
 * Instructs the parser to parse some HTML
 * @param string HTML to parser
 * @return void
 * @access public
 */
function parse($html)
{
    $this->parser->parse($html);
}
}
```

Now, to use the class:

File: **2.php**

```php
<?php
// Include the PEAR::XML_HTMLSax
require_once 'XML/XML_HTMLSax.php';

// Include the ParseHTML class
require_once 'XML/ParseHTML.php';

// A Classic violation of XML rules...
$html = <<<EOD
```

```
<p>If you've ever trawled the PHP listings over at Hotscripts in
search of a content management system to save you from writing
your own, you've probably run into
<a href="http://developer.ez.no/">eZ publish</a>, a PHP-based CMS
application, and thought <i><b>"Wow!"</i></b> Jubilant, you tried
to install it... to no avail. Desperately, you tried reading the
code, only to discover it made no sense whatsoever. Finally, you
skulked away to a quiet corner to lick your wounds, resorting to
PHP Nuke instead.

<p>This series is all about eZ publish and why it deserves the
title of "PHP's killer app." We'll start from the ground up:
first, we'll install eZ publish in your development environment.
EOD;

// Create the parser
$parseHTML = new ParseHTML();

// Parse the HTML
$parseHTML->parse($html);
?>
```

The output at the moment is simply a breakdown of the HTML document as
XML_HTMLSax sees it, but we can use this approach to "respond" to HTML tags
in a manner that preserves the formatting as we render a PDF document.

Laying the Foundations

Before we set to work generating PDF from the content in our database, we need
some classes that will do the work of fetching articles in the first place, called
Articles and Article. The Articles class will fetch data from the database,
while the Article class will store the data and provide an API for fetching it.
With this in place, we can then render on top of the data stored by the Article
class any content type we like.

Looking at the public methods in the Articles class, the constructor takes an
instance of the MySQL class from Volume I, Chapter 3 that will be used by the
methods to fetch data:

File: **ExampleApps/Articles.php (in SPLIB) (excerpt)**

```
/**
 * Articles constructor
 * @param object instance of MySQL class
 * @access public
```

```
 */
function Articles(&$db)
{
  $this->db = &$db;
}
```

The `getArticles` method is used to tell the class to get a selection of articles. It can take the optional argument `$numRows` (the number of rows to fetch) and the argument `$startRow`, which is the row number from which to begin fetching. Internally, this method builds an array from the result, each element of the array corresponding to a row of article data. What's important to notice is that this method doesn't actually return any data—it simply prepares it for retrieval via another method.

File: **ExampleApps/Articles.php (in SPLIB) (excerpt)**

```
/**
 * Fetches a list of articles into the local array
 * @param int (optional) number of rows to fetch
 * @param int (optional) row to start from
 * @return boolean
 * @access public
 */
function getArticles($numRows = false, $startRow = false)
{
  $sql = "SELECT
              article_id, title, intro, body,
              author, published, public
            FROM articles
            ORDER BY published DESC";

  if ($numRows && $startRow) {
    $sql .= " LIMIT $startRow, $numRows";
  } else if ($numRows) {
    $sql .= " LIMIT $numRows";
  }

  $result = $this->db->query($sql);

  if ($result->isError()) {
    trigger_error('Articles::fetchArticles: ' .
                  'Unable to fetch articles');
    return FALSE;
  }

  while ($row = $result->fetch()) {
```

```
    $this->articles[] = $row;
  }

  return TRUE;
}
```

The getArticle method instructs the Articles class to collect a **single article**
from the database, given its article_id, then store the result in the internal array.

File: **ExampleApps/Articles.php (in SPLIB) (excerpt)**

```
/**
 * Fetches a single article into the local array
 * @param int article_id
 * @return boolean
 * @access public
 */
function getArticle($articleID)
{
  if (!is_numeric($articleID)) {
    trigger_error(
      'Articles::fetchArticle: Numeric value for ' .
      '$articleID required');
  }

  $articleID = addslashes($articleID);

  $sql = "SELECT
            article_id, title, intro, body,
            author, published, public
          FROM articles
          WHERE article_id = '$articleID'";
  $result = $this->db->query($sql);

  if ($result->isError()) {
    trigger_error('Articles::fetchArticle: ' .
                  'Unable to fetch article');
    return FALSE;
  }

  $this->articles[] = $result->fetch();
  return TRUE;
}
```

The fetch method acts as the iterator for fetching the articles from the array
that the Articles class has built. It returns a single object instance of the **Article**
class (see below), or FALSE when the end of the list has been reached.

File: **ExampleApps/Articles.php (in SPLIB) (excerpt)**

```
/**
 * Returns the current article from the internal array
 * and moves the internal array point forward
 * @return object instance of Article
 * @access public
 */
function fetch()
{
  $article = each($this->articles);
  if ($article) {
    return new Article($article['value']);
  } else {
    reset($this->articles);
    return FALSE;
  }
}
```

Note that the SQL queries in the above class are designed to be used with the articles table defined in Volume I, Chapter 3. The SQL queries to create this table and fill it with sample data may be found in the sql directory of the code archive.

The Article class is simply a store for the article data. The constructor stores in local variables all the article data it is given:

File: **ExampleApps/Article.php (in SPLIB) (excerpt)**

```
/**
 * Article constructor
 * @param array data from database contain an Article
 * @access public
 */
function Article($data)
{
  $this->article_id = isset($data['article_id']) ?
    $data['article_id'] : FALSE;
  $this->title = isset($data['title']) ?
    $data['title'] : FALSE;
  $this->title = isset($data['intro']) ?
    $data['intro'] : FALSE;
  $this->body = isset($data['body']) ?
    $data['body'] : FALSE;
  $this->author = isset($data['author']) ?
    $data['author'] : FALSE;
  $this->published = isset($data['published']) ?
```

```
    $data['published'] : FALSE;
  $this->public = isset($data['public']) ?
    $data['public'] : FALSE;
  }
```

This is followed by the methods that fetch the data from the class:

File: **ExampleApps/Article.php (in SPLIB) (excerpt)**

```
/**
 * Returns the article_id
 * @return int
 * @access public
 */
function id()
{
  return $this->article_id;
}

/**
 * Returns the article title
 * @return string
 * @access public
 */
function title()
{
  return $this->title;
}

/**
 * Returns the article intro
 * @return string
 * @access public
 */
function intro()
{
  return $this->intro;
}

/**
 * Returns the article title
 * @return string
 * @access public
 */
function body()
{
  return $this->body;
```

```php
    }

    /**
     * Returns the author
     * @return string
     * @access public
     */
    function author()
    {
      return $this->author;
    }

    /**
     * Returns the data published like "October 1st 2001"
     * @param string (optional) date format
     * @return string
     * @access public
     */
    function published($format = 'F jS Y')
    {
      return date($format, $this->published);
    }

    /**
     * Whether the article is "public" or not
     * @return boolean
     * @access public
     */
    function public()
    {
      return $this->public == 1 ? TRUE : FALSE;
    }
}
?>
```

The accessor methods above give us an API to the data in the article. Although this class is relatively simplistic right now, the reason we made it a class was to give us an easy way to apply transformations on the data, such as those made with the `published` method, which converts the UNIX timestamp stored in the database to a human-readable timestamp.

Putting it Together

Now that we have classes to help us access the data and, from earlier in the chapter, a general design for our PDF documents, we need a class to act as the interface to R&OS PDF and reduce the process of building the PDF document to a few simple methods. We can then use these methods in conjunction with XML_HTMLSax to render documents directly from the content we've stored in the database.

This class is designed specifically for the PDF format we designed earlier in this chapter, but it shouldn't be difficult to modify it for your own purposes, while keeping the method names the same. Here are the key parts of the class.

The constructor takes the URL at which the original article can be found, as well as an optional value for the fonts and image directory paths.

File: **ExampleApps/ArticlePDF.php (in SPLIB) (excerpt)**

```
/**
 * ArticlePdf constructor
 * @param string URL of the article
 * @param string font path
 * @param string image path
 */
function ArticlePdf($url, $fontPath, $imagePath = '')
{
  $this->articleUrl = $url;
  $this->fontPath   = $fontPath;
  $this->imagePath  = $imagePath;
  $this->pdf        = &new Cezpdf();
  $this->pdf->ezSetMargins(40, 40, 155.28, 90);
  $this->addObjects();
}
```

The addInfo method is used to add the Acrobat summary information about the document.

File: **ExampleApps/ArticlePDF.php (in SPLIB) (excerpt)**

```
/**
 * Adds the PDF summary information
 * @param string title of document
 * @param string author of document
 * @param string producer of document
 * @param string date
 * @return void
 * @access public
 */
function addInfo($title, $author, $producer, $date)
{
  $info = array (
```

```
      'Title' => $title,
      'Author' => $author,
      'Producer' => $producer,
      'CreationDate' => $date
    );
    $this->pdf->addInfo($info);
}
```

The addTitlePage method builds the first page of the document.

File: **ExampleApps/ArticlePDF.php (in SPLIB) (excerpt)**

```
/**
 * Adds the title page
 * @param string title of document
 * @param string author of document
 * @param string date
 * @param string introduction
 * @return void
 * @access public
 */
function addTitlePage($title, $author, $date, $intro) {
    $this->pdf->selectFont($this->fontPath .
        'Helvetica-Bold.afm');
    $this->pdf->ezSetY(650);
    $this->pdf->saveState();
    $this->pdf->setColor(1, 0.4, 0);
    $this->pdf->ezText($title, 20,
        array('justification' => 'center'));
    $this->pdf->restoreState();
    $this->pdf->ezSetDy(-50);
    $this->pdf->ezText('by ' . $author, 15,
        array('justification' => 'center'));
    $this->pdf->ezSetDy(-50);
    $this->pdf->ezText("<c:alink:" . $this->articleUrl . ">" .
        $this->articleUrl . "</c:alink>",
        11, array('justification' => 'centre'));
    $this->pdf->ezSetDy(-50);
    $this->pdf->ezText($date, 13,
        array('justification' => 'center'));
    $this->pdf->ezSetDy(-50);
    $this->pdf->selectFont($this->fontPath . 'Helvetica.afm');
    $this->pdf->ezText($intro, 10,
        array('justification' => 'full'));
    $this->pdf->ezNewPage();
    $this->pdf->ezStartPageNumbers(505, 24, 6);
}
```

The `addText` method wraps the `ezText` method to provide a method for use with `XML_HTMLSax` (coming shortly).

File: **ExampleApps/ArticlePDF.php (in SPLIB) (excerpt)**

```php
/**
 * Adds the text to the page
 * @param string text
 * @param int (optional) size of text
 * @param string (optional) justification
 * @return void
 * @access public
 */
function addText($text, $size = 10, $justification = 'full')
{
  $this->pdf->ezText($text, $size,
    array('justification' => $justification));
}
```

The `display` method wraps the `ezStream` method, which sends the PDF document to the browser. It provides a filename that will be given to the document once the format of that filename is checked.

File: **ExampleApps/ArticlePDF.php (in SPLIB) (excerpt)**

```php
/**
 * Sends the PDF document to the visitors browser
 * @param string (optional) filename
 * @return void
 * @access public
 */
function display($fileName = 'file.pdf')
{
  $fileName = explode(',', chunk_split($fileName, 1, ','));
  foreach ($fileName as $key => $char) {
    if (preg_match("/^[A-Za-z0-9_\.]$/",
        $char, $matches) == 0) {
      unset($fileName[$key]);
    }
  }
  $fileName = implode('', $fileName);
  $options = array('Content-Disposition' => $fileName);
  $this->pdf->ezStream($options);
}
```

As you can see, the process of building the PDF document is now wrapped up in three simple methods, plus the constructor, and precludes any code that uses the class from having to work directly with the R&OS PDF API. As well as making it much easier to generate documents to our design, this also helps us should we decide we want to switch to FPDF, or one of the native PHP extensions. We can use an adapter pattern (see Chapter 7) to deal with the specifics of those libraries, while still conforming to the `ArticlePDF` class's API, which means that any code using `ArticlePDF` shouldn't require much modification.

Note that in the case of R&OS PDF, the author provides a special markup for constructing links in the PDF document that's too tempting to ignore, so the principle of building a library-independent API for generating PDF document does not quite hold true here. However, with some further effort you could, no doubt, make it possible to switch libraries, should you need to, with minimal requirement for code modifications.

Let's take `ArticlePDF` for a little test drive:

File: **3.php**

```php
<?php
// Include the PdfArticle class
require_once 'ExampleApps/ArticlePDF.php';

// Define font path - MODIFY THIS!!!
$fontPath = 'c:/htdocs/phpanth/SPLIB/ThirdParty/rospdf/fonts/';

// Some information about the article
$title      = 'Build your own Database Driven Website using ' .
              'PHP & MySQL';
$author     = 'Kevin Kank';
$producer   = 'SitePoint';
$articleUrl = 'http://www.sitepoint.com/article/228';
$date       = 'October 1st 2001";

// Get the intro from a text file
$intro = file('intro.txt');
$intro = implode('', $intro);

// Get the body from a text file
$body = file('body.txt');
$body = implode('', $body);

$pdfArticle = new ArticlePDF($articleUrl, $fontPath);
$pdfArticle->addInfo($title, $author, $producer, $date);
$pdfArticle->addTitlePage($title, $author, $date, $intro);
$pdfArticle->addText($body);
```

```
$pdfArticle->display();
?>
```

With that class ready, next, we need to put together a handler class that will use **XML_HTMLSax** and listen for HTML tags. This class will also use the **ArticlePDF** class and, as it encounters HTML tags, will use the **ArticlePDF** API to generate the PDF document. The handler itself builds up a text buffer of the HTML it has parsed, adding any R&OS PDF markup for links, bold, and italic tags as it finds them. The text buffer will then be committed to the document every time an opening p or br tag is encountered. HTML header tags (e.g. h5) will be treated as a special case, as they're committed to the document immediately.

Here are the key parts of this class from the point of view of how we'd use it. The constructor takes an instance of the **ArticlePDF** class as its only parameter. This allows us to use **ArticlePDF** to start creating the document (such as adding the title page) *outside* of HTMLtoPDF, then pass it to the constructor in preparation for writing HTML content to the PDF. The constructor instantiates XML_HTMLSax as we saw before with the **ParseHTML** class.

File: **XML/HTMLtoPDF.php (in SPLIB) (excerpt)**

```
/**
 * HTMLtoPDF Constructor
 * @param ArticlePDF instance of ArticlePDF
 * @access public
 */
function HTMLtoPDF(&$articlePDF)
{
  $this->articlePDF = &$articlePDF;
  $this->parser = new XML_HTMLSax();
  $this->parser->set_object($this);
  $this->parser->set_element_handler('open', 'close');
  $this->parser->set_data_handler('data');
}
```

The two remaining public methods are the **parse** method, which tells the parser to begin work, and the **getPdf** method, which returns the completed document after parsing is finished.

File: **XML/HTMLtoPDF.php (in SPLIB) (excerpt)**

```
/**
 * Triggers parsing and converts newlines to &lt;br /%gt;
 * @param string HTML document
 * @return void
 * @access public
```

```
*/
function parse($html)
{
  $this->parser->parse(nl2br($html));
}

/**
 * Adds any remaining text in the buffer then
 * returns the ArticlePDF object
 * @return object instance of ArticlePDF
 * @access public
 */
function getPdf()
{
  $this->articlePDF->addText($this->buffer);
  return $this->articlePDF;
}
```

The internals of the class—the handler methods themselves—look like this:

File: **XML/HTMLtoPDF.php (in SPLIB)** (excerpt)

```
/**
 * Opening tag event "listener"
 * @param XML_HTMLSax instance of the parser
 * @param string HTML tag name
 * @param array of tag attributes
 * @return void
 * @access private
 */
function open($parser, $tag, $attr)
{
  $tag = strtolower($tag); // Convert tag to lower case
  switch ($tag) {
    case 'a':
      if (isset($attr['href'])) {
        $this->open  = '<c:alink:' . $attr['href'] . '>';
        $this->close = '</c:alink>';
      }
      break;
    case 'b':
      $this->open  = '<b>';
      $this->close = '</b>';
      break;
    case 'br':
      $this->articlePDF->addText($this->buffer);
      $this->buffer = '';
```

```
        break;
    case 'h1':
      $this->header = '12';
      break;
    case 'h2':
      $this->header = '10';
      break;
    case 'h3':
      $this->header = '8';
      break;
    case 'h4':
      $this->header = '6';
      break;
    case 'h5':
      $this->header = '4';
      break;
    case 'i':
      $this->open  = '<i>';
      $this->close = '</i>';
      break;
    case 'p':
      $this->articlePDF->addText($this->buffer);
      $this->buffer = '';
      break;
    case 'strong':
      $this->open  = '<b>';
      $this->close = '</b>';
      break;
  }
}
/**
 * Character data event "listener"
 * @param XML_HTMLSax instance of the parser
 * @param string character data
 * @return void
 * @access private
 */
function data($parser, $data)
{
  $data = str_replace(
    array('&gt;', '&lt;', '&quot;', '&amp;', ' '),
    array('>', '<', '"', '&', ' '),
    $data);
  if (isset($this->open) && isset($this->close)) {
    $this->buffer .= $this->open . $data . $this->close;
    $this->open   = NULL;
```

```
      $this->close  = NULL;
   } else if (isset($this->header)) {
      $this->articlePDF->addText($data, 10 + $this->header,
         'left');
      $this->header = NULL;
   } else {
      $this->buffer .= $data;
   }
}
/**
 * Closing tag event "listener"
 * @param XML_HTMLSax instance of the parser
 * @param string HTML tag name
 * @return void
 * @access private
 */
function close($parser, $tag)
{
   // Do nothing
}
```

We won't go into the handlers too deeply here, but suffice it to say that the strategy we've employed deals with tags in either the open or data handler, ignoring the close handler. This helps us cope with HTML such as unclosed p and br tags.

Now we're ready. Using together all the classes we've defined so far, we have a collection of code that allows us to render articles as both HTML and PDF:

File: **4.php (excerpt)**

```php
<?php
// No time limit for large documents
set_time_limit(0);

// Include the MySQL class
require_once 'Database/MySQL.php';

// Include the two data fetching article classes
require_once 'ExampleApps/Articles.php';

// Include the ArticlePDF class
require_once 'ExampleApps/ArticlePDF.php';

// Include the HTMLtoPDF converter
require_once 'XML/HTMLtoPDF.php';
```

```
// Define font path - MODIFY THIS!!!
$fontPath = 'c:/htdocs/phpanth/SPLIB/ThirdParty/rospdf/fonts/';
```

First, we set the time limit of the execution of this code to unlimited; rendering large PDF documents can take more than PHP's default thirty-second execution time.

Then, we include all the classes we need. Some of these include other classes in turn, such as the R&OS PDF classes and PEAR::XML_HTMLSax, so that a total of eight classes are involved in the process of turning our HTML-based content into a PDF document. Despite the number, the code that uses the classes is very simple and again exemplifies why object oriented programming is a Good Thing[8]; in developing each class, we were able to focus on each problem we were trying to solve "in a box", without having to struggle through reams of procedural code. The classes hide the complexity of the problem behind their API, making the code that finally delivers a document to an end user fairly simple.

Next, we set up a couple of variables that we need for PDF generation, then we start up the `MySQL` and `Articles` classes, which allow us to fetch articles from the database.

File: **4.php (excerpt)**

```
// Define variables for MySQL class
$host   = 'localhost'; // Hostname of MySQL server
$dbUser = 'harryf';    // Username for MySQL
$dbPass = 'secret';    // Password for user
$dbName = 'sitepoint'; // Database name

// Settings for PDF generation
$baseUrl =
'http://localhost/phpanth/AlternativeContentTypes/4.php?id=';
$producer = 'SitePoint';

// Instantiate MySQL class
$db = &new MySQL($host, $dbUser, $dbPass, $dbName);

// Instantiate Articles class
$articles = new Articles($db);
```

We use simple `if-else` constructs to decide which content to display. In a production environment, we might consider building a class to handle these decisions,

---

[8] http://info.astrian.net/jargon/terms/g/Good_Thing.html

but for this example `if-elses` will suffice. As you can see, if the URL ends with `?id=3&mime=pdf`, it will display the article with the ID 3 in PDF format.

File: **4.php (excerpt)**

```php
// If viewing an article
if (isset($_GET['id'])) {

  // Get the article from the client class
  if ($articles->getArticle($_GET['id'])) {

    // Fetch the article object
    $article = $articles->fetch();

    // If PDF format has been requested
    if (isset($_GET['mime']) && $_GET['mime'] == 'pdf') {
```

Here's how the PDF generation code works:

File: **4.php (excerpt)**

```php
    // Instantiate the PdfArticle class
    $articlePDF = &new ArticlePDF($baseUrl . $article->id(),
      $fontPath);

    // Add the "meta" information
    $articlePDF->addInfo($article->title(),
                         $article->author(),
                         $producer,
                         $article->published());

    // Add the title page
    $articlePDF->addTitlePage($article->title(),
                              $article->author(),
                              $article->published(),
                              $article->intro());

    // Instantiate the HTMLtoPDF class
    $htmlToPdf = new HTMLtoPDF($articlePDF);

    // Parse the article body
    $htmlToPdf->parse($article->body());

    // Get back the ArticlePDF object
    $articlePDF = $htmlToPdf->getPdf();

    // Display the PDF document
    $articlePDF->display($article->title() . '.pdf');
```

```
    // Terminate execution to avoid mixed headers
    exit();
} else {
```

It's very simple. You can examine the rest of the code on your own, as it's pure HTML and very similar to examples we've seen in earlier chapters, such as Chapter 2.

We now have the option of displaying either HTML, as shown in Figure 3.2...

Figure 3.2. Article as HTML

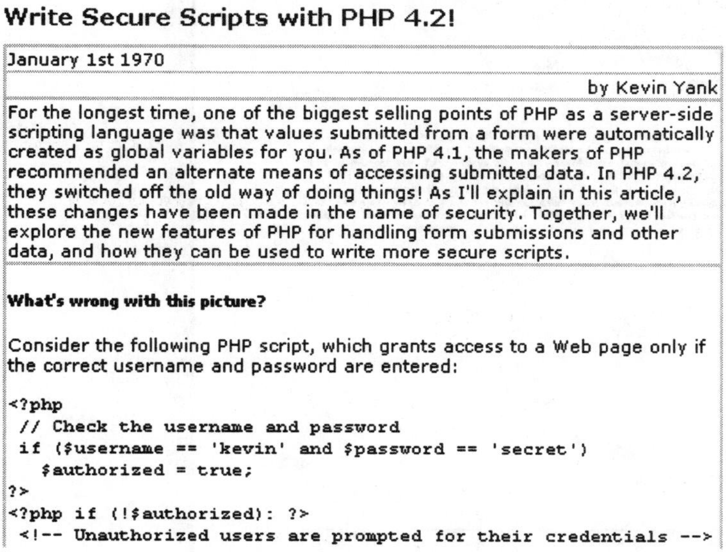

Write Secure Scripts with PHP 4.2!

January 1st 1970	
	by Kevin Yank

For the longest time, one of the biggest selling points of PHP as a server-side scripting language was that values submitted from a form were automatically created as global variables for you. As of PHP 4.1, the makers of PHP recommended an alternate means of accessing submitted data. In PHP 4.2, they switched off the old way of doing things! As I'll explain in this article, these changes have been made in the name of security. Together, we'll explore the new features of PHP for handling form submissions and other data, and how they can be used to write more secure scripts.

What's wrong with this picture?

Consider the following PHP script, which grants access to a Web page only if the correct username and password are entered:

```php
<?php
 // Check the username and password
 if ($username == 'kevin' and $password == 'secret')
    $authorized = true;
?>
<?php if (!$authorized): ?>
 <!-- Unauthorized users are prompted for their credentials -->
```

...or PDF, as shown in Figure 3.3!

Figure 3.3. Article as PDF

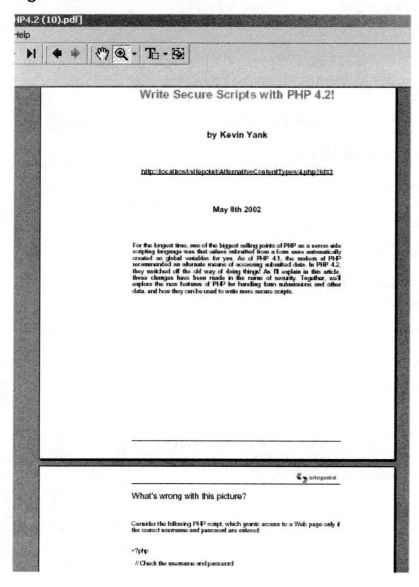

It's also important to realize that creating the correct **layers** in our application helped us reuse the data we fetched from the database to deliver multiple (and radically different) content types. This organization is illustrated in Figure 3.4.

Figure 3.4. Layered Application

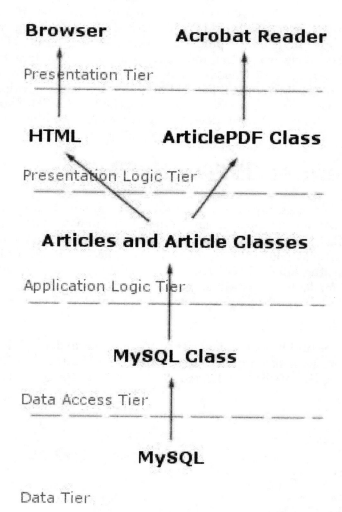

Using the layering in this application, we were able to take the data delivered from the application logic tier and render *both* HTML and PDF at the presentation logic tier. For a more detailed discussion of layering and N-Tier applications, see Chapter 6.

An alternative, and potentially more powerful approach to that presented here would be to take advantage of **XSL Formatting Objects**[9] (XSL-FO), an XML standard designed to provide page-based formatting for XML documents. By using XML_HTMLSax to convert the stored HTML into XML-FO formatting instructions, you could use an XSL-FO processor, such as the Apache FOP[10] (Formatting Objects Processor) project, to render it directly to PDF format. You could even get away from XML_HTMLSax, thanks to an interesting open source project that converts HTML to XSL-FO, HTML2FO[11], which is written in C++ and is available for most platforms. To use Apache FOP in PHP, you can look to PEAR::XML_fo2pdf[12]. This does, however, require use of the PHP Java extension as well as the Java SDK, which few hosts offer.

How do I render SVG with PHP?

Scalable Vector Graphics[13] (SVG) is a W3C XML standard for describing graphics. As a technology, it represents an alternative to animated GIFs or Flash movies. Being XML, it is more easily renderable with PHP than are binary formats such as Flash. To display your SVG creations, a visitor needs a browser plug-in, which today means the Adobe SVG Viewer[14]. Adobe is one of the main promoters of SVG. Mozilla browsers will also have SVG support built right in[15] relatively soon, and the Apache Group provides a Java-based SVG viewer known as Batik[16].

It's beyond the scope of this book to look at the SVG format in detail, but you'll find an excellent resource listed under the section called "Further Reading" at the end of this chapter. A worthwhile, and free, tool for drawing simple SVG images is Dia[17].

[9] http://www.w3.org/TR/xsl/
[10] http://xml.apache.org/fop/index.html
[11] http://html2fo.sourceforge.net/
[12] http://pear.php.net/XML_fo2pdf
[13] http://www.w3.org/TR/SVG/
[14] http://www.adobe.com/svg/viewer/install/main.html
[15] http://www.mozilla.org/projects/svg/
[16] http://xml.apache.org/batik/index.html
[17] http://www.lysator.liu.se/~alla/dia/

Here's a simple example of a PHP script that renders an SVG image (you'll need a viewer to see it):

File: **5.php**

```php
<?php
header('Content-type: image/svg+xml');
echo '<?xml version="1.0" encoding="ISO-8859-1" standalone="no"?>';
?>
<!DOCTYPE svg PUBLIC "-//W3C//DTD SVG 20010904//EN"
  "http://www.w3.org/TR/2001/REC-SVG-20010904/DTD/svg10.dtd">
<svg xmlns="http://www.w3.org/2000/svg"
     xmlns:xlink="http://www.w3.org/1999/xlink">
  <circle cx="50" cy="50" r="40" fill="navy"/>
</svg>
```

First, we send the SVG `Content-type` header to tell the client browser what it's dealing with, then we simply display the SVG document as plain text.

 Tip

XML Processing Instructions and PHP

The XML specification recommends that all XML documents should begin with a `<?xml ?>` processing instruction that identifies the version of XML in use and a number of options, like the character set. In the case of XHTML documents, it is currently prudent to leave out this optional element, because it interferes with Internet Explorer 6 for Windows' ability to identify the document type.

In other documents, like the SVG document above, this element should be included, however. Unfortunately, the default configuration will cause the PHP engine to attempt to process XML processing instructions as if they contain PHP code, producing nasty error messages.

To get around this, you need to write the processing instruction with a PHP `echo` statement, as demonstrated in the example above.

Viewing this page displays a circle in navy blue with a radius of forty pixels, which is centered at x = 50, y =50 from the top left of the image, as shown in Figure 3.5.

Figure 3.5. Join the Dots

The following tag embeds an SVG image in an HTML document:

```
<object data="image.svg" width="100" height="100"
  type="image/svg+xml" />
```

 Tip

SVG and Netscape 4

Since Netscape 4 doesn't support the `object` tag, you need to use an `embed` tag to display SVG in this antiquated browser:

```
<embed src="image.svg" width="100" height="100"
    type="image/svg+xml" />
```

Be aware that `embed` is not standards-compliant HTML, and should therefore be avoided if you can spare Netscape 4 support.

What makes SVG a potentially powerful tool when combined with PHP is its ability to render fully interactive images that not only look good but, with some help from JavaScript, are able to "do" things such as communicate with a Website using simple HTTP GET/POST requests, or even take advantage of the Web services protocols XML-RPC and SOAP. The implementation of such functionality relies on the viewer and, where Web services are concerned, there is still some more work to do. Adobe is planning to release version 4 of the viewer, while the Batik project is making steady progress and will likely reach the same point as Adobe eventually. Mozilla is further ahead, providing SOAP and XML-RPC support courtesy of the XPCom library (more on that later). Some early adopters have had success implementing SOAP and XML-RPC clients in JavaScript.

Where SVG has really taken off, though, is in rendering online maps. An example that shows the potential is the Open SVG Map Server[18], which provides some fascinating examples of what SVG and PHP can do together. I've also heard of a company using PHP and SVG to implement a nationwide IP router monitoring tool, which displays network status against an interactive SVG map from a Website. For an interactive map of Canada, try http://www.svgmapper.com/example/example3/North_America.htm.

SVG Network Clock

To give you a feel for SVG's potential, here's an SVG digital clock that gets the time from a PHP script:

---

[18] http://www.carto.net/projects/open_svg_mapserver/

```php
<?php
// Send SVG header
header('Content-type: image/svg+xml');
echo '<?xml version="1.0" encoding="ISO-8859-1" standalone="no"?>';

// Edit this line
$timeUrl =
  'http://localhost/sitepoint/AlternativeContentTypes/7.php';
?>
<!DOCTYPE svg PUBLIC "-//W3C//DTD SVG 20010904//EN"
  "http://www.w3.org/TR/2001/REC-SVG-20010904/DTD/svg10.dtd">
<svg width="100%" height="100%" xmlns="http://www.w3.org/2000/svg"
  xmlns:xlink="http://www.w3.org/1999/xlink"
  onload="init(evt);">
<script type="text/ecmascript">
<![CDATA[
  var clock;

  function init(e) {
    if (window.svgDocument == null) {
      svgDocument = e.target.ownerDocument;
    }
    clock = svgDocument.getElementById("clock").firstChild;
    getTime();
  }
  function getTime() {
    getURL('<?php echo $timeUrl; ?>', showTime);
  }
  function showTime(response) {
    clock.data = response.content;
    setTimeout('getTime()', 1000);
  }
]]>
</script>
<text id="clock" x="80" y="20" fill="navy" text-anchor="middle">
  Time goes here
</text>
</svg>
```

The SVG example above uses JavaScript (also known as ECMAScript) to fetch the contents of a URL using the SVG getUrl function. The SVG image updates itself every second, repeating the fetch from the script:

File: **7.php**

```php
<?php
echo date('H:i:s d M Y');
?>
```

To display, we use a simple piece of HTML:

File: **8.php**

```html
<!DOCTYPE html PUBLIC "-//W3C//DTD XHTML 1.0 Transitional//EN"
  "http://www.w3.org/TR/xhtml1/DTD/xhtml1-transitional.dtd">
<html xmlns="http://www.w3.org/1999/xhtml">
<head>
<title> SVG Network Clock </title>
<meta http-equiv="Content-Type"
  content="text/html; charset=iso-8859-1" />
</head>
<style type="text/css">
body {
    font-family: verdana;
    font-size: 13px;
    font-weight: bold;
    color: red;
}
</style>
<body>
<p>The time sponsored by SVG is<br />
<object data="6.php" width="200" height="30"
  type="image/svg+xml" />
</p>
</body>
</html>
```

The result is a clock that updates itself from your Web server every second (barring network delays), as shown in Figure 3.6

Figure 3.6. SVGWatch

19:00:54 11 Oct 2003

Obviously, this is a somewhat irritating example that will have your site's visitors running for miles, but it demonstrates the basic principle nicely. What's more, Adobe have been sure to implement JavaScript within their viewer to a degree that's comparable to Mozilla, so there are no hassles regarding browsers that don't support your code.

Most work editing SVG documents is likely to be done with tools like Adobe's Illustrator or GoLive, but as SVG is, in the end, just text, there's no reason why you shouldn't render a complete SVG using PHP. A solid basis for getting started is Charlie Killian's SVG classes[20], which were described in some detail in Wrox's *Professional PHP 4 XML*. The book has a full chapter on SVG, so if you're interested, grab a copy while they can still be found.

How do I render WML with PHP?

Wireless Markup Language (WML) is an XML format designed to allow hand held devices to access content on the Web using **Wireless Application Protocol** (WAP). As the first generations of WAP enabled devices use LCD displays and are usually grayscale, developing WML based sites may not seem too exciting, but the potential for teams of people on the go to work together via a WML-based site makes it an interesting technology.

The first problem to overcome when trying to develop WML-based sites is finding a browser that displays WML. Obviously, your mobile network provider would love you to do the testing with your own phone, but that's a fast track to a large bill. Thankfully, Opera (ideally version 7+) comes ripe with WML support and is perfect for designing a WML-based site. Not too far behind is Mozilla with a WML browser[21] that's currently a work in progress, but should be fairly handy in the not too distant future, thanks to the ease of developing XUL applications (see the next solution).

With that problem solved, it's time to build a WML page with a little help from PHP:

File: **9.php**

```php
<?php
header('Content-type: text/vnd.wap.wml');
echo '<?xml version="1.0"?>';
?>
<!DOCTYPE wml PUBLIC "-//WAPFORUM//DTD WML 1.1//EN"
  "http://www.wapforum.org/DTD/wml_1.1.xml">
<wml>
<card id="index" title="PHP and WAP in Action" newcontext="true">
  <big>Menu:</big><br />
  <a href="#news">News</a><br/>
  <a href="#products">Products</a><br/>
```

[20] http://www.phpclasses.org/browse.html/package/457.html
[21] http://wmlbrowser.mozdev.org/

```
</card>

<card id="news" title="News">
  <p align="right"><small><a href="#index">Back</a></small></p>
  <big>News:</big><br />
  <a href="#news1">Something happened</a><br />
  <a href="#news2">Something else happened</a><br />
</card>

<card id="news1" title="Something happened">
  <p align="right"><small><a href="#index">Back</a></small></p>
  Yep something happened.
</card>

<card id="news2" title="Something else happened">
  <p align="right"><small><a href="#index">Back</a></small></p>
  Oh and something else happened
</card>

<card id="products" title="For Sale">
  <p align="right"><small><a href="#index">Back</a></small></p>
  Here are some things to buy...
</card>
</wml>
```

WML is designed to limit the number of requests a browser has to make, which reflects the fact that mobile networks are not high speed, and makes using WML-based sites friendly on the thumb. Hence, a WML document is made up of **cards,** which are separate pages loaded at the same time. The above examples should give you a feel for the markup, which is very similar to HTML for the most part, though be warned—WML must conform to the rules of well formed XML (e.g. tags must be closed).

"Internal" links can be made between cards using #id_name, which points at the id attribute of another card. Links to other WML documents are handled in the same way as an HTML link, and there's even support for forms. An online reference is suggested at the end of this chapter.

Figure 3.7 shows what the front page of our simple example looks like in Opera.

Figure 3.7. A WML Article Listing

HAWHAW

Now that we understand the basics, it's time to meet HAWHAW[22] (the HTML and WML hybrid adapted Webserver), a PHP class library that makes serving WML pages easy. Using HAWHAW to construct WML pages is much like using the DOM extension to create XML, as we saw in Chapter 2. In the HAWHAW document model, the parent of all elements is the `HAW_deck` class, to which other elements are added, as described in the online documentation[23].

HAWHAW doesn't make use of multiple cards, but instead places all elements within a single card. This is to some extent a shortcoming, but helps HAWHAW provide support for older wireless formats, including HDML, as well as other formats such as MML, which is used by some Japanese devices.

The code for this chapter includes the HAWHAW library.[2]

At the start of this chapter, we looked at rendering PDF files from the `articles` table. Here's how we could render WML from the same data:

File: **10.php (excerpt)**

```php
<?php
// Switch off error notices - required for HAWHAW
error_reporting(E_ALL ^ E_NOTICE);

// Include MySQL, Articles and Article class
require_once 'Database/MySQL.php';
require_once 'ExampleApps/Articles.php';


// Include the HAWHAW library
require_once 'ThirdParty/hawhaw/hawhaw.php';

// Define variables for MySQL class
$host    = 'localhost'; // Hostname of MySQL server
$dbUser = 'harryf';     // Username for MySQL
$dbPass = 'secret';     // Password for user
$dbName = 'sitepoint'; // Database name

// (Modify this) Specify the root URL of the site
```

---

[22] http://www.hawhaw.de/
[23] http://www.hawhaw.de/ref/php/
[2]I've renamed the file from `hawhaw.inc` to `hawhaw.php`. Files that Apache doesn't recognize as being PHP have a nasty habit of being open to public viewing.

```
$url =
  'http://localhost/sitepoint/AlternativeContentTypes/10.php';
```

Note that we have to switch error notices off, otherwise HAWHAW will generate some minor complaints about undefined variables and ruin our austere WML output. The $url variable is used to make life simpler when we build links in the document.

Now, we must instantiate the MySQL and Articles classes as before. We then instantiate the root node class Haw_deck, passing it the document title. The set_waphome method is used to specify a URL that is only displayed to Web browsers. HAWHAW renders a simple HTML page (shown at the end of this code) with a "Powered by HAWHAW" link that points to the value specified by set_waphome, via a logging script on the HAWHAW Website. This link is only displayed to Web browsers, not to WAP devices.

File: **10.php (excerpt)**

```
// Instantiate MySQL class
$db = &new MySQL($host, $dbUser, $dbPass, $dbName);

// Instantiate Articles class
$articles = new Articles($db);

// Instantiate the HAW_Deck root node
$wml = new HAW_deck('SitePoint Articles');

// For Web browsers...
$wml->set_waphome('http://www.sitepoint.com/');
```

The HAW_Deck class comes with methods for the addition of other elements, so the next step is to create a HAW_Link node, give it some text to display and a URL to link to, and then add it using the add_link method. This demonstrates how we can add elements to the root node:

File: **10.php (excerpt)**

```
// Instantiate HAW_link for the "Home" url
$home = new HAW_link('Home', $url);

// Add the link to the WML document
$wml->add_link($home);
```

To display a single article, we've opted to use a table, adding each element from the table as a new row. Here we see the process of adding the title to the table:

File: **10.php** (excerpt)

```php
// If viewing a single article
if (isset($_GET['id'])) {
  // Prepare the article
  if ($articles->getArticle($_GET['id'])) {
    // Get the article object
    $article = $articles->fetch();

    // Create a HAW_Table
    $table = new HAW_table();

    // Create a HAW_Row
    $row = new HAW_row();

    // Create a text node for the title
    $title = new HAW_text($article->title(),
      HAW_TEXTFORMAT_BOLD);

    // Add the title to the row
    $row->add_column($title);

    // Add the row to the table
    $table->add_row($row);
```

The subsequent rows follow the same pattern. Finally, we add the table to the root node using the add_table method. Note that we've chosen not to display the body of the article, as many mobile devices can only handle a limited amount of text. We'll simply tease visitors with the introductory section, in which you'll note we used PHP's strip_tags function to ensure no HTML markup finds its way into the WML page.

File: **10.php** (excerpt)

```php
    // The author row
    $row = new HAW_row();
    $author = new HAW_text($article->author(),
      HAW_TEXTFORMAT_SMALL);
    $row->add_column($author);
    $table->add_row($row);

    // The date row
    $row = new HAW_row();
    $date = new HAW_text($article->published(),
      HAW_TEXTFORMAT_SMALL);
    $row->add_column($date);
    $table->add_row($row);
```

```
// The intro
$row = new HAW_row();
$intro = new HAW_text(strip_tags($article->intro()),
  HAW_TEXTFORMAT_SMALL);
$row->add_column($intro);
$table->add_row($row);

// Add table to document
$wml->add_table($table);
```

If there's any problem displaying the article, we can provide the visitor with an error message:

File: **10.php (excerpt)**

```
} else {
  // Error message
  $wml->add_text(new HAW_text('Sorry:', HAW_TEXTFORMAT_BIG));
  $wml->add_text(
    new HAW_text('Service unavailable at this time'));
}
```

If the visitor isn't viewing a single article, the following code handles the request:

File: **10.php (excerpt)**

```
} else {
  if ($articles->getArticles()) {
    // Build a table and loop through the rows
    $table = new HAW_table();
    while ($article = $articles->fetch()) {
      $row = new HAW_row();
      $title = new HAW_link($article->title(),
        $url . '?id=' . $article->id());
      $author = new HAW_text($article->author(),
        HAW_TEXTFORMAT_SMALL);
      $row->add_column($title);
      $row->add_column($author);
      $table->add_row($row);
    }
    $wml->add_table($table);
  } else {
    $wml->add_text(new HAW_text('Sorry:', HAW_TEXTFORMAT_BIG));
    $wml->add_text(
      new HAW_text('Service unavailable at this time'));
  }
}
```

Essentially, it's the same thing, but we build the rows within the `while` loop.

Finally, we display the page and HAWHAW takes care of the rest:

File: **10.php (excerpt)**

```
// Display the page
$wml->create_page();
?>
```

The result is shown in Figure 3.8.

Figure 3.8. A WML Table

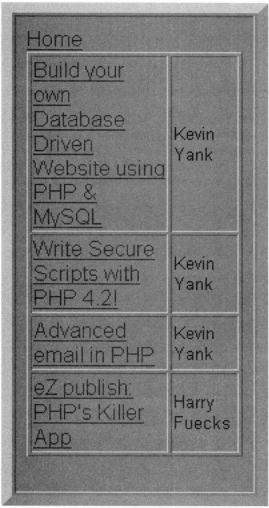

One point to note about HAWHAW is that in its downloadable form, it's a little too rigid to be convenient as an alternative content type in the sense of the applications we saw at the start of this chapter, which were capable of rendering HTML and PDF documents from the same data. The problem we have to solve for WAP-enabled devices is to detect them when they visit the site, and deliver them a WML document. They don't have the option of viewing an HTML page from which they could choose to view a WML version, as they would with PDF versions of the content. It would be nice if HAWHAW provided a convenient API so that you could detect the device yourself, but in its present form, it handles the client detection internally and needs some modification to be used this way.

WML, Sessions and Security

One aspect of WAP devices of which you need to be aware is that many are not able to save cookies locally, as they're not backed by a spare gigabyte or two of available disk space. This presents a problem for sessions, as you won't be able to use the cookie mechanism to allow clients to provide their session ID to you. The alternative mechanism PHP provides is to add the session ID as a GET variable, rewriting every URL in your page to add a variable typically named PHPSESSID. This can be invoked by HAW_deck's enable_session method, but comes at a price; non-relative URLs will not have the session ID added to them for the sake of security.

In cases where you need it, you can add the session ID yourself, like this:

```php
<?php
session_start();
?>

<a href="http://www.sitepoint.com/?<?php echo SID;
?>">SitePoint</a>
```

Be careful not to add the session ID to external links; this will broadcast it to those linked sites, and can potentially lead to session hijacking.

Overall, as you can see, building a WML-based site is very easy. Yet, you may be wondering whether it's worth it, given the limited number of people who surf that way. Let me just give you a tip—developers working in this area get paid almost twice what their HTML-based brethren receive. Enough said.

How do I render XUL with PHP?

XML User interface Language[24] (XUL) is the innovation of the developers working on the Mozilla project[25]. (X)HTML is easy, right? The idea behind XUL is to make building desktop applications (or **rich clients**) as easy as working with HTML. What's more, it allows rich clients to be launched from your Website. For an introduction to XUL, try SitePoint's *Introducing XUL: The Net's Biggest Secret*[26], which comes as a three-part series and provides plenty of resources to get you started.

Now, assuming you have a grasp of what XUL is about, the question is: can it be applied to your Website in a useful manner? Given the popularity of Internet Explorer, requiring visitors use Mozilla, Firebird, Camino, or one of the other Gecko-based browsers is obviously not going to be popular. But for the "back end"—the interface you provide for administering your site—there's much to be gained from XUL. You can reasonably require your site's administrators to use a Gecko-based browser, perhaps purely as a tool for administering your site. What's more, the work of administration often places a much heavier load on your bandwidth and resources, for example, as you switch numerous times between a list of your site's users and the detailed view of an individual user selected from the list. This is exactly where XUL can provide significant value.

The easiest way to launch an XUL application from your Website is to send the correct HTTP header, which a Gecko-based browser will recognize and respond to with the page it gets by building the XUL application. To demonstrate, let's put together a simple but effective XUL application that helps us administer users we have registered.

To start, we'll include the `MySQL` class and select a list of users from the `user` table (see Volume I, Chapter 9 for the structure of the table).

File: **11.php (excerpt)**

```php
<?php
// Include MySQL class
require_once 'Database/MySQL.php';

// Define the base URL for editing users - MODIFY THIS!!!
$baseUrl =
```

---

[24] http://www.mozilla.org/projects/xul/
[25] http://www.mozilla.org/
[26] http://www.sitepoint.com/article/1140

```
    'http://localhost/phpanth/AlternativeContentTypes/12.php';

// Define variables for MySQL class
$host   = 'localhost'; // Hostname of MySQL server
$dbUser = 'harryf';    // Username for MySQL
$dbPass = 'secret';    // Password for user
$dbName = 'sitepoint'; // Database name

// Instantiate MySQL class
$db = &new MySQL($host, $dbUser, $dbPass, $dbName);

// Select all the available users
$sql    = "SELECT * FROM user ORDER BY user_id";
$result = $db->query($sql);

// Send XUL content header
header("Content-type: application/vnd.mozilla.xul+xml");
echo '<?xml version="1.0"?>';
echo '<?xml-stylesheet href="chrome://global/skin/" type="text/css"?>';
?>
```

With the list ready, we send the XUL content type application/vnd.moz-
illa.xul+xml, followed by a couple of XML processing instructions, which are
recognized by Gecko based browsers. Now, let's render some XUL. I'll keep the
detail on XUL to a minimum, so if you're puzzled by any of the elements you
see, be sure to visit XULPlanet[27], where the Element Reference[28] should clear
things up.

File: **11.php (excerpt)**

```
<window id="admin" title="Admin Interface"
  xmlns:html="http://www.w3.org/1999/xhtml"
  xmlns=
"http://www.mozilla.org/keymaster/gatekeeper/there.is.only.xul">
  <script type="application/x-javascript">
  <![CDATA[
    var baseUrl = '<?php echo $baseUrl; ?>'; /* Base URL */
    /* Redirects XUL browser element to correct editing URL */
    function editUser(id) {
      var user_edit = document.getElementById('user_edit');
      user_edit.setAttribute('src', baseUrl + id);
    }
  ]]>
  </script>
```

[27] http://www.xulplanet.com/
[28] http://www.xulplanet.com/references/elemref/

The window element is typically the root element of all XUL applications. Beneath this, we've placed a simple JavaScript function that redirects a browser element (which we'll create momentarily) to a Web page; here, we'll place a form that will allow us to edit a single user.

Next, we lay out the user interface:

File: **11.php (excerpt)**

```
<grid flex="1" style="background-color: silver">
  <columns>
    <column flex="1" />
    <column flex="3" />
  </columns>
  <rows>
    <row flex="1">
      <browser id="user_edit" src="<?php echo $baseUrl; ?>"/>
      <listbox flex="1">
        <listhead>
          <listheader/>
          <listheader label="Login"/>
          <listheader label="Name"/>
          <listheader label="Email"/>
        </listhead>
        <listcols>
          <listcol flex="0.3"/>
          <listcol flex="1"/>
          <listcol flex="1"/>
          <listcol flex="1"/>
        </listcols>
```

The grid element is used to help position widgets on the user interface. Of note is the browser element, a special XUL widget that is a Web browser. Its src attribute is used to point it at a URL, the fetched Web page being displayed in the XUL application. The listbox is where we'll place a list of users. Notice the listhead element; here, we specify labels that correspond to column headers in the user table. You can probably see where this is going...

File: **11.php (excerpt)**

```
<?php
$alt = '#d3d3d3';
while ($user = $result->fetch()) {
    $alt = $alt == '#d3d3d3' ? 'silver' : '#d3d3d3';
?>
<listitem
  onclick="editUser('?id=<?php echo $user['user_id'];
```

```
                ?>')"
                style="background-color: <?php echo $alt; ?>">
                <listcell label="<?php echo $user['user_id']; ?>"/>
                <listcell label="<?php echo $user['login']; ?>"/>
                <listcell label="<?php echo $user['firstName'] . ' ' .
                  $user['lastName']; ?>" flex="1"/>
                <listcell label="<?php echo $user['email']; ?>"/>
            </listitem>
            <?php
            }
            ?>
          </listbox>
        </row>
      </rows>
    </grid>
</window>
```

Here, we've rendered with PHP multiple `listitem` elements that correspond to the rows from the database. Notice, in particular, the `onclick` attribute of the `listitem`; this calls the JavaScript function we defined earlier. Note also that the value it sends to the `editUser` JavaScript function begins with `?id=`. We're building a query string such as `?id=4`, which will identify a user to the PHP script where we'll place a form for editing users.

For the page with the editing form, we simply used QuickForm as you've seen before in Volume I, Chapter 9. Note the script in question, `12.php` is only a mock up; it's capable of fetching user details, but not updating them. I'll leave it to you to explore that code and deal with updating the database with changes, as you've seen it before in Volume I, Chapter 9.

When viewed with Mozilla or Firebird, it looks like Figure 3.9.

Figure 3.9. XUL Administration

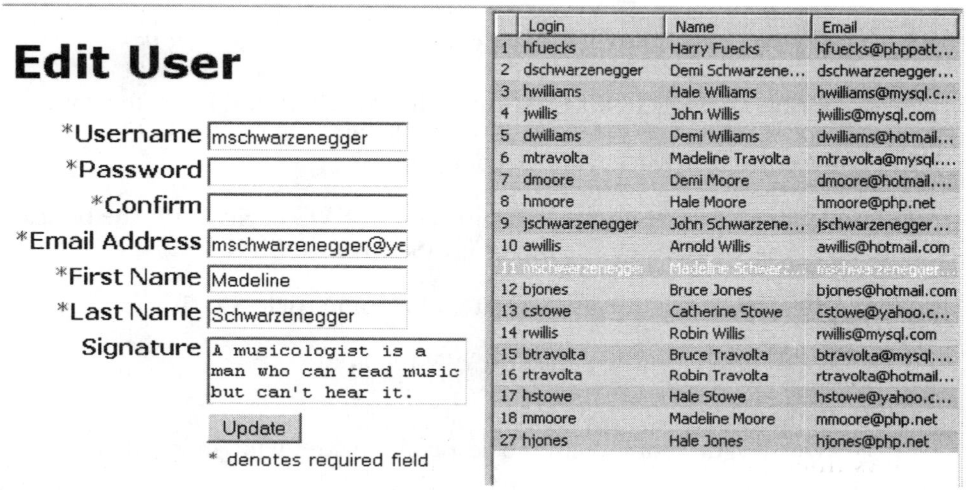

The left hand side shows the form generated (as HTML) by QuickForm and displayed thanks to the XUL browser element. On the right hand side is the list of users, built as an XUL listbox. Whenever we click on the name of a user in the list, a new page request is made to the form, showing the details for that user, while the entire user list remains available on the right hand side.

The advantage of using XUL here is that we need only perform the query that fetches the user list once. It then becomes part of the application running on my own computer, and does not need to be refreshed repeatedly as I perform routine administration tasks. Using other XUL elements like tabpanels, I could easily load a large part of the administration interface for the site in one go, which would allow me to swap between tabs to access each view available for administering the site.

A user interface that is part XUL and part HTML (via the browser element) is a little crude, but it makes a very adequate quick and dirty solution. As the "rendering engine" is effectively my Web browser, I can use sessions to secure the interface so that a valid user name and password combination is required to load it in the first place. The Mozilla team is also working on support for SOAP and WSDL, so, if you needed a more rigorous solution you could build an application that, once loaded, was capable of fetching data from a PHP script acting as a SOAP server (see Chapter 2 for details).

Further Reading

❑ Generate PDFs with PHP: http://www.sitepoint.com/article/1225

This tutorial discusses PDF generation with the PHP PDFLib extension.

❑ KevLinDev: http://www.kevlindev.com/

This excellent set of examples and tutorials on SVG begins with the basics and moves on to examine the use of JavaScript with SVG.

❑ *WML: An Introduction*: http://www.sitepoint.com/article/351/1

This tutorial provides a fast start on WML markup.

❑ WML Reference:
http://www.devguru.com/Technologies/wml/quickref/wml_index.html

This must-see reference has all the WML tags you need.

Stats and Tracking

Ever since Perl and CGI made their way onto the Internet, Webmasters have suffered an insatiable thirst for knowing who's visiting their site. Over time, gathering information about a site's visitors has become a discipline in itself; today, tracking tools offer advanced features such as the analysis of visitors' **click paths** through your site, and some even attempt to locate a visitor's geographical location based on the details of his or her ISP. This area of Webmastership has also gained a reputation for being part of the murkier side of the Internet, however, with advertising agencies using banner ads to monitor surfers' movements across multiple sites, wherever the agencies' banners are placed. There's a fine line between gathering data in order to help improve a site for its visitors and spying; I leave it up to you to make the value judgments.

Building a system that tracks visitors and logs their progress through our sites can be extremely valuable from the perspectives of both security and improving visitors' experience of the site. A tracking system can also help you determine the searches that brought visitors to your site, and identify sites that link to yours, helping you to place the site where people will find it.

In this chapter, we'll look at the basics of storing visitor information with some simple PHP scripts, then defer to phpOpenTracker[1]. This excellent tracking tool offers some "state of the art" features that any good tracker should provide,

---

[1] http://www.phpopentracker.de/

and uses a very well structured, object oriented design that makes it possible to customize the product without breaking a sweat.

We'll also be looking at phpSniff[2], a handy tool for the identification of Web browsers and their specific capabilities. A fairly complex task, browser sniffing is often important if you use some of the more advanced elements of CSS and JavaScript on your site, but want to be sure that people using older browsers aren't deterred.

What information can I gather about my site's visitors?

Assuming you're using Apache, you have access to a wealth of information about visitors—data that's communicated by their browsers to your Web server.

Here's a script which demonstrates the point:

File: **1.php**

```php
<?php
echo 'Nearest IP address: ' . @$_SERVER['REMOTE_ADDR'] . '<br />';
echo 'Nearest Hostname: ' .
  @gethostbyaddr(@$_SERVER['REMOTE_ADDR']) . '<br />';
echo 'Useragent: ' . @$_SERVER['HTTP_USER_AGENT'] . '<br />';
echo 'Request: ' . @$_SERVER['REQUEST_URI'] . '<br />';
echo 'Preferred Language: ' . @$_SERVER['HTTP_ACCEPT_LANGUAGE'] .
  '<br />';
echo 'Referer: ' . @$_SERVER['HTTP_REFERER'] . '<br />';

echo '<p>Click <a href="' . $_SERVER['PHP_SELF'] .
  '?link=referer">here</a>';
?>
```

The output this generates, if you click on the link, is as follows:

```
Nearest IP address: 127.0.0.1
Nearest Hostname: localhost
Useragent: Mozilla/4.0 (compatible; MSIE 6.0; MSIE 5.5; Windows NT
5.1) Opera 7.01 [en]
Request: /sitepoint/StatsAndTracking/1.php?link=referer
Preferred Language: en
Referer: http://localhost/sitepoint/StatsAndTracking/1.php
```

[2] http://phpsniff.sourceforge.net/

Tip

The Golden Rule

Remember the golden rule: *never trust anything from the browser.* There are ways to "spoof" almost anything that might come from a browser.

Be especially wary of the `$_SERVER['HTTP_REFERER']` value. I've seen some people build security mechanisms based around this—a very bad idea.

Also be aware, when dealing with these variables, that they are only created by PHP if they have a value, so you may need to be careful to check that they exist in your code before you do anything with them. In the example above, we used the error suppression operator (`@`) to handle this issue.

Given the basic information from the above script, we already have a foundation for building a stats and tracking system; we can store this information in a database, then use it later to display a report of what's been happening on the site.

The hostname of the visitor, obtained with the `gethostbyaddr` function[1], can be used to tell me the domain from which the visitor came. Running this example on my own machine, I'm told that `localhost` is the host name, but on a live site you'll get values such as `ottawa-hse-ppp266908.sympatico.ca`. The `.ca` at the end tells us the visitor came from Canada, so we could build a report that tells us which countries site visitors come from, with the exception of the `.com`, `.net` and `.org` domains, which tend to be used internationally.

The `$_SERVER['HTTP_USER_AGENT']` value tells us about the visitor's browser. In the example above, you'll notice this value contains information about both the Web browser (`Opera 7.01 [en]`) and the operating system (`Windows NT 5.1`, which is how Windows XP advertises itself). Of course, if you've built a site that's compatible with all browsers, you won't need to worry about this information...

The `$_SERVER['REQUEST_URI']` data can be used to determine exactly which page a user was viewing. This is important with PHP, where the difference between URLs like `index.php?view=news` and `index.php?view=articles` can be very significant. This is the basis of click path analysis.

`$_SERVER['HTTP_REFERER']` tells you whether the visitor followed a link to get to the current page. Although this information can't be relied upon, it generally does provide useful data about sites that are linked to yours.

---

[1]Please note that `gethostbyaddr` is quite slow as functions go, as it must contact another server to perform a reverse DNS lookup. Using this function heavily is one way to quickly bog down a speedy server.

`$_SERVER['HTTP_ACCEPT_LANGUAGE']` tells you which language the browser advertises as being the visitor's preferred choice; you can use this information to present content to visitors in different languages.

IP Addresses

Every computer surfing the Internet must have an IP address to be able to communicate. Although they're often compared to phone numbers, IP addresses are far easier to come by, and make it far more difficult to identify exactly who the user is (some say this is a very good thing). If you use a dial up Internet connection from home, you've probably already used *at least* 100 IP addresses, before we even begin to consider the times you surfed from the Internet café down the street, the local library, and so on. The story with IP addresses becomes even more convoluted when you take into account proxy servers, which act as "middle men" between your browser and a Website, network address translation, and more. One thing to be aware of is that AOL uses a particularly bizarre mechanism; their members are assigned a new IP address upon practically every page request, which basically defeats any IP-based security mechanism you might care to use (e.g. confining a user's session to a single IP address).

The `$_SERVER['REMOTE_ADDR']` variable tells you the nearest Internet IP address to the Web browser (i.e. it will not show the local address of the computer if it resides on a private network). What's important to realize is that this could be a proxy server; should this be the case, you need to check `$_SERVER['HTTP_X_FORWARDED_FOR']` to obtain the client's *actual* IP address. Of course, life is never that simple! Depending on the type of proxy server clients use, and whether they're using network address translation, there are other variables you may need to consider, such as `$_SERVER['HTTP_CLIENT_IP']`, which is sometimes used to advertise a client's IP address when a proxy server is used, along with `$_SERVER['HTTP_VIA']`, which identifies the type of proxy server in use.

Here's a function that can be used to obtain the Internet IP address nearest to the end user, based on the `REMOTE_ADDR`, `HTTP_X_FORWARDED_FOR` and `HTTP_CLIENT_IP` values:

```
function getAddress()
{
  if (!empty($_SERVER['HTTP_CLIENT_IP'])) {
    $ip_expl = explode('.', $_SERVER['HTTP_CLIENT_IP']);
    $referer = explode('.', $_SERVER['REMOTE_ADDR']);
    if ($referer[0] != $ip_expl[0]) {
```

```
    $ip = array_reverse($ip_expl);
    $return = implode('.', $ip);
  } else {
    $return = $client_ip;
  }
} elseif (!empty($_SERVER['HTTP_X_FORWARDED_FOR'])) {
  if (strstr($_SERVER['HTTP_X_FORWARDED_FOR'], ',')) {
    $ip_expl = explode(',', $_SERVER['HTTP_X_FORWARDED_FOR']);
    $return = end($ip_expl);
  } else {
    $return = $_SERVER['HTTP_X_FORWARDED_FOR'];
  }
} else {
  $return = $_SERVER['REMOTE_ADDR'];
}
return $return;
}
```

Note that you can't rely completely upon this information either; it's possible for a visitor to fake these details, which will allow a determined hacker to get past nearly any security system that's based purely on checking the IP address. But 99.9% of your visitors will provide accurate information, which will be handy for later analysis.

How do I store visitor statistics with PHP?

Although most Web hosts provide tools for viewing your site's statistics—one of the most popular tools for the job being AWStats[3]—typically, these will not be under your control (i.e. you can only view the results), and they may not meet the needs of a site owner hoping to analyze in detail the path a visitor takes through his or her site (known as the **click path**). Also, you may have need for a logging mechanism that's integrated with your application, and is capable of capturing detailed information related to the *actions* a user can perform, rather than simply logging all traffic to your server in an application-agnostic fashion.

If you've built an ecommerce system based on PHP and MySQL, for example, and you believe your navigation system could be improved to help customers explore your site, being able to see exactly which pages visitors are viewing, and how they got there, may help boost your site's sales.

---

[3] http://awstats.sourceforge.net/

Logging Strategy

There are a few practical tips you should be aware of when using PHP to log traffic from your site. These points usually become obvious only after you've been gathering traffic information for a while.

First of all, be aware that tracking can generate a *lot* of data. A visitor who views five pages on your site may generate at least five new rows in your database—possibly more in other tables, depending on your implementation. Make sure before you "go live" with any logging system that you also have a mechanism in place for archiving and purging old data, otherwise you'll quickly have a massive database on your hands. In practice, this might mean something like a cron job, which executes a command line PHP script on a regular basis, the script "dumping" data older than a certain age to some useful file format (e.g. XML), then purging it from the database. You can then move the files off your server for digestion at your leisure.

The data itself can be categorized as **raw data**, such as an IP address, a hostname, or a user agent, or **derived data**, such as the identity of a visitor's browser and operating system, derived from the user agent field, or even a daily total of visits from a particular country, based on the host name. It may be a wise decision to store the raw data in one table, then populate other, related tables with the derived data. As the size of your logs grows, asking PHP or MySQL to re-execute calculations on the raw data to generate derived data every time you request the report page will result in a long wait, not to mention the process overhead it will place on your server. It may also be worth regarding the building of a report from your log data as a task that's best performed "offline"—on your desktop PC, for example. If you're feeling adventurous, perhaps consider building a SOAP server (see Chapter 2) on your site from which you can fetch the data, and then store and analyze it locally.

How you *capture* the data itself requires a little consideration. One approach is simply to include in every page you want monitored a logging PHP script that stores usage data in the database as each page is viewed. If you use this approach, you'll need to take care not to slow your site with logging processes and queries. In other words, it's best to store only the raw data, and leave the processing associated with derived data generation until later—to be handled by a cron job, perhaps, or dealt with the first time a report on the data is requested.

An alternative approach is to get the visitors' browsers to execute the logging script separately from the page itself, meaning the task of storing the data occurs independently of the main script. "How?" you may ask. In Volume I, Chapter 9, we looked at how to display an image with a PHP script that had been fetched from a database. To execute this script, you would use an ordinary HTML `img` tag:

```
<img src="logo.php" />
```

`logo.php` would contain something like the code below, which sends an image file to the browser:

```
header('content-type: image/gif');
readfile('/home/username/www/images/logo.gif');
```

But what's to stop you putting other PHP code in there? Nothing! And if the logo is being displayed on every page, it's also the perfect tool to capture Web traffic information.

Note that it's a good idea to call PHP's `flush` function right after `readfile`, before you begin a time consuming number crunching routine. Otherwise, the image may only finally be sent to the client Web browser after the script has finished execution, which will have people wondering where the logo went. Some cunning is needed to allow the "real page" being viewed to pass information to the script that displays the image, for example, giving it the `REQUEST_URI` data from the page on which the image is displayed:

```
<img src="logo.php?page=<?php
echo urlencode($_SERVER['REQUEST_URI']); ?>" />
```

An alternative mechanism (that's less reliable, as it depends upon the browser passing on the information), is to use the `HTTP_REFERER` value, which should contain the URL of the page in which the `img` tag was used.

The rest is just a database query to store the information. As this approach will have no impact on the rendering of the main page, you might even consider doing some of the calculations that create the derived data from the raw data here. A further advantage of this approach is that it allows you to log statistics from any type of Web page, including static HTML pages. The only downside is that it relies on the browser fetching the image; a PHP or Perl script that is pretending to be a browser will generally only load the HTML of the page, and will skip fetching the image, which means the statistics-gathering script is never executed.

Don't worry too much if this isn't clear right now. phpOpenTracker[4] solves most of these problems, allowing you to concentrate on the specifics of your online

---

[4] http://www.phpopentracker.de/

application. In addition to basic logging functionality, some of the advanced features that phpOpenTracker offers are:

☐ logging for multiple sites

☐ reports are generated as images (with JpGraph[5])

☐ click path analysis reports (requires Graphviz[6] to generate the click path diagrams)

☐ automatic exit link generation (no need to modify your HTML)

☐ tracking the number of users online at a given instant

☐ incoming search phrases from search engines

As it has a solid object oriented design, it's possible to utilize phpOpenTracker in many ways without having to alter radically your site's code. We'll focus here on the basics of phpOpenTracker to get you started; covering all the advanced features are beyond the scope of this book, but I hope you've already got the (accurate) impression that phpOpenTracker is a very mature package, and one of the best you could build your Web traffic logging around.

Installing phpOpenTracker

The version of phpOpenTracker used here was 1.0.2.

To install phpOpenTracker, you can use the PEAR package manager (see Appendix D), which, assuming you have the PEAR directory in your include path, will make phpOpenTracker available to any script on your server. You can also install phpOpenTracker manually without too much trouble. The main script, `phpOpenTracker.php`, includes some further files, which it expects will reside, by default, in a directory named `phpOpenTracker` that's placed in some other directory on the include path (typically, the PEAR directory). You can get around this in your code by defining the following constant:

```
define('POT_INCLUDE_PATH', '/home/username/lib/phpOpenTracker/');
```

---

[5] http://www.aditus.nu/jpgraph/
[6] http://www.research.att.com/sw/tools/graphviz/

If you place the code in any public directory on your site, make sure you place a .htaccess file in the conf subdirectory of the installation with the following contents[2]:

```
<Files ~ "\.ini$">
  Order deny,allow
  Deny from all
</Files>
```

The configuration files use the extension .ini, which will not be handled by the PHP engine if anyone views them; your database password could quickly become the latest topic for discussion on Slashdot[7] if you don't take the above measure!

In the docs/sql/mysql subdirectory of the phpOpenTracker package, you'll find a query, mysql.sql, which you can run to create the tables needed for phpOpenTracker, using either a tool like phpMyAdmin[8], or by typing the following from the command line:

```
mysql database_name < mysql.sql
```

Now, edit the file phpOpenTracker.ini.dist in the conf directory and save it as phpOpenTracker.ini. To start with, all you need to do is modify the database settings. For example:

```
; Database Connection

db_type     = "mysql"
db_host     = "localhost"
db_port     = "default"
db_socket   = "default"
db_user     = "harryf"
db_password = "secret"
db_database = "sitepoint"
```

With that done, all that remains is to add phpOpenTracker to your own page, and tell it to log all views:

File: **2.php**

```
<?php
// Include phpOpenTracker
```

---

[2]This code is of course Apache specific. If you use IIS or some other Web server, you'll need to use it's access control facilities to block access to your .ini files.
[7] http://www.slashdot.org/
[8] http://www.phpmyadmin.net/

```
include 'phpOpenTracker.php';

// Log
phpOpenTracker::log();

echo 'This page view was logged!';
?>
```

The alternative approach is to use a PHP script masquerading as an image, known as a **Web bug** in the phpOpenTracker documentation. You first need to copy the file **image.php** from **docs/scripts** (under the phpOpenTracker directory) to a public directory on your Website. Here's an example of a page that uses the Web bug:

File: **3.php**

```
<?php
$webbugUrl = 'image.php?document_url=' . $_SERVER['REQUEST_URI'] .
             '&referer=' . @$_SERVER['HTTP_REFERER'];
?>
<!DOCTYPE html PUBLIC "-//W3C//DTD XHTML 1.0 Transitional//EN"
  "http://www.w3.org/TR/xhtml1/DTD/xhtml1-transitional.dtd">
<html xmlns="http://www.w3.org/1999/xhtml">
<head>
<meta http-equiv="Content-type"
  content="text/html; charset=iso-8859-1" />
<title> phpOpenTracker Web Bug </title>
</head>
<body>
<img alt="" src="<?php echo $webbugUrl; ?>" />
This page is logged.
</body>
</html>
```

That's it; phpOpenTracker is now installed and logging traffic to your site! Notice that when we built the **$webbugUrl** variable, we passed two variables via the query string—the (relative) URL of the above script itself, and the referer field, which the Web bug needs as the referer it "sees" will be the above script, rather than the true referer.

Be aware that phpOpenTracker, when used "inline" in your scripts, will log the complete URI, such as **page.php?var1=Hello&var2=World**. This may not be particularly easy to read when it comes to viewing the log, so you might like to override this behavior by defining an array that contains a **document** element, and giving it a value that will make sense when you view the log. For example:

File: **4.php**

```php
<?php
// Include phpOpenTracker
include 'phpOpenTracker.php';

// Redefine document name
$params = array('document' => 'Article: Stats with PHP');

// Log
phpOpenTracker::log($params);

echo 'This page view was logged!';
?>
```

If you want to log traffic for multiple sites, usually all you need to do is pass in the array a unique `client_id` value, which will be used to identify the site in question. Here's how it would look for the first site:

```php
$params = array('client_id' => 1);
phpOpenTracker::log($params);
```

You probably won't be in a position to include the phpOpenTracker code in the scripts on the remote site, so the preferred mechanism is to use the Web bug method to record data for you. The example provided with phpOpenTracker is already primed to accept the client ID via a query string variable:

```html
<img alt="" src="phpOpenTracker/image.php?client_id=1" />
```

The phpOpenTracker API

When you include the `phpopentracker.php` file in your script, you can use one of three methods:

`phpOpenTracker::log()`	As you've seen, this method instructs phpOpenTracker to log an entry in its database.
`phpOpenTracker::get()`	This method is used to build reports, including click path analysis.
`phpOpenTracker::plot()`	This method is used for drawing graphs from phpOpenTracker.

So far, we've seen the `log` method, which is the simplest to use. We'll look at the other two methods as this chapter progresses. For full details, be sure to examine the documentation on the phpOpenTracker Website[9].

How do I recognize returning visitors?

As mentioned earlier in this chapter, IP addresses are easy to come by, and frequently change. As a result, they cannot be used as a reliable source of information for recognizing returning visitors—they may not even be useful for gathering stats as visitors progress through your site. If they're using a dial up connection, for example, they may disconnect while reading downloaded content, then reconnect to surf further.

Should you wish to be able to recognize a returning visitor, or monitor a visitor's path across your site, you'll need to make use of **cookies**.

Sessions vs. Cookies

Although PHP sessions *use* cookies to pass an identifying token to a client, the session and cookie functionality provided by PHP is best applied to other problems.

Sessions are intended for use on a "per visit" basis. They store data that's required only for the *current visit*, and the data "belongs to" the Web server only (the session files being stored locally), as we saw in Chapter 1.

Cookies are best applied to data that should persist across *multiple visits* to your site, such as viewing preferences or the visitor's name. Cookies should *not* be used to store sensitive information, as this data is stored on the client, and may be subject to interception if you're not using SSL; it's also available to anyone who has access to the client machine's file system.

Some may argue this is an overly paranoid point of view, and certainly, sites that use cookies to ensure regular visitors are "always logged in" would lose this feature without them. The problem is that, should someone gain access to my computer, in theory, he or she could use the cookies I have stored to log in as me, without requiring my user name or password.

Using a cookie, you can store for visitors a unique identifier (assigned on their first visit), which you can use to identify them on subsequent visits. For example:

---

[9] http://www.phpopentracker.de/

File: **5.php**

```php
<?php
// Note rand() must be seeded for PHP < 4.2.0
// see: http://www.php.net/rand
$uniqueId = md5('example' . uniqid(rand(), TRUE));

// Set the cookie
if (!isset($_COOKIE['MyIdentifier'])) {
  setcookie('MyIdentifier', $uniqueId,
    time() + 60 * 60 * 24 * 120, "/");
  echo 'Cookie Set';
} else {
  echo 'MyIdentifier: ' . $_COOKIE['MyIdentifier'];
}
?>
```

Once it's set, the cookie identifier can be stored in the raw log data for every page viewed. This allows you to build reports that display an individual visitor's progress across your site for current and future visits, and perform queries that order or group results by the unique ID; this can prove invaluable for understanding how visitors use your site.

Setting this up with phpOpenTracker is easy. Modify the following section in your phpopentracker.ini file:

```
; Returning Visitors Handling

track_returning_visitors            = On
returning_visitors_cookie           = "pot_visitor_id"
returning_visitors_cookie_lifetime = 365
```

The track_returning_visitors setting is used to switch this functionality on. The returning_visitors_cookie setting specifies a name for the cookie, while returning_visitors_cookie_lifetime assigns it a lifetime in seconds. With the phpOpenTracker database, the pot_visitors table will use the same ID (visitor_id) to record page views for visitors that have a cookie, so reports that are built from the database will be able to identify a given user.

We'll be looking at how to take advantage of this later in the chapter.

How do I track exit links?

It's fine to know where visitors are coming from, courtesy of the HTTP_REFERER value Apache makes available to PHP, but what about where they go when they *leave* your site? Such information can be valuable in building "networks" with other sites to which you're providing traffic.

The solution to this problem is to use a script through which all external links are passed. For example, a link to http://www.sitepoint.com/ might use a URL like this:

http://www.mydomain.com/exit.php?url=http://www.sitepoint.com/

The script exit.php first logs the URL of the link to which the visitor is being sent, then sends an HTTP location header to forward them to the new site, in this case http://www.sitepoint.com/.

Among the example scripts provided with phpOpenTracker, the following (exit.php) demonstrates how this works:

File: **6.php**

```php
<?php
// Include the phpOpenTracker code
require_once 'phpOpenTracker.php';

// The link for forward to is passed using the GET variable "url"
if (isset($_GET['url'])) {
  // Convert HTML entities back to URI entities
  $exitURL = str_replace('&amp;', '&',
    base64_decode($_GET['url']));

  // Set up the config, database and container objects
  $config    = &phpOpenTracker_Config::singleton();
  $db        = &phpOpenTracker_DB::singleton();
  $container = &phpOpenTracker_Container::singleton(
    array(
      'initNoSetup' => true
    )
  );

  // Perform the query which logs the exit URL
  $db->query(
    sprintf(
      'UPDATE %s
```

```
          SET exit_target_id = %d
        WHERE accesslog_id   = %d
          AND document_id    = %d
          AND timestamp      = %d',

    $config['accesslog_table'],
    $db->storeIntoDataTable($config['exit_targets_table'],
        $exitURL),
    $container['accesslog_id'],
    $container['document_id'],
    $container['timestamp']
    )
);


// Redirect to the new site
header('Location: http://' . $exitURL);
}
?>
```

If the code above is a little confusing, don't worry. phpOpenTracker implements its own database classes, which makes it very easy to fit into any site, but does take a little effort to understand when you need to modify it. The examples provided are generally ready to use, which should help matters a lot.

Note that the example expects you to have used **base64_encode** to encode the URL *and* have stripped out the leading **http://**. This has the advantage of "forcing" visitors to use the link, rather than simply copying the address straight into their browsers' address bars. It is intended for use with a function like this:

File: **7.php**

```
<?php
// Modifies links to point an exit handling script
function encodeExitUrls($content, $exitScript)
{
  return preg_replace(
    "#<a href=(\"|')http://([^\"']+)(\"|')#ime",
    '"<a href=\"$exitScript?url=" . base64_encode(\'\\2\') . "\""'
    , $content);
}

$content = <<<EOD
This is some text containing a <a href="http://www.sitepoint.com/"
>link to sitepoint.com</a>
EOD;
```

```
echo encodeExitUrls($content, '6.php');
?>
```

This can be used automatically to format content as it is displayed, so that links can be entered normally, but are altered when they're sent to a visitor's browser to pass through the exit script. Note that the above regular expression in the `encodeExitUrls` function leaves room for improvement. It will "catch" the vast majority of links but there are some exceptions, the most obvious being a link to an FTP site, for example.

How do I record search engine queries?

Wouldn't it be nice if you knew which searches being performed on Google lead people to your site? Well, the good news is that you can—and, even better, phpOpenTracker has a plug-in that takes care of all the work for you.

The general trick that Webmasters employ when gathering this data is to examine the referer field made available from the browser and mine it for the search keywords the visitor used to find your site. If you visit Google, for example, and search for "php and mysql," the following URL will display your search results:

http://www.google.com/search?hl=en&lr=&ie=ISO-8859-1**&q=php+and+m ysql**&btnG=Google+Search

Hard as it may be to see, in the above URL you'll find the string `&q=php+and+mysql`, which contains the search string you gave to Google. Now, when a user is referred to our site from Google, all we need to do is extract that information from the URL and store it in our database.

Installing the phpOpenTracker Search Engine Plug-in

The Search Engine plug-in is available as a separate download via the same SourceForge project space[11] from which you downloaded phpOpenTracker itself. You can either install it with the PEAR installer (see Appendix D), or manually place the files in your phpOpenTracker directory. If you extract the plug-in ZIP file, you'll find that the directory structure is the same as it should be in the main phpOpenTracker directory; simply copy the files over as you find them. Then,

---

[11] http://sourceforge.net/projects/phpopencounter/

run the SQL script `./phpOpenTracker/docs/sql/mysql/mysql.sql` against your MySQL database.

Now, modify your `phpopentrack.ini` file to tell it about the plug-in:

```
; Plugins

logging_engine_plugins = "search_engines"
```

That's it! Your site is now recording search engine queries. Later, we'll look at how to access the data that's collected.

How do I exclude search engines from my logs?

Chances are, once you're over the novelty of having your Website spidered by a search engine robot, you won't want the logs of the robot's movements cluttering up your Weblogs. Although you could filter out the logs you don't want to see, why waste valuable disk space with data you don't need? A mechanism is needed to tell the logging engine what not to log, based on the user agent supplied by the robots.

Handling this with phpOpenTracker is, as always, wonderfully simple. Just head to your `phpopentracker.ini` file and edit the following:

```
; Locking

locking       = On
log_reload    = Off
```

With locking switched on, phpOpenTracker watches for robots and excludes them from the database. Note also the `log_reload` setting here, which is used to control whether refreshed (reloaded) pages are logged.

What actually determines the robots that phpOpenTracker ignores is defined by the file `lock.ini`, found in the same directory as `phpopentracker.ini`. By default it's named `lock.ini.dist`, so you'll need to rename it. The content is a list of user agents used by search engine robots. For a useful list of further robots, try http://www.jafsoft.com/searchengines/webbots.html.

How do I get reports on my site's statistics?

What good are all the stats if you can't view them in a useful report? Again, phpOpenTracker makes mining your Web statistics easy; it provides the **get** method to simplify the process of getting the information you need. Provided with phpOpenTracker is an example that's useful as a general, simple report much like that provided by Webalizer, and as a reference for setting up your own reports.

Building reports can be a little tricky to begin with. In conjunction with other packages, phpOpenTracker offers a range of features. These include visual click path analysis, with help from PEAR::Image_GraphViz[13] and the GraphViz software; XML tree generation, with the aid of PEAR::XML_Tree[14]; and chart generation with the assistance of jpGraph, which we examined in Volume I, Chapter 7. Providing an in-depth discussion is beyond the scope of this book (and could even become a book in itself, when you consider the statistical manipulation involved in the creation of detailed reports). Here, I'll give a rough guide to the reporting API so you know your way around.

All requests to the phpOpenTracker report API are made via the `phpOpenTracker::get` method; this accepts an array which itself specifies further method calls. The generalized form of this array is:

```
array(
   'api_call' => 'method_name',
   '1st_param_name' => 'value',
   '2nd_param_name' => 'value',
   /* etc. */
);
```

It's worth delving into the phpOpenTracker documentation to spend some time experimenting with what's on offer. Here are a couple of simple examples.

An easy task is to find out how many visitors are currently online:

File: **8.php**

```
<?php
// Include phpOpenTracker
require_once 'phpopentracker.php';
```

---

[13] http://pear.php.net/Image_GraphViz
[14] http://pear.php.net/XML_Tree

```
$visitors_online = phpOpenTracker::get(
  array(
    'api_call' => 'visitors_online'
  )
);

echo 'There are currently ' . count($visitors_online) .
  ' visitors online';
?>
```

The $visitors_online variable is assigned an array of arrays, each element of the "main" array corresponding to a single online visitor. Each of the "sub" arrays contains information about a particular visitor, such as the operating system in use, the time of last access, and the browser type.

Most other information available from phpOpenTracker requires you to specify a time range over which you want data returned. For example, how might you ascertain the total number of visitors and page impressions your site clocked up today?

File: **9.php**

```
<?php
// Include phpOpenTracker
require_once 'phpopentracker.php';

$page_count = phpOpenTracker::get(
  array(
    'api_call' => 'page_impressions',
    'range' => 'today'
  )
);

$num_visitors = phpOpenTracker::get(
  array(
    'api_call' => 'visits',
    'range' => 'today'
  )
);

echo 'Total page impressions for ' . date('d M Y') . ': ' .
  $page_count . '<br />';
echo 'Total visitors for ' . date('d M Y') . ': ' .
  $num_visitors . '<br />';
?>
```

The parameters we specify to the `phpOpenTracker::get` method depend on the value of the first array element, `api_call`. The parameters include `range`, as seen in the example above, which is used to specify a time range (e.g. the current month). `constraints` is itself an array in which you can specify the criteria by which the report should be built, such as page or browser. `result_format` allows you to specify how the data should be output, such as XML, CSV, or GraphViz.

An additional method, `phpOpenTracker::plot` is used to generate charts with jpGraph.

Usually, the report API will give you most of the tools you need, but in rare cases you may have to build your own SQL queries in order to get precisely what you want. Make sure you examine the documentation that explains the relationships between the tables phpOpenTracker uses.

Further Reading

❏ *Take Web data Analysis to the next level with PHP*:
http://www.ibm.com/developerworks/web/library/wa-phpolla/?ca=dgr-lnxw06PHPchi

Analyzing your Web traffic can be high powered stuff, as this article explains.

5

Caching

In the good old days, back when building Websites was as easy as knocking up a few HTML pages, the delivery of a Web page to a browser was a simple matter of having the Web server fetch a file. A site's visitors would see its small, text-only pages almost immediately, unless they were using particularly slow modems. Once the page was downloaded, the browser would **cache** it somewhere on the local computer so that, should the page be requested again, after performing a quick check with the server to ensure the page hadn't been updated, the browser could display the locally cached version. Pages were served as quickly and efficiently as possible, and everyone was happy (except those using 9600 bps modems).

The advent of dynamic Web pages spoiled the party, effectively "breaking" this model of serving pages by introducing two problems:

❑ When a request for a dynamic Web page is received by the server, some intermediate processing, such as the parsing of scripts by the PHP engine, must be completed. This introduces a delay before the Web server begins to deliver the output to the browser. For simple PHP scripts this may not be significant, but for a more complex application, the PHP engine may have a lot of work to do before the page is finally ready for delivery. This extra work results in a noticeable lag between the users' requests and the actual display of pages in their browsers.

❏ A typical Web server, such as Apache, uses the time of file modification to correctly inform a Web browser of a requested page's cache status. With dynamic Web pages, the actual PHP script may change only occasionally, while the content it displays, which is perhaps fetched from a database, will change frequently. The Web server has no way of knowing about updates to the database, however, so it doesn't send a last modified date. If the client (browser) has no indication of how long the data is valid, it will take a guess, which usually means it will request the same page again. The Web server will always respond with a fresh version of the page, regardless of whether the data has changed. To avoid this shortcoming, most Web developers use a `meta` tag or HTTP headers to tell the browser never to use a cached version of the page. However, this negates the Web browser's natural ability to cache Web pages, and involves some serious disadvantages. For example, the content delivered by a dynamic page may change once a day, so there's certainly a benefit to be gained by having the browser cache a page—even if only for twenty four hours.

It's usually possible to live with both problems given a small PHP application, but as the complexity of, and traffic to, your site increases, you may run into difficulties. However, both these issues *can* be solved, the first with **server side caching**, the second, by taking control of **client side caching** from within your application. The exact approach you use to solve the problem will depend on your application, but in this chapter, we'll see how you can solve both using PHP and a number of class libraries from PEAR.

Note that in this chapter's discussions of caching, we'll look at only those solutions implemented in PHP. These should not be confused with some of the script caching solutions that work on the basis of optimizing and caching compiled PHP scripts. Included in this group are the Zend Accelerator[1], iconCube PHP Accelerator[2], and Turck MMCache[3], the latter being the only accelerator that's ready for use with Windows based PHP installations today.

How do I prevent Web browsers caching a page?

Before we look at the approaches you can take to client and server side caching, the first thing we need to understand is how to prevent Web browsers (and proxy

[1] http://www.zend.com/store/products/zend-performance-suite.php
[2] http://www.phpaccelerator.co.uk/
[3] http://www.turcksoft.com/en/e_mmc.htm

servers) from caching pages in the first place. The most basic approach to doing this utilizes HTML `meta` tags:

```
<meta http-equiv="Expires" content="Mon, 26 Jul 1997 05:00:00 GMT"
/>
<meta http-equiv="Pragma" content="no-cache" />
```

By inserting a past date into the `Expires meta` tag, we can tell the browser that the cached copy of the page is always out of date. This means the browser should never cache the page. The `Pragma: no-cache meta` tag is a fairly well-supported convention that most Web browsers follow. Upon encountering this tag, they usually won't cache the page (although there's no guarantee; this is just a convention).

It sounds good, but there are two problems associated with the use of `meta` tags:

1. If a tag wasn't present when the page was first requested by a browser, but appears later (for example, you modified the included `pageheader.php` file, which contains the top of every Web page), the browser will remain blissfully ignorant and keep its cached copy of the original.

2. Proxy servers that cache Web pages, such as those common to ISPs, generally will *not* examine the HTML documents themselves. Instead, they rely purely on the Web server from which the documents came, and the HTTP protocol. In other words, a Web browser might know that it shouldn't cache the page, but the proxy server between the browser and your Web server probably doesn't—it will continue to deliver the same out-of-date page to the client

A better approach is to use the HTTP protocol itself, with the help of PHP's `header` function, to produce the equivalent of the two `meta` tags above:

```php
<?php
header('Expires: Mon, 26 Jul 1997 05:00:00 GMT');
header('Pragma: no-cache');
?>
```

We can go one step further, using the `Cache-Control` header that's supported by HTTP 1.1 capable browsers:

```php
<?php
header('Expires: Mon, 26 Jul 1997 05:00:00 GMT');
header('Cache-Control: no-store, no-cache, must-revalidate');
header('Cache-Control: post-check=0, pre-check=0', FALSE);
header('Pragma: no-cache');
?>
```

This essentially guarantees that no Web browser or intervening proxy server will cache the page, so visitors will always receive the latest content. In fact, the first header should accomplish this on its own; this is the best way to ensure a page is not cached. The `Cache-Control` and `Pragma` headers are added for "insurance" purposes. Though they don't work on all browsers or proxies, they will catch some cases in which the `Expires` header doesn't work as intended (e.g. if the client computer's date is set incorrectly).

Of course, to disallow caching entirely introduces the problems we discussed at the start of this chapter. We'll look at the solution to these issues in just a moment.

Internet Explorer and File Download Caching

Our discussion of PDF rendering in Chapter 3 explained that issues can arise when you're dealing with caching and file downloads. In serving a file download via a PHP script that uses headers such as `Content-Disposition: attachment, filename=myFile.pdf` or `Content-Disposition: inline, filename=myFile.pdf`, you'll have problems with Internet Explorer if you tell the browser not to cache the page.

Internet Explorer handles downloads in a rather unusual manner, making two requests to the Website. The first request downloads the file, and stores it in the cache before making a second request (without storing the response). This request invokes the process of delivering the file to the end user in accordance with the file's type (e.g. it starts Acrobat Reader if the file is a PDF document). This means that, if you send the cache headers that instruct the browser not to cache the page, Internet Explorer will delete the file between the first and second requests, with the result that the end user gets nothing. If the file you're serving through the PHP script will not change, one solution is simply to disable the "don't cache" headers for the download script.

If the file download will change regularly (i.e. you want the browser to download an up-to-date version), you'll need to use the `last-modified` header, discussed later in this chapter, and ensure that the time of modification remains the same across the two consecutive requests. You should be able to do this without affecting users of browsers that handle downloads correctly. One final solution is to write the file to your Web server and simply provide a link to it, leaving it to the Web server to report the cache headers for you. Of course, this may not be a viable option if the file is supposed to be secured by the PHP script, which requires a valid session in order to provide users access to the file; with this solution, the written file can be downloaded directly.

How do I capture server side output for caching?

It's time to look at how we can reduce server side delay by caching output. The general approach begins by rendering the page as normal, performing database queries and so on with PHP. However, before sending it to the browser, we **capture** and store the finished page somewhere, for instance, in a file. The next time the page is requested, the PHP script first checks to see whether a cached version of the page exists. If it does, the script sends the cached version straight to the browser, avoiding the delay involved in rebuilding the page.

What about Template Caching?

Template engines such as Smarty[4] often talk about template caching. Usually, these engines offer an in-built mechanism for storing a compiled version of a template (i.e. the native PHP generated from the template), which prevents us having to recompile the template every time a page is requested. This should *not* be confused with output caching, which refers to the caching of the rendered HTML (or other output) that PHP sends to the browser. You can successfully use both types of caching together on the same site.

Here, we'll look at PHP's in-built caching mechanism, the output buffer[5], which can be used with whatever page rendering system you prefer (templates or no templates). Consider a situation in which your script displays results using, for example, `echo` or `print`, rather than sending the data *directly* to the browser. In these cases, you can use PHP's output control functions to store the data in an in-memory buffer, which your PHP script has both access to and control over.

Here's a simple example:

File: **1.php**

```php
<?php
// Start buffering the output
ob_start();

// Echo some text (which is stored in the buffer);
echo '1. Place this in the buffer<br />';
```

[4] http://smarty.php.net/
[5] http://www.php.net/outcontrol

245

```
// Get the contents of
$buffer = ob_get_contents();

// Stop buffering and clean out the buffer
ob_end_clean();

// Echo some text normally
echo '2. A normal echo<br />';

// Echo the contents from the buffer
echo $buffer;
?>
```

The buffer itself stores the output as a string. So, in the above script, we commence buffering with ob_start and use echo to display something. We then use ob_get_contents to fetch the data the echo statement placed in the buffer, and store it in a string. The ob_end_clean function stops the output buffer and trashes the contents; the alternative is ob_end_flush, which displays the contents of the buffer.

The above script displays:

```
2. A normal echo
1. Place this in the buffer
```

In other words, we captured the output of the first echo, then sent it to the browser after the second echo. As this simple example suggests, output buffering can be a very powerful tool when it comes to building your site; it provides a solution for caching, as we'll see in a moment, and is an excellent way to hide errors from your site's visitors (see Volume I, Chapter 10). It even provides a possible alternative to browser redirection in situations such as user authentication.

Tip

HTTP Headers and Output Buffering

Output buffering can help solve the most common problem associated with the header function, not to mention session_start and set_cookie. Normally, if you call any of these functions after page output has begun, you'll get a nasty error message. With output buffering turned on, the only output types that can escape the buffer *are* HTTP headers. Using ob_start at the very beginning of your application's execution, you can send headers at whichever point you like, without encountering the usual errors. You can then write out the buffered page content all at once, when you're sure there are no more HTTP headers required.

Using Output Buffering for Server Side Caching

Now you've seen a basic example of output buffering, here's the next step, in which the buffer is stored as a file:

File: **2.php**

```php
<?php
// If a cached version exists use it...
if (file_exists('./cache/2.cache')) {

  // Read and display the file
  readfile('./cache/2.cache');
  exit();

}

// Start buffering the output
ob_start();

// Display some HTML
?>
<!DOCTYPE html PUBLIC "-//W3C//DTD XHTML 1.0 Strict//EN"
  "http://www.w3.org/TR/xhtml1/DTD/xhtml1-strict.dtd">
<html xmlns="http://www.w3.org/1999/xhtml">
<head>
<title> Cached Page </title>
<meta http-equiv="Content-Type"
  content="text/html; charset=iso-8859-1" />
</head>
<body>
This page was cached with PHP's
<a href="http://www.php.net/outcontrol">Output Control
Functions</a>
</body>
</html>

<?php
// Get the contents of the buffer
$buffer = ob_get_contents();

// Stop buffering and display the buffer
ob_end_flush();

// Write a cache file from the contents
$fp = fopen('./cache/2.cache', 'w');
```

```
fwrite($fp, $buffer);
fclose($fp);
?>
```

First, the above script checks to see if a cached version of the page exists and, if it does, the script reads and displays it. Otherwise, it uses output buffering to create a cached version of the page. It stores this as a file, while using `ob_end_flush` to display the page to the visitor.

The file `2.cache` looks exactly like the HTML that was rendered by the script:

```
<!DOCTYPE html PUBLIC "-//W3C//DTD XHTML 1.0 Strict//EN"
   "http://www.w3.org/TR/xhtml1/DTD/xhtml1-strict.dtd">
<html xmlns="http://www.w3.org/1999/xhtml">
<head>
<title> Cached Page </title>
<meta http-equiv="Content-Type"
   content="text/html; charset=iso-8859-1" />
</head>
<body>
This page was cached with PHP's
<a href="http://www.php.net/outcontrol">Output Control
Functions</a>
</body>
</html>
```

Chunked Buffering

A simplistic approach to output buffering is to cache an entire page. However, this approach forfeits the real opportunities presented by PHP's output control functions to improve your site's performance in a manner that's relevant to the varying lifetimes of your content.

No doubt, some parts of the page you send to visitors change very rarely, such as the page's header, menus and footer. But other parts, such as the table containing a forum discussion, may change quite often. Output buffering can be used to cache *sections* of a page in separate files, then rebuild the page from these—a solution that eliminates the need to repeat database queries, while loops, and so on. You might consider assigning each block of the page an expiry date after which the cache file is recreated, or alternatively, you may build into your application a mechanism that deletes the cache file every time the content it stores is changed.

Here's an example that demonstrates the principle:

File: **3.php (excerpt)**

```php
<?php
/**
 * Writes a cache file
 * @param string contents of the buffer
 * @param string filename to use when creating cache file
 * @return void
 */
function writeCache($content, $filename)
{
  $fp = fopen('./cache/' . $filename, 'w');
  fwrite($fp, $content);
  fclose($fp);
}

/**
 * Checks for cache files
 * @param string filename of cache file to check for
 * @param int maximum age of the file in seconds
 * @return mixed either the contents of the cache or false
 */
function readCache($filename, $expiry)
{
  if (file_exists('./cache/' . $filename)) {
    if ((time() - $expiry) > filemtime('./cache/' . $filename)) {
      return FALSE;
    }
    $cache = file('./cache/' . $filename);
    return implode('', $cache);
  }
  return FALSE;
}
```

The first two functions we've defined, writeCache and readCache, are used to create cache files and check for their existence, respectively. The writeCache function takes rendered output as its first argument, as well as a filename that should be used when creating the cache file. The readCache function takes a filename of a cache file as its first argument, along with the time in seconds after which the cache file should be regarded as having expired. If it finds a valid cache file, the script will return it; otherwise it returns FALSE to instruct the calling file that either no cache file exists, or it's out of date.

For the purposes of this example, I used a procedural approach. However, I wouldn't recommend doing this in practice, as it will result in very messy code (see later solutions for better alternatives) and is likely to cause issues with file locking (e.g. what happens when someone accesses the cache at the exact moment it's being updated?).

Let's continue this example. After the output buffer is started, processing begins. First, the script calls `readCache` to see whether the file `3_header.cache` exists; this contains the top of the page—the HTML `head` section and the start of the body. We've used PHP's `date` function to display the time at which the page was actually rendered, so you'll be able to see the different cache files at work when the page is displayed.

File: **3.php (excerpt)**

```
// Start buffering the output
ob_start();

// Handle the page header
if (!$header = readCache('3_header.cache', 604800)) {
  // Display the header
  ?>

  <!DOCTYPE html PUBLIC "-//W3C//DTD XHTML 1.0 Strict//EN"
    "http://www.w3.org/TR/xhtml1/DTD/xhtml1-strict.dtd">
  <html xmlns="http://www.w3.org/1999/xhtml">
  <head>
  <title> Chunked Cached Page </title>
  <meta http-equiv="Content-Type"
    content="text/html; charset=iso-8859-1" />
  </head>
  <body>
  The header time is now: <?php echo date('H:i:s'); ?><br />

  <?php
  $header = ob_get_contents();
  ob_clean();
  writeCache($header,'3_header.cache');
}
```

Note what happens when a cache file isn't found. Some content is output and assigned to a variable with `ob_get_contents`, after which the `ob_clean` function empties the buffer. This allows us to capture the output in "chunks" and assign it to individual cache files with `writeCache`. The header of the page is now stored as a file, which can be reused without our needing to re-render the page. Look back to the start of the `if` condition for a moment. When we called `readCache`, we gave it an expiry time of 604800 seconds (one week); `readCache` uses the file modification time of the cache file to determine whether the cache is still valid.

For the body of the page, we'll use the same process as before. However, this time, when we call readCache, we'll use an expiry time of five seconds; the cache file will be updated whenever it's more than five seconds old:

File: **3.php (excerpt)**

```
// Handle body of the page
if (!$body = readCache('3_body.cache', 5)) {
  echo 'The body time is now: ' . date('H:i:s') . '<br />';
  $body = ob_get_contents();
  ob_clean();
  writeCache($body, '3_body.cache');
}
```

The page footer is effectively the same as the header. After this, the output buffering is stopped and the content of the three variables that hold the page data is displayed:

File: **3.php (excerpt)**

```
// Handle the footer of the page
if (!$footer = readCache('3_footer.cache', 604800)) {
  ?>

  The footer time is now: <?php echo date('H:i:s'); ?><br />
  </body>
  </html>

  <?php
  $footer = ob_get_contents();
  ob_clean();
  writeCache($footer, '3_footer.cache');
}
// Stop buffering
ob_end_clean();

// Display the contents of the page
echo $header . $body . $footer;
?>
```

The end result looks like this:

```
The header time is now: 17:10:42
The body time is now: 18:07:40
The footer time is now: 17:10:42
```

The header and footer are updated on a weekly basis, while the body is updated whenever it is more than five seconds old.

The diagram in Figure 5.1 summarizes the chunked buffering methodology.

Figure 5.1. Chunked Buffering Flow Diagram

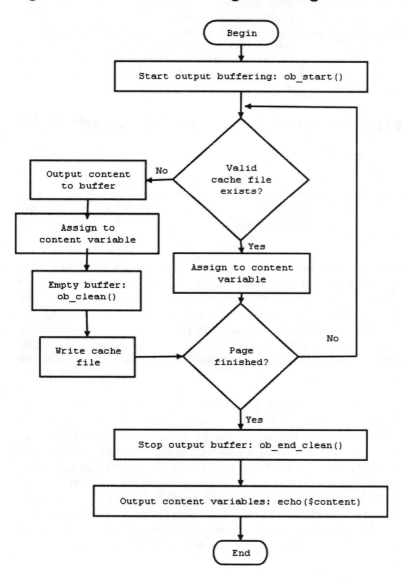

Nesting Buffers

You can **nest** one buffer within another practically *ad infinitum* simply by calling `ob_start` more than once. This can be useful if you have multiple operations that use the output buffer, such as one that catches the PHP error messages, and another that deals with caching. Care needs to be taken to make sure that `ob_end_flush` or `ob_end_clean` is called every time `ob_start` is used.

How do I implement a simple server side caching system?

Now that we have a grasp of the ideas behind output buffering, it's time to see how we can put this process into action in a manner that will be easy to maintain. To do this, we'll use a little help from PEAR::Cache_Lite (version 1.1 was used in the examples here).

As I mentioned, in the interests of keeping your code maintainable and having a reliable caching mechanism, it's a good idea to delegate the responsibility of caching logic to classes you trust. Cache_Lite provides a solid but easy to use library for caching, handling issues such as file locking, creating, checking for, and deleting cache files, controlling the output buffer, and directly caching the results from function and class method calls. More to the point, Cache_Lite should be relatively easy to apply to an existing application, requiring only minor code modifications.

There are three main classes in Cache_Lite. First is the base class, `Cache_Lite`, which deals purely with creating and fetching cache files, but makes no use of output buffering. This class can be used alone for caching operations in which you have no need for output buffering, such as storing the contents of a template you've parsed with PHP. The examples here will not use `Cache_Lite` directly, but will instead focus on the two subclasses. `Cache_Lite_Function` can be used to call a function or class method and cache the result; this might prove useful for storing a MySQL query result set, for example. The `Cache_Lite_Output` class uses PHP's output control functions to catch the output generated by your script, and store it in cache files; it allows you to perform tasks such as those we completed in the previous solution.

Here's an example of how you might use Cache_Lite to accomplish the task we completed in the last solution. When instantiating any of Cache_Lite's classes, we must first provide an array of options that determine the behavior of

Cache_Lite. We'll look at these in detail in a moment. Note that the cacheDir directory specified must be one to which the script has read and write access.

File: **4.php (excerpt)**

```php
<?php
// Include the PEAR::Cache_Lite Output class
require_once 'Cache/Lite/Output.php';

// Define options for Cache_Lite
$options = array(
  'cacheDir'        => './cache/',
  'writeControl'    => 'true',
  'readControl'     => 'true',
  'readControlType' => 'md5'
);

// Instantiate Cache_Lite_Output
$cache = new Cache_Lite_Output($options);
```

For each chunk that we want to cache, we need to set a lifetime (in seconds) for which the cache should live before it's refreshed. Next, we use the start method, available only in the Cache_Lite_Output class, to turn on output buffering. The two arguments passed to the start method are an identifying value for this particular cache file, and a **cache group**. This is an identifier that allows a collection of cache files to be acted upon; it's possible to delete all cache files in a given group, for example (more on this in a moment). Once the output for this chunk has finished, we use the end method to stop buffering and store the content as a file.

File: **4.php (excerpt)**

```php
// Set lifetime for this "chunk"
$cache->setLifeTime(604800);

// Start the cache with an id and group for this chunk
if (!$cache->start('header', 'Static')) {
  ?>
  <!DOCTYPE html PUBLIC "-//W3C//DTD XHTML 1.0 Strict//EN"
    "http://www.w3.org/TR/xhtml1/DTD/xhtml1-strict.dtd">
  <html xmlns="http://www.w3.org/1999/xhtml">
  <head>
  <title> PEAR::Cache_Lite example </title>
  <meta http-equiv="Content-Type"
    content="text/html; charset=iso-8859-1" />
  </head>
  <body>
```

```
<h2>PEAR::Cache_Lite example</h2>
The header time is now: <?php echo date('H:i:s'); ?><br />
<?php
// Stop and write the cache
$cache->end();
}
```

Caching the body and footer follows the same procedure as the header. Note that we again specify a five second lifetime when caching the body:

File: **4.php (excerpt)**

```
$cache->setLifeTime(5);
if (!$cache->start('body', 'Dynamic')) {
  echo 'The body time is now: ' . date('H:i:s') . '<br />';
  $cache->end();
}

$cache->setLifeTime(604800);
if (!$cache->start('footer', 'Static')) {
  ?>
  The footer time is now: <?php echo date('H:i:s'); ?><br />
  </body>
  </html>
  <?php
  $cache->end();
}
?>
```

On viewing the page, Cache_Lite creates in the `cache` directory files with these names:

```
./cache/cache_Static_header
./cache/cache_Dynamic_body
./cache/cache_Static_footer
```

When the same page is requested later, the code above will use the cached file if it is valid and has not expired.

Protect your Cache Files

Make sure that the directory in which you place the cache files is not publicly available, or you may be offering your site's visitors access to more than you realize.

Cache_Lite Options

When instantiating `Cache_Lite` (or any of its subclasses, such as `Cache_Lite_Output`), there are a number of ways to control its behavior. These should be placed in an array and passed to the constructor as in the previous example:

File: **4.php (excerpt)**

```
// Define options for Cache_Lite
$options = array(
  'cacheDir'        => './cache/',
  'writeControl'    => TRUE,
  'readControl'     => TRUE,
  'readControlType' => 'md5'
);

// Instantiate Cache_Lite_Output
$cache = new Cache_Lite_Output($options);
```

In the current version (1.1) the available options are:

`cacheDir`	This is the directory in which the cache files will be placed. This defaults to the current script execution directory.
`caching`	This option switches on or off the caching behavior of Cache_Lite. If you have numerous Cache_Lite calls in your code and want to disable the cache for debugging, for example, this will be important. The default value is TRUE (caching enabled).
`lifetime`	This represents the default lifetime (in seconds) of cache files. It can be changed using the `setLifeTime` method. The default value is 3600 (one hour).
`fileNameProtection`	With this option activated, Cache_Lite uses an MD5 encryption hash to generate the filename for the cache file. This protects you from error when you try to use IDs or group names containing characters that aren't valid for filenames; it must be turned on when you use `Cache_Lite_Function`. The default is TRUE (enabled).

`fileLocking`	This is used to switch the file locking mechanisms on or off. The default is `TRUE` (enabled).
`writeControl`	This checks that a cache file has been written correctly immediately after it has been created, and throws a `PEAR::Error` if it finds a problem. Obviously, this would allow your code to attempt to rewrite a cache file that was created incorrectly, but comes at a cost in terms of performance. The default is `TRUE` (enabled).
`readControl`	This checks cache files that are being read for corruption. Cache_Lite is able to place inside the file a value, such as the string length of the file, which can be used to confirm that the cache file isn't corrupted. There are three alternative mechanisms for checking that a file is valid, and they're specified using the `readControlType` option. These mechanisms come at the cost of performance, but should help guarantee your visitors aren't seeing scrambled pages. The default value is `TRUE` (enabled).
`readControlType`	This specifies the type of read control mechanism to use. The available mechanisms are a cyclic redundancy check (`'crc32'`, the default value) using PHP's `crc32` function, an MD5 hash using PHP's `md5` function (`'md5'`), or a simple and fast string length check (`'strlen'`). Note that this mechanism is not intended to provide security from people tampering with your cache files; it's just a way to spot corrupt files.
`pearErrorMode`	This tells Cache_Lite how it should return PEAR errors to the calling script. The default is `CACHE_LITE_ERROR_RETURN`, which means Cache_Lite will return a `PEAR::Error` object
`memoryCaching`	With memory caching enabled, every time a file is written to the cache, it is stored in an array in Cache_Lite. The `saveMemoryCachingState` and `getMemoryCachingState` methods can be used to store and access the memory cache data between requests. The advantage of this is that the complete set of cache files can be stored in a single file, reducing the number

of disk read/writes by reconstructing the cache files straight into an array to which your code has access. We'll be sticking to the normal Cache_Lite mechanism here, but `memoryCaching` may be worth further investigation if you run a large site. The default value is TRUE (disabled).

`onlyMemoryCaching` — If this is enabled, only the memory caching mechanism will be used. The default value is TRUE (disabled).

`memoryCachingLimit` — This places a limit on the number of cache files that will be stored in the memory caching array. The more cache files you have, the more memory will be used up by memory caching, so it may be a good idea to enforce a limit that prevents your server from having to work too hard. Of course, this places no restriction on the *size* of each cache file, so just one or two massive files may cause a problem. The default value is 1000.

Purging the Cache

Cache_Lite's in-built lifetime mechanism for cache files provides a good foundation for keeping your cache files up to date, but there will be some circumstances in which you need the files to be updated immediately. For such cases, the methods `remove` and `clean` come in handy. The `remove` method is designed to delete a specific cache file; it takes the cache ID and group name of the file. To delete the page body cache file we created above, we'd use:

```
$cache->remove('body', 'Dynamic');
```

Using the `clean` method, we can delete all the files in our `cache` directory simply by calling the method with no arguments; alternatively, we can specify a group of cache files to delete. If we wanted to delete both the header and footer created above, we could do so like this:

```
$cache->clean('Static');
```

The `remove` and `clean` methods should obviously be called in response to events within an application. For example, if you have a discussion forum application, you probably want to remove the relevant cache files when a visitor posts a new message. Although it may seem like this solution entails a lot of code modifications, with some care it can be applied to your application in a global manner.

If you have a central script that's included in every page a visitor views, you can simply watch for incoming events (e.g. a variable like $_GET['newPost']) and have some code respond by deleting the required cache files. This keeps the cache file removal mechanism central and easier to maintain. You might also consider using the php.ini setting auto_prepend_file to include this code in every PHP script.

Caching Function Calls

In Chapter 2, we looked at accessing remote Web services with SOAP and XML-RPC. Because Web services are accessed over a network, it's often a very good idea to cache results so that they can be fetched locally, rather than repeating the same slow request multiple times. A simple approach might be to use PHP sessions, as we considered in that chapter, but as this solution operates on a per visitor basis, the opening requests for each visitor will still be slow. This is where Cache_Lite can come in very handy.

PEAR uses Cache_Lite

The PEAR Web installer (see Appendix D) takes advantage of Cache_Lite by caching the XML-RPC requests it makes to the PEAR Web server.

In "How do I consume SOAP Web services with PHP?" in Chapter 2, we built a client for a SOAP Web service based on its WSDL file; the service provided weather information for airports around the world. Here's the code that fetched the data from the remote server:

```
$countries = $stationInfo->listCountries();
```

and

```
$country = $stationInfo->searchByCountry($_GET['country']);
```

In both cases, these calls correspond to a request for data that's made over the network. Using Cache_Lite_Function, we could cache the results so the data returned from the service could be reused; this would avoid unnecessary network calls and significantly improve performance. Note that we're focusing on only the relevant code here. At the top, we include Cache_Lite_Function:

File: **5.php (excerpt)**

```
// Include PEAR::Cache_Lite_Function
require_once 'Cache/Lite/Function.php';
```

Further down, we instantiate the `Cache_Lite_Function` class with some options:

File: **5.php (excerpt)**

```
// Define options for Cache_Lite_Function
// NOTE: fileNameProtection = TRUE!
$options = array(
  'cacheDir'           => './cache/',
  'fileNameProtection' => TRUE,
  'writeControl'       => TRUE,
  'readControl'        => TRUE,
  'readControlType'    => 'strlen',
  'defaultGroup'       => 'SOAP'
);

// Instantiate Cache_Lite_Function
$cache = new Cache_Lite_Function($options);
```

It's important that the `fileNameProtection` option is set to `TRUE` (this is in fact the default value, but in this case I've set it manually to emphasize the point). If it were set to `FALSE`, the filename will be invalid, so the data will not be cached.

Here's how we make the calls to our SOAP client class:

File: **5.php (excerpt)**

```
$countries = $cache->call('stationInfo->listCountries');
```

And:

File: **5.php (excerpt)**

```
$country = $cache->call('stationInfo->searchByCountry',
  $_GET['country']);
```

If the request is being made for the first time, `Cache_Lite_Function` stores the results as serialized arrays in cache files (not that you need to worry about this), and this file is used for future requests until it expires. The `setLifeTime` method can again be used to specify how long the cache files should survive before they're refreshed; right now, the default value of 3,600 seconds (one hour) is being used.

In general Cache_Lite provides a solid, easy-to-implement library for solving caching issues. As we move to the "next level" of caching, for sites with particularly high traffic, it's worth examining PEAR::Cache[6], Cache_Lite's big brother. PEAR::Cache is a complete caching framework that offers greater flexibility than

[6] http://pear.php.net/package/CACHE

Cache_Lite, and ties in with database abstraction libraries such as PEAR::DB[7]. It also offers advanced features such as caching to shared memory, as an alternative to the file system, or, with help from the Msession PHP extension[8], storing cache data in load balanced sessions, which is particularly useful for load balanced Web servers. Further PEAR::Cache reading material is recommended for at the end of this chapter. Cache_Lite, however, offers more than enough functionality to meet the requirements of the majority of sites.

How do I control client side caching with PHP?

Having seen how to disable client side caching and deal with server side caching, it's time to look at a mechanism that allows us to take advantage of client side caches in a way that can be controlled from within a PHP script. This approach will *only* work if you are running PHP with an Apache Web server, because it requires use of the function `getallheaders` to fetch the HTTP headers sent by a Web browser. This function only works with Apache.

New Function Names

If you're using PHP version 4.3.0+ on Apache, HTTP headers are available with the functions `apache_request_headers`[9] and `apache_response_headers`[10]. The function `getallheaders` has become an alias for the new `apache_request_headers` function.

The mechanism for dealing with Web browser caches is again HTTP. A number of headers are involved in instructing Web browsers and proxy servers whether to cache a page; the situation is further complicated by the fact that some are only available with HTTP 1.1.

Examine HTTP Headers in your Browser

A simple but very handy tool for examining request and response headers is LiveHttpHeaders[11], which is an add-on to the Mozilla browser. It's worth knowing exactly what headers your script is sending, particularly when you're dealing with HTTP cache headers.

[7] http://pear.php.net/package/DB
[8] http://www.php.net/msession
[9] http://www.php.net/apache_request_headers
[10] http://www.php.net/apache_response_headers
[11] http://livehttpheaders.mozdev.org/

From the point of view of keeping it simple, we'll concentrate here on the HTTP 1.0 caching headers only, namely `Expires`, `Last-Modified`, and `If-Modified-Since`, as well as HTTP status code 304 (Not Modified).

Those headers available with HTTP 1.1, such as `Cache-Control` and `ETAG`, are intended to provide an advanced mechanism that can be used in conjunction with a Web session's state; in other words, the version of a given page displayed to a visitor who's not logged in may differ vastly from that displayed to a logged-in user. The HTTP 1.1 headers were added primarily to allow the caching of such pages.

Page Expiry

The header that's easiest to use is the `Expires` header, which sets a date (presumably in the future) on which the page will expire. Until that time, Web browsers are allowed to use a cached version of the page.

An example:

File: **6.php**

```php
<?php
/**
 * Sends the Expires HTTP 1.0 header.
 * @param int number of seconds from now when page expires
 */
function setExpires($expires)
{
  header('Expires: ' .
    gmdate('D, d M Y H:i:s', time() + $expires) . 'GMT');
}

// Set the Expires header
setExpires(10);

// Display a page
echo 'This page will self destruct in 10 seconds<br />';
echo 'The GMT is now ' . gmdate('H:i:s') . '<br />';
echo '<a href="' . $_SERVER['PHP_SELF'] .
  '">View Again</a><br />';
?>
```

The `setExpires` function sets the HTTP `Expires` header to a future time, defined in seconds. The above example shows the current time in GMT and provides a link that allows you to view the page again. Using your browser's Refresh button, you might tell the browser to refresh the cache. Using this link, you'll notice the time updates only once every ten seconds.

Dates and Times in HTTP

HTTP dates are always calculated relative to Greenwich Mean Time (GMT). The PHP function gmdate is exactly the same as the date function, except it automatically offsets the time to GMT, based on your server's system clock and regional settings.

When a browser encounters an Expires header, it caches the page. All further requests for the page that are made before the specified expiry time use the cached version of the page; no request is sent to the Web server.

The Expires header has the advantage of being easy to implement, but for most cases, unless you're a highly organized person, you won't know exactly when a given page on your site will be updated. Because the browser will only contact the server *after* the page has expired, there's no way to tell browsers that the page they've cached is out of date. You also lose some knowledge of the traffic to your Website, as the browser will not make contact with the server when requesting a page that has been cached.

Page Modification Time

A more useful approach is to make use of the Last-Modified and If-Modified-Since headers, both of which are available in HTTP 1.0. Technically, this is known as performing a **conditional GET**; whether you return any content is based on the condition of the incoming If-Modified-Since request header.

Using this approach, you need to send a Last-Modified header *every* time your PHP script is accessed. The next time the browser requests the page, it sends an If-Modified-Since header containing a time; your script can then identify whether the page has been updated since the time provided. If it hasn't, your script sends an HTTP 304 status code to indicate that the page has not been modified, and exits before sending the body of the page.

Providing a simple example of conditional GETs is tricky, but PEAR::Cache_Lite is a handy tool to show how this works. Don't get confused though; this is *not* meant to show server side caching; it simply provides a file that's updated periodically.

Here's the code:

```php
<?php
// Include PEAR::Cache_Lite
require_once 'Cache/Lite.php';

// Define options for Cache_Lite
$options = array(
  'cacheDir' => './cache/'
);

// Instantiate Cache_Lite
$cache = new Cache_Lite($options);

// Some dummy data to store
$id = 'MyCache';

// Initialize the cache if first time the page is requested
if (!$cache->get($id)) {
  $cache->save('Dummy', $id);
}

// A randomizer...
$random = array(0, 1, 1);
shuffle($random);

// Randomly update the cache
if ($random[0] == 0) {
  $cache->save('Dummy', $id);
}

// Get the time the cache file was last modified
$lastModified = filemtime($cache->_file);

// Issue an HTTP last modified header
header('Last-Modified: ' .
  gmdate('D, d M Y H:i:s', $lastModified) . ' GMT');

// Get client headers - Apache only
$request = getallheaders();

if (isset($request['If-Modified-Since'])) {
  // Split the If-Modified-Since (Netscape < v6 gets this wrong)
  $modifiedSince = explode(';', $request['If-Modified-Since']);

  // Turn the client request If-Modified-Since into a timestamp
  $modifiedSince = strtotime($modifiedSince[0]);
```

```
} else {
  // Set modified since to 0
  $modifiedSince = 0;
}

// Compare time the content was last modified with client cache
if ($lastModified <= $modifiedSince) {
  // Save on some bandwidth!
  header('HTTP/1.1 304 Not Modified');
  exit();
}

echo 'The GMT is now ' . gmdate('H:i:s') . '<br />';
echo '<a href="' . $_SERVER['PHP_SELF'] .
  '">View Again</a><br />';
?>
```

Remember to use the "View Again" link when you run this example (clicking Refresh usually clears your browser's cache). If you click on the link repeatedly, eventually the cache will be updated; your browser will throw out its cached version and fetch a new page rendered by PHP.

In the above example we used PEAR::Cache_Lite to create a cache file that is updated randomly. We ascertain the file modification time of the cache file with this line:

```
$lastModified = filemtime($cache->_file);
```

Technically speaking, this *is* a hack, as PEAR::Cache_Lite intends its `$_file` member variable to be private. However, we must use it to get the name of the cache file so that we can fetch its modification time.

Next, we send a `Last-Modified` header using the modification time of the cache file. We need to send this for *every* page we render, to cause visiting browsers to send us the `If-Modifed-Since` header upon every request.

```
// Issue an HTTP last modified header
header('Last-Modified: ' .
  gmdate('D, d M Y H:i:s', $lastModified) . ' GMT');
```

Use of the `getallheaders` function ensures that PHP gives us all the incoming request headers as an array. We then need to check that the `If-Modified-Since` header actually exists; if it does, we have to deal with a special case caused by older Mozilla browsers (below version 6), which appended an (illegal) extra field to their `If-Modified-Since` headers. Using PHP's `strtotime` function, we generate a timestamp from the date the browser sent us. If there is no such header, we set this timestamp to zero, forcing PHP to give the visitor an up-to-date copy of the page.

```
// Get client headers - Apache only
$request = getallheaders();

if (isset($request['If-Modified-Since'])) {
    // Split the If-Modified-Since (Netscape < v6 gets this wrong)
    $modifiedSince = explode(';', $request['If-Modified-Since']);

    // Turn the client request If-Modified-Since into a timestamp
    $modifiedSince = strtotime($modifiedSince[0]);
} else {
    // Set modified since to 0
    $modifiedSince = 0;
}
```

Finally, we check to see whether the cache has been modified since the last time the visitor received this page. If it hasn't, we simply send a **Not Modified** response header and exit the script, saving bandwidth and processing time by instructing the browser to display its cached copy of the page.

```
// Compare the time the content was last modified with cache
if ($lastModified <= $modifiedSince) {
  // Save on some bandwidth!
  header('HTTP/1.1 304 Not Modified');
  exit();
}
```

If you combine the Last-Modified approach with time values that are already available in your application (e.g. the time of the most recent news article, or expiry times from the server side caching system we saw in the last solution), you should be able to take advantage of Web browser caches and save bandwidth, while being able to gather your site's traffic information and improve its *perceived* performance.

Be *very* careful to test any caching performed in this manner, though; if you get it wrong, you may cause your visitors to have permanently out of date copies of your site.

Further Reading

❑ *Caching Tutorial for Web Authors and Webmasters*:
http://www.mnot.net/cache_docs/

This article represents the definitive discussion of Web caching.

❑ *Issuing Correct HTTP Headers*:
http://perl.apache.org/docs/general/correct_headers/correct_headers.html

This tutorial provides a useful discussion of HTTP headers in Perl, which can be readily applied to PHP.

❑ HTTP 1.1 RFC 2616 on Cache Control:
http://www.w3.org/Protocols/rfc2616/rfc2616-sec14.html#sec14.9

Here, you'll find a precise description of HTTP 1.1 cache control headers.

❑ *Output Buffering, and how it can Change Your Life*:
http://www.zend.com/zend/art/buffering.php

Zeev Suraski gives a short tour of what can be done with PHP's output buffering in this great article.

❑ *Output Buffering with PHP*:
http://www.devshed.com/Server_Side/PHP/OutputBuffering/

this article provides another look at PHP's output buffering, with notes on using it to capture PHP errors.

❑ *Caching PHP Programs with PEAR*:
http://www.onlamp.com/pub/a/php/2001/10/11/pearcache.html

Sebastian Bergmann introduces PEAR::Cache.

6

Development Technique

In this chapter, we take a step out away from solving particular problems, to look at general techniques that can make you and me better developers. "Better" may mean many things: more productive, more relaxed, able to take on more complex projects, able to deliver reliable and maintainable code... or able to sleep at night.

Some of what you read here may be obvious to you. Other parts may seem unusual, and others, completely foreign. In the end, what suits you is a matter of personal taste, but by trying some of the suggestions here you may find that a few things grow on you and become part of your development habits.

How do I optimize my code?

"Premature optimization is the root of all evil."
—Donald E. Knuth

When developing applications, the first stage should be to make design your top priority; we should sacrifice performance in favor of a well designed application architecture, and allow our code to be flexible and maintainable. When it comes to putting your application online, though, performance becomes an issue.

In general, assuming you haven't made any critical mistakes in your code, performance is really a hardware issue (i.e. you have the option to throw memory, faster processors etc. at the problem); it may also be solved with Caching (see Chapter 5).

That said, it's important to know the techniques you can use to optimize your code without either breaking it or sacrificing the design. Looking for ways to optimize code should be a final stage of design.

Here, we'll look at some specific examples that are common to PHP applications, and suggest alternative approaches to structure the code and help performance.

I'll also be introducing you to the **Xdebug extension**[1], which, aside from being a very handy script debugging tool, also allows you to profile your code—a powerful technique for finding bottlenecks in your development. Profiling involves examining what your code does at runtime from the perspective of the work the PHP engine has to perform in order to execute it. With Xdebug you can generate a report of how your code performs; perhaps you'll format it to show the function calls that take the most time to execute first, so you can focus on optimizing those functions without breaking your overall design.

The online documentation does a good job of explaining how to install Xdebug; it should be easy to set up on all common operating systems where PHP is used—Linux, Windows and MacOS. Note that on Windows systems, Xdebug often requires that you have the latest stable release of PHP installed; to this, Xdebug can be installed as an extension like any other. For example, you could simply add the following to your `php.ini` file:

```
extension = xdebug-4.3.2-1.2.0-win32.dll
```

Some of the "common optimizations" suggested here have popped up elsewhere in this book, in highlighting mistakes, or in presenting specific solutions for problems that, while obscure, yield better performance without requiring radical alterations to your code.

---

[1] http://www.xdebug.org/

> **The Performance Cost of OOP**
>
> Some people writing PHP applications still rail against the idea of using classes and objects to build applications. They're opposed to this philosophy because of the cost in performance it entails, and yes, it's true—using an object oriented approach to solve a problem will be a little slower than the equivalent procedural code. What is important to remember about OOP is that it improves radically your performance as a developer; if you have infinite time to waste, lucky you! But for the rest of us, the object oriented paradigm far outstrips procedural coding in terms of reduced development times.

Most Probable First

A core aspect of any PHP application will typically be some sort of control structure, such as an `if-else` statement. Often, these are written in a manner that suits the way humans think, but this may not produce the most effective code in terms of speed and performance. By placing the most *probable* condition first, you can help PHP complete an `if-else` statement faster.

For example, let's say we have a function, `isBlue`, which checks to see if a variable passed to it has the value `'blue'`. If, most of the time, the value is given the function `'red'`, rather than `'blue'`, it would be better to react to that condition first.

The following example serves as a test to prove this:

File: **1.php (excerpt)**

```php
<?php
// Check Xdebug is installed
if (!extension_loaded('xdebug')) {
  die('<a href="http://xdebug.derickrethans.nl/">Xdebug</a> ' .
      'required');
}

// Start Xdebug profiling
xdebug_start_profiling();

// A array of colors "weighted" to red
$colors = array('red', 'red', 'red', 'red', 'red', 'red', 'red',
  'blue');

// The slow way
function isBlueSlow($color)
{
```

```php
  if ($color == 'blue') {
    return TRUE;
  }
  return FALSE;
}

// The fast way - test for red first
function isBlueFast($color)
{
  if ($color != 'blue') {
    return FALSE;
  }
  return TRUE;
}
```

To start with, we tell Xdebug to begin profiling. Using the $colors array, we have some sample data over which we can iterate to prove the point; note that most of the elements of the array have the value 'red', so this will be the most probable. The isBlueSlow function is written the way a human being would probably think about the problem; it simply checks whether the color is blue, and if not, it returns FALSE. The isBlueFast function first tests that the color *isn't* blue, and is based on prior knowledge of the data that's being tested; otherwise, it's logically the same as the isBlueSlow function, from the point of view of the values it will return.

To test the functions, we can use the following code:

File: **1.php (excerpt)**

```php
for ($i = 0; $i < 50; $i++) {
  if (!$color = each ($colors)) {
    reset($colors);
    $color = each($colors);
  }
  if (isBlueSlow($color['value'])) {
    // Do something here
  }
}

for ($i = 0; $i < 50; $i++) {
  if (!$color = each($colors)) {
    reset($colors);
    $color = each($colors);
  }
  if (isBlueFast($color['value'])) {
    // Do something here
```

```
    }
}

// Display the Xdebug report grouped by function call
xdebug_dump_function_profile(XDEBUG_PROFILER_NC);
?>
```

We test each of the functions with fifty function calls, iterating over the $colors array using PHP's each function. The report generated by Xdebug should look something like Figure 6.1, though of course, the absolute times will depend on the speed of your server.

Figure 6.1. Most Probably Faster

Execution Time Profile (sorted by number of calls to each function)			
Time Taken	Number of Calls	Function Name	Location
0.0019927025	50	*isblueslow()	c:\htdocs\phprecipes\developmenttechnique\1.php:32
0.0008553267	50	*isbluefast()	c:\htdocs\phprecipes\developmenttechnique\1.php:43

As you can see, when tested over fifty iterations, isBlueSlow turned out to take almost twice as long as isBlueFast. Of course, in a real application, the results would be unpredictable; it could be that on a particular run all the values were 'blue', which would make isBlueSlow quicker. But by designing the code to reflect the most *probable* input, you can improve the overall performance of the application on *average*.

Note that when we called xdebug_dump_function_profile, we passed it the constant XDEBUG_PROFILE_NC, which tells XDebug to merge all function calls from the same line in the script into a single entry in the output. There are a number of different profiling modes which XDebug provides to give you different "views" of what's actually happening in your PHP script. These modes range from a list of slowest function calls in order of execution time, to averages for each function. See the XDebug documentation for further details.

Although this example may seem trivial, it's common for applications to have many such "probable conditions"; by weighting all code to the most probable outcome, the end effect for a large application can be a significant increase in performance.

The for Loop

Another common pattern in PHP code is to use a for loop to step through the elements of an array until the end of the array is reached. PHP provides the function count to test the size of an array and, although it may look like nice, clean coding practice to place the count function call in the for loop, consider the following script:

File: **2.php**

```php
<?php
// Check Xdebug is installed
if (!extension_loaded('xdebug')) {
  die('<a href="http://xdebug.derickrethans.nl/">Xdebug</a> ' .
      'required');
}

// Create an array with element values from 1 to 50000
$numbers = range(1, 50000);

// Start Xdebug profiling
xdebug_start_profiling();

// For with count function call in loop
for ($i=0; $i < count($numbers); $i++) {
  // Do something here
}

// Place count() outside for loop
$size = count($numbers);
for ($i=0; $i < $size; $i++) {
  // Do something here
}

// Display the Xdebug line by line report
xdebug_dump_function_profile();
?>
```

Notice that in the first for loop, the count function is called each time the condition in the for loop is checked. In the second, we call the function only once and store the result in the variable $size. Xdebug tells me the total time in each case; the report from my testing is shown in Figure 6.2.

Figure 6.2. Taking Forever

Execution Time Profile (sorted by line numbers)			
Time Taken	Number of Calls	Function Name	Location
0.3070683479	50001	count()	c:\htdocs\phprecipes\developmenttechnique\2.php:13
0.0000029802	1	count()	c:\htdocs\phprecipes\developmenttechnique\2.php:18

The first loop wastes about 0.3 seconds by making 50001 calls to the `count` function. This is clearly improved by calling the function only once and storing the value in a variable.

Don't Be Greedy

Always be on the lookout for queries like this:

```
SELECT * FROM table
```

Generally speaking, you will never need to display the *complete* contents of a table to a user and, more importantly, queries like this endanger your application. If you have a table that gathers visitor stats, for example, it will grow very quickly. A `SELECT * FROM stats`, which looked fine when you developed your application, will eventually bring it to a grinding halt.

You should always be able to apply a limiting clause to a query, such as a `WHERE` clause, which fetches results for the last week only, or, if you're using MySQL, a `LIMIT` clause, which returns a limited set of results, allowing you to build a paged result set interface for your visitors.

Using `SELECT * FROM table` will select all the columns from a table. For a table with many fields, this may be unnecessary; consider limiting the query to the columns you need only (e.g. `SELECT title, date FROM articles`).

Lazy Inclusion

Including at the start of a script, or in some central include file, all the files you'll need to execute your script can make understanding the code easier. However, where classes are concerned, it may result in a large overhead as you load classes that aren't actually used for the current execution. It's perfectly reasonable to include the class files at the point at which they're required. For example:

```php
<?php
class LazyInclude {
  var $session;
  function LazyInclude()
  {
    // Include the class as it's needed
    require_once 'Session/Session.php';
    $this->session = &new Session();
  }
}

$li = new LazyInclude();
?>
```

Notice that in the above example we've used the `require_once` statement immediately before we actually needed to instantiate the `Session` class.

The trade off here is that it's harder to see which classes your code uses.

Quotes

Using double quotes when assigning values to strings causes PHP to check the contents for variables and special character codes; using single quotes tells PHP simply to regard the contents as a literal string.

Consider this code:

```php
$string = "<b>This string is searched for PHP variables</b>";
```

The above code is a little slower than this:

```php
$string = '<b>This string is taken as is</b>';
```

If you don't need to place variables in the string, or use escaped characters like \n (new line), stick to single quotes.

Reference or Copy?

In Volume I, Chapter 2 you learned about the ins of outs of references in PHP. In general, it takes longer to pass variables by reference than it does to use the default copying behavior of PHP. This is because the PHP engine has to trace to the original value in memory when references are used. In some cases that involve the use of OOP in PHP, references are essential to the design of the application, but if you're *sure* that for a particular problem you can legitimately use a copy of the object, doing so will result in a saving.

Note that copying variables uses up memory for each copy. This won't slow down a simple application under moderate load, but, implemented in large applications that deal with a lot of requests, could use up the physical memory of your server. The impact of this could be very significant, as the server must dip into virtual memory to run your application.

Xdebug

Where Xdebug is particularly useful is in examining applications that are near completion. The documentation explains the available reports it can generate, which can give an excellent overview of where the main bottlenecks lie, and help you focus your effort on specific functions and routines. It also encourages you to take a more systematic approach to optimizing your application, rather than using educated guesses in an *ad hoc* manner.

You can also log Xdebug data to a file, which will allow you to gather profile information while your application is online. Sometimes, problems won't show up until you're running in a live environment; the impact to a database table which now contains many megabytes of data, for example, might make itself clear only once your application's live and online.

How do I structure my application into layers?

The term **N-Tier** may or may not be familiar to you, but it's definitely a concept that's worth being aware of, as it makes a very useful measure of the design of your application. The "N" means "some number of", while "tier" refers to the layers in your application being like tiers on a wedding cake.

Let's step back into the past for a moment. In the old days of client-server computing on corporate networks, applications shared by multiple users were generally built with two tiers: a central database or file server, and a desktop application that accessed the central resource. This worked well for small groups of users, but as applications were distributed across regional and international networks and user bases grew, all sorts of problems ensued. The database might be overloaded, client side upgrades and maintenance became more expensive, and network latency delivered poor performance to users—and this was before people thought about putting their applications online!

These days, five is a generally accepted number of tiers for distributed and Web-based applications. What defines the tiers themselves is open to discussion, but if we think about a typical PHP application, the tiers could be described as shown in Figure 6.3.

Figure 6.3. N-Tier PHP

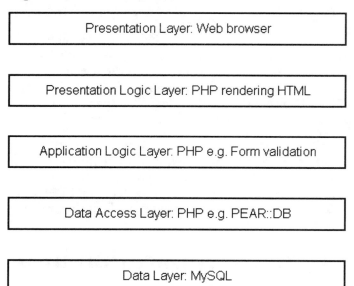

The names of the tiers themselves vary, as N-Tier is not a well-defined standard. For example, the application logic layer is sometimes referred to as the business logic layer, while the presentation layer is often confused with the presentation logic layer. In general, though, what happens at each layer is fairly well agreed upon, as the diagram suggests; vendors like Sun and Microsoft will generally refer to a very similar five tier structure, using their own technologies, of course.

The Principles of N-Tier

When we talk about an N-Tier application, a few general principles are inferred; these principles apply to the tiers themselves.

☐ Each layer *must* be able to exist on a physically independent system and be able to communicate over a network. Having said that, the layers do not *have* to be separate systems—they need only be designed in such a way that this is *possible*. Communication between layers on separate systems must be able to be handled over a network, with the help of some intermediate technology like SOAP or XML-RPC. In other words, this principle is something of a thought experiment for developers: "Is this layer distributable?" By applying this principle, the architecture as a whole becomes scalable, for example, allowing it to be expanded with load balancing technologies as site traffic increases.

☐ Each layer should exchange information only with the layers above and below it. For example, the presentation logic tier may not exchange information directly with the data access tier, but must communicate only with the business tier; this will act as the interface to the data access tier.

☐ Each layer should be replaceable with other equivalent technologies. At the presentation layer, this means that Mozilla or Opera should function just as well as Internet Explorer when viewing a site. For the presentation logic layer, it should be possible to render alternative content types to HTML, such as WML (wireless mark up language) or SOAP. Down at the data tier, this might mean being able to replace MySQL with PostgreSQL. Two further principles stem from this one:

    ☐ Each layer should have a clearly defined interface, or API.

    ☐ Layers should expect nothing of other layers, except that they conform to the defined APIs.

But What's the point?

The concepts behind N-Tier deliver three key benefits.

First, by designing in accordance with the N-Tier principles, an application has a better chance of coping with future traffic and performance demands, as it's able to scale well within each tier. For example, as traffic increases, you may need to run multiple MySQL servers with data replication, or use multiple load balanced Web servers to serve content. When doing this, the preservation of PHP sessions, for example, becomes a problem, but with a reasonable N-Tier design it should be possible to adapt the application to the new requirements without any significant code rewriting. Perhaps you simply modify your session handling logic so that, instead of accessing session data from the local file system, it shares session data with the help of PHP's Msession extension[2].

Secondly, N-Tier aims to make developers independent of specific vendors, other than the vendor of your programming language (the PHP Group and Zend). It should be possible to swap MySQL for another database server with minimal impact on your code. It should also be possible for users running browsers other than Internet Explorer to have the same experience as IE users browsing your site. Note that database abstraction layers like PEAR::DB go some of the way to making you independent of a specific database, but, vendors being vendors, all have their own implementations of SQL, to "keep the punters coming back for more." In some cases, the nonstandard syntax, such as MySQL's LIMIT clause or FULLTEXT searching, is too tempting to ignore, but be aware that these will come back to bite you if you wish to move to another database at some point in the future.

Thirdly, and perhaps most importantly, is that the N-Tier model can help developers design well structured, flexible applications that are easy to maintain. By considering your application in terms of "which layer should this code be in?", a large chunk of the design decisions fall into place.

Consider the following, fairly typical, procedural PHP script:

File: **4.php**

```php
<?php
// Start Data Access Layer
if (!mysql_connect('localhost', 'harryf', 'secret')) {
  die('Could not connect to database server');
}
if (!mysql_select_db('sitepoint')) {
  die('Could not select database');
}
// End Data Access

// Start Presentation Logic
if (isset($_GET['id'])) {

  // Start Application logic
  $sql = "SELECT title, body, published FROM articles
          WHERE article_id='" . $_GET['id'] . "'";
  // End Application logic
```

---

[2] http://www.php.net/msession

```php
// Start Data Access
$result = mysql_query($sql);
$row = mysql_fetch_array($result);
// End Data Access Layer

// Start Application logic
$date = date('Y m d', $row['published']);
// End Application logic

// Start Presentation Logic
echo "<h1>" . $row['title'] . "</h1>\n";
echo "Published: $date<br />";
echo $row['body'] . "<br />\n";
// End Presentation Logic

} else {

// Start Application logic
$sql = "SELECT article_id, title FROM articles LIMIT 0, 5";
// End Application logic

// Start Data Access
$result = mysql_query($sql);
while ($row = mysql_fetch_array($result)) {

// Start Application logic
$date = date('Y m d', $row['published']);
// End Application logic

// Start Presentation Logic
echo "<a href=\"" . $_SERVER['PHP_SELF'] . "?id=" .
    $row['article_id'] . "\">" . $row['title'] . "</a>" .
    $date . "<br />\n";
// End Presentation Logic

}
// End Data Access

}
// End Presentation Logic
?>
```

Now, the three of the five tiers in the N-Tier model that are typically written in PHP are the data access layer, the application logic layer and the presentation logic layer. In the above script, I've marked the sections of the code that could be regarded as being parts of one layer or another. Even at a quick glance, it's clear that the layers are mixed together, and there's no clear order to N-Tier terms.

Taking a step towards implementing the above code in an N-Tier fashion, the following example moves as many of the layers as possible into separate classes. We'll reuse the `Articles` and `Article` classes we developed to render PDFs in Chapter 3, this time, to render HTML. This is, after all, part of the point of N-Tier—it helps make code reusable for solving different problems.

File: **5.php**

```php
<?php
// Data Access Layer Classes
require_once 'Database/MySQL.php';
require_once 'ExampleApps/Articles.php';

// Application Logic Class
require_once 'ExampleApps/Article.php';

// Presentation Logic Classes
require_once 'ExampleApps/ArticlesView.php';
require_once 'ExampleApps/ArticleView.php';

$db = &new MySQL('localhost', 'harryf', 'secret', 'sitepoint');

if (isset($_GET['id'])) {
  $articles = &new Articles($db);
  $articles->getArticle($_GET['id']);
  $article = $articles->fetch();
  $view = &new ArticleView($article);
} else {
  $articles = &new Articles($db);
  $articles->getArticles();
  $view = &new ArticlesView($articles);
}

echo $view->render();
?>
```

The `if-else` condition is still present, which is part of the application logic (replacing it completely would make the example overly complicated), but otherwise, you can see from the classes we've included at the start how we've broken the code into a data access layer, an application logic layer, and a presentation logic layer.

If we want to access an alterative data source, such as PostgreSQL, all we should need to do is write a `PostgreSQL` class with the same API as the `MySQL` class, then modify the `require_once` statement to include the correct file, and modify the class name when we instantiate it.

The same applies to the presentation logic layer. The classes `ArticlesView` and `ArticleView` are currently geared to rendering HTML. If we write with the same API two classes that render WML instead of HTML, again, all we need to do is modify the included file names and the names of the classes we instantiate so that it's easy to exchange one presentation logic layer for another. Also, we're able to use the underlying `Articles` and `Article` classes, originally created to render PDF documents; the presentation logic was very different here, but there was no need to reproduce the database queries, thanks to these reusable classes.

So, where the presentation logic, in particular, is concerned, the benefit of using an N-Tier approach to application design is clear. With some care, we can render all sorts of content types, such as PDF, XHTML, XML, and so on, simply by "slotting in" the correct class. Achieving the same result with the procedural example with which we began would potentially involve writing a completely new version, reproducing the data access and application logic layers, and would probably result in many files containing more or less the same code. The moment we modify a column name in the table, for example, we have to modify all the files that access the table, whereas with my abstracted, N-Tier version, we'd only need to change one or perhaps two files, making only minor modifications.

How do I read API documentation?

API documentation is a nicely formatted reference to a set of classes, which a program has automatically generated based on the source code of those classes.

If you're used to reading the excellent PHP manual with its detailed function descriptions, understanding API documentation can be confusing—especially if your OOP skills are uncertain. Once you grasp the concept, however, reading this documentation can help make object oriented programming more accessible to you, and can open you up to the wealth of freely available open source PHP classes found in various online repositories. No longer will you need to trawl through the source code, scratching your head...

The first thing to understand is how API documentation is generated. When writing classes, most developers place comments in the code. One of the many tools that generates PHP documentation then uses these comments to build the

API documents automatically. This approach to generating API documentation from source code comments was first introduced to the mainstream by Sun's launch of the Javadoc utility, which produces (now famous) API documentation such as the Java API Reference[3]. Most PHP documentation generation tools use a similar approach to Javadoc (there's even a modified version of Javadoc for PHP, called PHPDoc[4]).

Let's look at a simple PHP example:

File: **6.php**

```php
<?php
/**
 * @abstract
 */
class Something {

}
/**
 * This class does something.
 */
class DoesSomething extends Something {
  /**
   * Stores some string
   * @access private
   * @var string
   */
  var $someString;
  /**
   * Constructs DoesSomething
   * @param string Some string
   */
  function DoesSomething($someString)
  {
    $this->someString = $someString;
  }
  /**
   * Returns the stored someString
   * @param boolean whether to format XML entities
   * @return string
   * @access public
   */
  function getSomeString($specialChars = FALSE)
```

[3] http://java.sun.com/j2se/1.4.2/docs/api/
[4] http://www.callowayprints.com/phpdoc/

```
{
  if (!$specialChars) {
    return $this->someString;
  } else {
    return htmlspecialchars($this->someString);
  }
}
}
?>
```

Notice the comment lines that begin with the @ symbol? These describe the behavior of the class, and are extracted by the **documentation parser** to generate the API documentation. For more detail, see " How do I generate API documentation? "

The upshot is that, passed through the right documentation generation tool, the above classes can be used to generate documentation like that shown in Figure 6.4.

Figure 6.4. Generated API Documentation

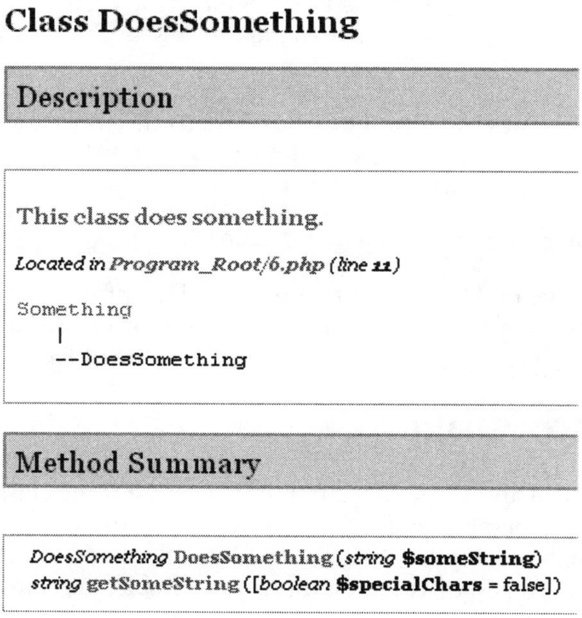

Class DoesSomething

Description

This class does something.

Located in Program_Root/6.php (line 11)

```
Something
   |
   --DoesSomething
```

Method Summary

DoesSomething DoesSomething (*string* **$someString**)
string getSomeString ([*boolean* **$specialChars** = false])

What good API documentation should do is tell you what "goes in" to a class, and what "comes out", as well as explaining what the available methods are meant to be used for. Assuming the API documentation is adequate and the class design is acceptable (e.g. it involves no undeclared dependence on global variables), API documentation should provide all the information you need to use a class—there's no need to worry about what's happening "behind the scenes" in the source code itself.

This development experience is much the same as most people's use of the built-in PHP functions; when was the last time you looked at the C source code of the PHP function you just called? If the code is adequately designed, there's no need to look under the hood.

The difficult part of dealing with class API documentation is that, if you're uncertain of OOP in PHP, it may make you more confused than enlightened. API documentation does assume a general knowledge of the use of classes and objects (so make sure you've read Volume I, Chapter 2), but you don't need to be an OOP guru to be able to benefit from a class someone else has written.

Once you've grasped the basics of OOP, the next step is to understand how classes are normally depicted in API documentation. In Figure 6.4 above, for example, notice the lines connecting the DoesSomething class to the Something class. This represents the fact that DoesSomething extends Something (i.e. it's a subclass of Something).

Also, the API documentation describes class methods similarly to the way functions are explained in the PHP manual. The getSomeString method in my DoesSomething class would be described with a **signature** like this:

```
string getSomeString([boolean $specialChars = false])
```

The word "string" identifies the type of data the method returns. The information inside the parentheses tells us we can pass a Boolean value (TRUE or FALSE) as an argument to this method, but that the argument has a default value of FALSE.

Private, Protected and Public

In programming languages like Java and C++, it's common to define some class methods and member variables as being **private** (or sometimes, as **protected**. where Java is concerned). This tells a compiler that any code that accesses object instances of the class is not allowed to use these methods or variables directly. Attempts to do so will usually generate some kind of error at compile time. This enforces the notion of **encapsulation** that's advocated by the object oriented paradigm: that users of a class should only access objects of that class via the public doorways—its public methods and variables.

PHP 4 does not restrict what you can and can't access inside an object. You're free to "talk" to any method or member variable you want to. Whether you *should* access them directly is another question altogether. Often, the developer who built the class will provide member variables and methods that are meant for internal use only, for example, storing some temporary data about the state of the object while it's in use. As a result, while there's no enforcement of object privacy in PHP 4, many developers will use comments to mark a method or class variable as private, thereby telling other developers not to use it.

These access control markers will be spotted by an API documentation parser; the generated documentation will indicate which methods and variables are intended for public use, and which are private.

Access Control in PHP 5

Note that PHP 5 will support the Java convention of being able to declare private, protected, and public class members, and will enforce those restrictions.

Practice Makes Perfect

It's fine to talk about API documentation, but, unless you've got some staring you in the face, it's unlikely to make sense. The best approach is to get your hands dirty by picking some well-known PHP classes and examining the documentation. Here are some suggestions:

PHPMailer

In Volume I, Chapter 8, we looked at `PHPMailer` in detail, as a tool for creating advanced emails that can easily be managed using PHP's `mail` function. Because practically all PHP coders will be very familiar with the issues of sending email from PHP, this makes a great project to start learning how to use API documentation and classes in general. `PHPMailer` also has a fairly simple class hierarchy, so you won't need to worry about issues such as inheritance. Looking at "How do I simplify the generation of complex emails?" in Volume I, Chapter 8, we had:

```php
<?php
// Include the phpmailer class
require 'ThirdParty/phpmailer/class.phpmailer.php';
```

```php
// Instantiate it
$mail = new phpmailer();

// Define who the message is from
$mail->From = 'you@yourdomain.com';
$mail->FromName = 'Your Name';

// Set the subject of the message
$mail->Subject = 'Test Message';

// Add the body of the message
$body = 'This is a test';
$mail->Body = $body;

// Add a recicient address
$mail->AddAddress('you@yourdomain.com', 'Your Name');

// Send the message
if (!$mail->Send()) {
  echo 'Mail sending failed';
} else {
  echo 'Mail sent successfully';
}
?>
```

The PHPMailer API documentation[5] says that the AddAddress method used above has the following signature:

```
void AddAddress(string $address[, string $name = ""])
```

This means that calling this method will return a value of type void (i.e. it doesn't return anything). It accepts two strings as arguments, the first being required (the email address), and the second being optional (the name of the person you're sending the email to). Now, let's look at how we used this method in the example:

```
$mail->AddAddress('you@yourdomain.com', 'Your Name');
```

Is it starting to make sense yet? What about the Send method? The documentation says:

```
bool Send()
```

---

[5] http://phpmailer.sourceforge.net/docs/

That is, this method returns a Boolean value (either TRUE or FALSE), depending on the success or failure of the attempt to send the email.

HAWHAW

In Chapter 3, we looked at how to use HAWHAW to generate WML (Wireless Markup Language) pages for handheld devices. HAWHAW represents another good way to become more comfortable with API documentation. The HAWHAW classes have no inheritance relationships, but do involve multiple classes between which relationships exist.

In "How do I render WML with PHP?" in Chapter 3, we considered an example that used the HAWHAW library to make articles available to handheld devices. Let's look at a small piece of that code now:

```
// Instantiate the HAW_Deck root node
$wml = new HAW_deck('SitePoint Articles');

// For Web browsers...
$wml->set_waphome('http://www.sitepoint.com/');

// Instantiate HAW_link for the "Home" url
$home = new HAW_link('Home', $url);

// Add the link to the WML document
$wml->add_link($home);
```

Two classes are instantiated here—the Haw_deck and Haw_link classes. Let's first take a glance at the API documentation[6] for the constructor of the Haw_deck class.

This documentation has a slightly different format from what we've seen so far—the signatures are a little less descriptive than they were for PHPMailer—but here's what the API documentation has to say about the constructor:

```
public HAW_deck(var $title,
                var $alignment,
                var $output)
```

As you know, constructors never return values, hence there's no return value described here. The word public tells us that we're free to instantiate the class (thereby using the constructor). In some cases, we may see private or protected

---

[6] http://www.hawhaw.de/ref/php/index.html

for a constructor; this means the class is supposed to be created automatically by some other class, not your code. The three parameters this constructor takes are not clear in the signature, but if we consult the description that comes with the constructor, we'll find noted there the values we're expected to provide, as well as the fact that they're all optional.

More interesting is the point at which the `add_link` method is used to add the `Haw_link` object to the `Haw_deck` object:

```
$wml->add_link($home);
```

The API documentation shows the signature for this method as:

```
public void add_link(var $link)
```

We have also to look at the method description, which tells us that this method "Adds a `HAW_link` object to `HAW_deck`."

Eclipse

The Eclipse PHP library[7] provides a prime example of many of the principles of the object oriented paradigm, expressed in PHP. It was developed by Vincent Oostindie, occasional visitor to the SitePoint Forums[8], as part of the course work for his University studies. Hence, the design is as "by the book" as possible, making it an excellent library with which to spark your own ideas.

Eclipse "Community Edition"

The Eclipse library is also available on SourceForge[9], where work is in progress to develop the "Community Edition" of the library and expand on its functionality.

Among the classes it provides is a database abstraction layer; the API document-ation[10] for this layer demonstrates how class hierarchies are portrayed. A prime example is the `MyDatabase` (MySQL) class, which inherits from the abstract `Database` class. Figure 6.5 shows how the API documentation illustrates this re-lationship.

---

[7] http://www.students.cs.uu.nl/people/voostind/eclipse/
[8] http://www.sitepointforums.com/
[9] http://sourceforge.net/projects/eclipselib/
[10] http://www.students.cs.uu.nl/people/voostind/eclipse/api/index.html

Figure 6.5. **MyDatabase Extends Database**

Class Tree Index
PREV CLASS   NEXT CLASS
SUMMARY: INNER | FIELD | CONSTR | METHOD

Class MyDatabase

```
Database
  |
  +--MyDatabase
```

Also in the MyDatabase class is the factory method, query, which returns an object created from a class called MyQueryResult. This class has the following signature:

```
public MyQueryResult query(var $sql)
```

The signature tells us that the query method returns a value of type MyQueryResult (in other words, an object of class MyQueryResult).

Looking at the source code for that method, we see:

```
/***
 * @returns MyQueryResult
 ***/
function &query($sql)
{
  return new MyQueryResult($this,
    mysql_query($sql, $this->getLink()));
}
```

How do I generate API documentation?

Generating your own API documentation for classes you've written is surprisingly easy, and PHP has some excellent tools for the job. The main issue is getting into the habit of adding to your comments the tags that the documentation generator extracts and uses to describe the classes, methods, and member variables in your code. Once you get into the swing of things, you might realize that the types of comments you currently provide to explain what your code is doing are, in many ways, unnecessary; a well designed class will be structured so that the names of the methods themselves suggest what a section of code does. You'll likely keep each method streamlined, rather than writing large blocks of procedural code, and you'll come to realize that all that really matters is letting users know what goes in, what comes out, and a general idea of how to use the class.

The writing of API documentation may lead you to one other healthy practice. It will encourage you to begin by writing a "blank" class that just defines the method and member variable names and documents what they do without filling in any code. This makes a useful hands-on design stage that forces you to consider your class "from the outside", that is, from the perspective of the code that will use it.

All in all, if you're writing PHP code that's intended for consumption by others, publishing API documentation is one of those essential steps without which your project will be incomplete.

Choose your Weapons

The first problem is which documentation generation tool to choose. This is important, so it's worth investigating the options to work out which you prefer. The documentation syntax used by each tool varies; writing documentation for one will, at best, be only partially compatible with another. Of the *actively* developed alternatives, you have:

Doxygen: http://www.doxygen.org/
Doxygen is a documentation generation tool for multiple languages, including PHP. It's popular in the Linux community and is used by eZ systems to generate the documentation for the eZ publish framework[12]. If you program with C/C++, Java, or C#, as well as PHP, Doxygen is a great "one size fits all" solution, though the learning curve required to grasp it is probably slightly steeper than the alternatives.

PHP Edit: http://www.phpedit.net/
PHP Edit is a Windows IDE for writing PHP code, which comes with a documentation generation tool. If Windows is your chosen home, PHP Edit is on its way to becoming a very mature PHP development tool, even providing support for the generation of XMI (an XML format for UML diagrams).

---

[12] http://ez.no/developer

Umbrello UML Modeller: http://uml.sourceforge.net/

Although it's not a tool for generating API documentation per se, Umbrello is worthy of note (if you're a Linux user), as it's capable of generating PHP code from UML diagrams; in other words, it codes by drawing. You put together UML diagrams for your code and specify the APIs, then Umbrello generates "blank" classes that you fill with code. The problem with tools like this arises when you want to go in the other direction—from source code to UML diagram. However, Umbrello can make a very handy first stage in putting together a whole PHP project.

phpDocumentor: http://www.phpdoc.org/

phpDocumentor is rapidly becoming the standard tool for API documentation in PHP, and is my own tool of choice. What gives it the edge is that the documentation it produces is excellent—a very good sign for a tool that's supposed to generate documentation! The standard tag library (the @ tags you've seen in code throughout this book) is rich, and there's also a very friendly Web-based interface that can have you generating your first API docs within minutes of unzipping the phpDocumentor download. It's mature and stable, and it's endorsed by PEAR, which means the level of effort going into further development is higher than the average open source project. What's more, it's capable of generating output in numerous formats, and provides a range of HTML documentation styles with the base install, as well as PDF, Windows CHM, and DocBook XML. If you don't like any of those, no problem—you can create your own output format, which entails some template editing. Finally, the documentation attributes production of this tool to no less than sixteen authors, which means it's a very well supported project that's unlikely to fizzle out in the near future.

For the rest of this solution, we'll walk through a quick start guide to using php-Documentor, to start you generating your own API documentation. This isn't intended as a comprehensive guide; browsing the phpDocumentor site will provide you with extensive tutorials and detailed explanations of how to use the software. Here, we'll cover only the most common **doc tags**, so that you can begin using them straight away to build a class in stages.

We'll start with an empty class definition prefaced by a couple of sizable comments:

File: **7.php (excerpt)**

```php
<?php
/**
 * @package MyFirstDocumentedPackage
```

```
 */
/**
 * Randomizer Class
 *
 * Given an array this class allows you fetch random
 * elements from it.
 *
 * <code>
 * $randomizer = new Randomizer($array);
 * $randomElement = $randomizer->get();
 * </code>
 *
 * @author  Joe Bloggs <joe.bloggs@example.com>
 * @access  public
 * @package MyFirstDocumentedPackage
 */
class Randomizer {

}
?>
```

Sections of comments are called **DocBlocks**, and are identified with a special form of the /* */ PHP comment syntax:

```
/**
 * DocBlock comment here
 */
```

Each DocBlock is used to describe one element of the code within the file (or the file itself), such as a class member variable or method. Procedural PHP functions, the family of include functions, constants, and global variables can also be documented by phpDocumentor.

First of all, every PHP source file needs to start with a DocBlock that contains an @package comment to identify which **package** the file (but not the classes within the file, only the functions, includes and defines) belongs to. In the above example, the file belongs to the MyFirstDocumentedPackage package. A package is no more than a collection of related classes, and the concept of a package is virtual in PHP (i.e. PHP doesn't support packages as a language construct). The idea of grouping classes this way is inspired by Java; you might use it, for example, to group your database abstraction layer under a package called **Database**.

The second DocBlock above describes the Randomizer class itself. PHPDocumentor requires the use of the @package doc tag to identify the package the class belongs to, allowing it to distinguish the class from any procedural code in the script. The @access tag refers to the point in the code from which the class should be accessed. In this case, the class is declared public, meaning that this class may be used by code outside your application (see the previous solution for more information on public, private, and protected access). Note the code HTML tag we've used. This behaves in much the same way as the equivalent HTML element; in this case, it allows us to provide an example of how the class should be used. There are a few HTML-like tags available for use with phpDocumentor, such as b, ul, and ol, which help make comment text more readable.

Figure 6.6 shows the output phpDocumentor generates from what we've got so far.

Figure 6.6. The Randomizer Class Documentation

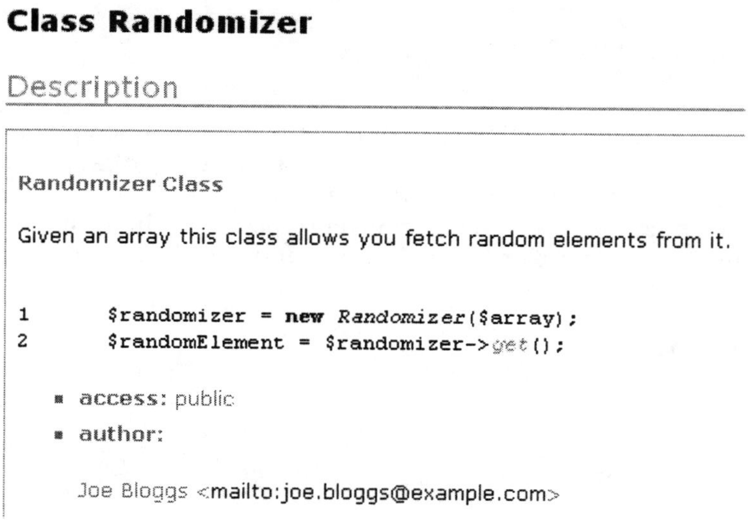

Class Randomizer

Description

Randomizer Class

Given an array this class allows you fetch random elements from it.

```
1        $randomizer = new Randomizer($array);
2        $randomElement = $randomizer->get();
```

- access: public
- author:

    Joe Bloggs <mailto:joe.bloggs@example.com>

Now, let's define a member variable with its own DocBlock:

File: **7.php (excerpt)**

```
class Randomizer {
  /**
   * Stores the array to be randomized
   * @var array
   * @access private
   */
  var $array = array();
}
```

The @var tag is used to define the **type** of a declared class member variable, the convention being to use one of PHP's native data types, or the name of a class if the variable will contain an object reference. We don't want people accessing the array directly, so we use @access private to mark it as such.

Let's move on to the constructor:

File: **7.php (excerpt)**

```
/**
 * Constructs Randomizer
 * @param array the array to be randomized
 * @access public
 */
function Randomizer($array)
{
  $this->array = $array;
  srand((float)microtime() * 1000000);
}
```

The @param doc tag is used to define the parameters a method accepts. For methods that accept multiple arguments, we use a series of @param tags in the order in which the parameters are defined in the method. The word occurring after the @param describes the type of the parameter (types being the same as for @var tags); any further text is used to provide a human-readable description of the parameter.

Now, let's see a method:

File: **7.php (excerpt)**

```
/**
 * Gets an element value from the array at random
 * @return mixed
 * @access public
 */
function get()
{
  shuffle($this->array);
  return $this->array[0];
}
}
?>
```

Here, we've used the @return tag to specify the data type that's being returned. In this case, the type is mixed because we don't know what type of array elements will be passed to the constructor.

It's now time to document. Simply extract phpDocumentor 1.2.0 (stable) to your local Web server, then point your browser at it. This will bring up the Web-based interface, as shown in Figure 6.7.

Figure 6.7. phpDocumentor Web Interface

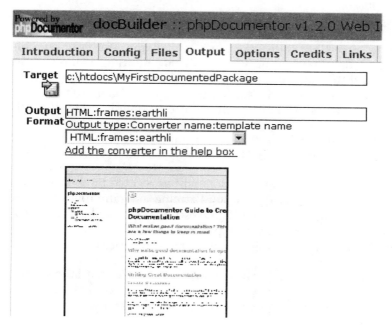

On the *Files* tab, specify the name of the file to be documented in the *Files to Parse* text area. Then, on the *Output* tab, specify the *Target* to point to the directory in which you want the documentation generated, and the *Output Format* to HTML:frames:earthli, which is the name of the desired documentation template (i.e. the look and feel of the documentation). Then, simply hit the Create button on the same tab and hey presto—instant documentation!

It really doesn't get much easier. Of course, phpDocumentor supports alternative interfaces, such as the command line (with help from the PHP command line binary), which would allow you to complete tasks such as running the document-ation generation process using a cron job.

The benefit of generating documentation this way is that it becomes very easy to make your code accessible to other developers with a minimum of hassle and effort.

How do I set up automated tests of my code?

"If it's not tested, it's broken."
—Bruce Eckel, *Thinking in Java*

Next time you write some PHP code—even just a small app—for your own interest, keep a note of how much time you spend bug hunting. I don't mean finding parse errors and the like, but actual situations in which the logic of your code doesn't perform as you expected it to. My guess is that you'll probably find yourself horrified by the amount of energy you waste troubleshooting. What if I told you that, by putting in a little extra effort up-front, you could more or less completely eliminate the time you waste on bug hunts, and end up with code about which you feel a lot more secure? All you need to become is test infected...

Unit Testing is a practical approach to development advocated by the **Extreme Programming** (XP) methodology[16]. Much of Extreme programming addresses issues related to project management, but Unit Testing, in particular, has struck a nerve among developers in practically every programming language you care to name—and is rapidly becoming a required development practice.

In the crudest terms, Unit Testing involves writing test code that sticks some data into your real code, and examines what it gets back to see if the result is what it's supposed to be. Before we go any further with the theory, though, let's put Unit Testing in context.

The general **testing lifecycle** of a good software project could be characterized as follows:

Unit testing	testing each piece of code
System or integration testing	testing the code within the type of environment in which it will be used
Acceptance testing	testing the application from an end user perspective

---

[16] http://www.extremeprogramming.org/

That theory probably doesn't apply to the majority of PHP projects, where you knock up a simple application in a matter of minutes. However, unless you're planning to delete the source file at the end of the day, it's likely that the code will gradually take on a life of its own, becoming a critical component of your site and a source of panic when you realize you didn't test it carefully enough.

What Unit Testing can do for you is automate the code testing process. Near the start of any new piece of code, you write a script that is designed to test it based on what you want the code in question to do. With the tests in place, you're able to re-execute them as many times as you like; they'll give you a very good idea of whether the code is broken, and, if there is a problem, a clear indication of where it lies.

As your projects grow to comprise numerous integrated components that rely on one another to work properly, being able automatically to test each piece becomes essential to the success of the project. All you have to do is invest the energy in writing the test scripts up-front...

There are two approaches to unit testing: **black box testing** (which is really what I'm talking about here) and **white box testing**.

Black box testing works outside the code that's being tested (the code is referred to as a black box), passing data to the code and examining what it gets back. This approach is particularly useful for classes that have a clear API. It also means that you don't have to mess with the code you're testing.

White box testing takes the view that everything can, and perhaps should, be tested, so there's no hiding behind APIs for those nasty bugs! It generally requires implanting the tests directly into the code being tested. In some cases it's essential—a class method may return the correct value but some operation it performed "behind the scenes" could have gone horribly wrong. You may already have used white box testing without realizing it, for instance, when using `print` statements inside a class to find out what it's doing internally.

 Tip

Gray Box Testing

The weaker encapsulation of PHP 4 (i.e. its lack of support for private/protected class members) provides one potential advantage here. It makes it possible for us to use a hybrid of black box and white box testing (gray box?) by accessing class member variables directly for test purposes, which can help pinpoint problems more accurately. You probably won't impress any object oriented purists, though...

Test Infected

Using Unit Testing as a development habit involves more than just adding tests to a project as an afterthought. In fact, the Extreme Programming methodology advocates writing the test scripts *before* you start developing the meat of your code. The argument behind this is that writing the test scripts helps you analyze the design of your classes' APIs without having to sit down and decide, "now, I'm going to analyze the API."

The general process of developing with Unit Tests looks like this:

1. Design your class API, perhaps with blank classes.

2. Create a test suite, modifying your API design as required to take into account this deeper insight.

3. Fill in the "blanks" of your class; write the code that does the real work.

4. Execute the test suite.

5. Fix logic errors, then repeat step 4 *ad infinitum*.

At first glance, this is clearly more work than the sort of development process you'll be used to if you're not writing Unit Tests today. The mission you have to set yourself is to become "test infected" by continually trying it until you can't code without the warm glow it gives you. Gradually, this approach will start to become a habit and, I promise you, you'll be wondering how you ever managed to code anything without it! If it all goes to plan, you will become so good at Unit Testing that it will *save* you time over the old trial-and-error coding method!

Test Drive

Now that we know roughly what Unit Testing is supposed to involve, it's time to put it into practice with an example. The first problem to overcome, though, is selecting a Unit Test framework to help you. There are at least five that I'm aware of, which can be confusing, as they all have more or less the same name. On the list of either "very stable or actively developed" are:

PhpUnit: http://phpunit.sourceforge.net/
This is probably the most stable test framework in PHP, though seemingly no longer being developed.

PEAR::PHPUnit: http://pear.php.net/package/PHPUnit

Intended as the test framework for PEAR, PHPUnit is likely to become the de facto Unit Test tool once PHP 5 arrives. However, the current version (0.6.2) has a number of bugs and is on hold, pending the release of PHP 5.

SimpleTest: http://www.lastcraft.com/simple_test.php

Developed by Marcus Baker, this is my own test framework of choice, and the one I used to test the code for this book. Although the current version is still Alpha, what's missing is advanced functionality; I've found the core to be very stable, as well as an excellent study of design patterns applied in PHP. More importantly, it has some important features, in particular Mock Objects (see below) and "Web test" tools (these are still work in progress), which, at a trivial level, can help you find broken links on your site, for example. More importantly, they can be an essential element in checks to confirm your site's security.

SimpleTest is the test framework we'll be using here, to demonstrate how unit testing works.

First, here are a couple of classes—one with a problem:

File: **8.php**

```php
<?php
/**
 * A Class for Collecting Stamps
 * @access public
 */
class StampCollection {
  /**
   * An array of Stamp objects
   * @var Stamp
   * @access private
   */
  var $collection = array();

  /**
   * Adds a stamp to the collection
   * @param Stamp
   * @return void
   * @access public
   */
  function add($stamp)
  {
    $this->collection[] .= $stamp;
```

```php
    }

    /**
     * Fetches a stamp to the collection
     * @return mixed
     * @access public
     */
    function fetch()
    {
      $stamp = each($this->collection);
      if ($stamp) {
        return $stamp;
      } else {
        reset($this->collection);
        return FALSE;
      }
    }
}

/**
 * Stores details of a single stamp
 * @access public
 */
class Stamp {
    /**
     * Name of the stamp
     * @var string
     * @access public
     */
    var $name;

    /**
     * Stores the price of the stamp
     * @var int
     * @access public
     */
    var $price;

    /**
     * Constructs Stamp
     * @param string name of stamp
     * @param int price of stamp
     * @access public
     */
    function Stamp($name, $price)
    {
```

```
    $this->name = $name;
    $this->price = $price;
  }
}
?>
```

Don't look too hard—you'll spoil the fun!

OK, let's write a test script for the `Stamp` class. The general process is to create another class that extends SimpleTest's `UnitTestCase` class, then place into it methods beginning with the word "test," which SimpleTest will use to identify and execute them. First, the necessary includes:

File: **9.php (excerpt)**

```
<?php
if (!defined('SIMPLE_TEST')) {
  // Modify this line to point at your simpletest installation
  define('SIMPLE_TEST', '../../simpletest/');
}
require_once SIMPLE_TEST . 'unit_tester.php';
require_once SIMPLE_TEST . 'reporter.php';
require_once '8.php'; // The StampCollection and Stamp classes
```

Here, the constructor for the class extends `UnitTestCase` and calls the `UnitTestCase` constructor:

File: **9.php (excerpt)**

```
// Create the test class
class TestOfStamp extends UnitTestCase {
  function TestOfStamp()
  {
    $this->UnitTestCase('Stamp');
  }
}
```

Next, we define a test method, `testName`, within which we create a `Stamp` object, then use SimpleTest's `assertEqual` method to check whether the name was set correctly. Pretty simple, don't you think?

File: **9.php (excerpt)**

```
// Test the name of the stamp
function testName()
{
  // Create a Stamp object
  $stamp = new Stamp('Penny Black', 3500);
```

```
// Compare the names of the stamps
$this->assertEqual($stamp->name, 'Penny Black');
}
```

Here's another test method:

File: **9.php (excerpt)**

```
// Test the name of the stamp is a string
function testNameType()
{
    // Create a Stamp object
    $stamp = new Stamp('Penny Black', 3500);

    // Compare the names of the stamps
    $this->assertTrue(is_string($stamp->name));
}
```

Here, we create a fresh `Stamp` object, and check the type of the `$name` member variable with PHP's `is_string` function. We use SimpleTest's `assertTrue` method to check that `is_string` is returning a true value.

Next, we do the same thing to set the contents and type of the stamp price:

File: **9.php (excerpt)**

```
// Test the price of the stamp
function testPrice()
{
    // Create a Stamp object
    $stamp = new Stamp('Penny Black', 3500);

    // Compare the names of the stamps
    $this->assertEqual($stamp->price, 3500);
}

// Test the price of the stamp is an int
function testPriceType()
{
    // Create a Stamp object
    $stamp = new Stamp('Penny Black', 3500);

    // Compare the names of the stamps
    $this->assertTrue(is_int($stamp->price));
}
}
```

Now, you may be fairly underwhelmed by the tests we've completed here. Why bother testing simple variable assignments like this? The Stamp class is very basic, after all. While that's true at the moment, this test script defines how we expect the Stamp API to behave, and by having the test written for it, we've essentially set the API "in concrete." This is important because other code will depend on the Stamp class to perform in a particular way. At some point in the future, we could decide to make a few minor modifications to the Stamp constructor which, for instance, change the type of the price from an integer to a string; although, technically, this won't *break* the Stamp class, it will change the API (remember the tags in the method comments that describe the types), which may cause other code using the class to break. Simple Unit Tests like these will catch these kinds of mistakes.

In short, the idea is to *write the simplest set of tests that will ensure that the behavior of the class will exactly match its API documentation.*

To execute the tests, we finish the script by instantiating the test class, and then, using an HtmlReporter object (provided by SimpleTest), which displays the test results in HTML format, we call the run method to execute the tests.

File: **9.php (excerpt)**

```
$test = &new TestOfStamp();
$test->run(new HtmlReporter());
?>
```

Viewed with a browser, the result looks like Figure 6.8.

Figure 6.8. Congratulations! You've Passed!

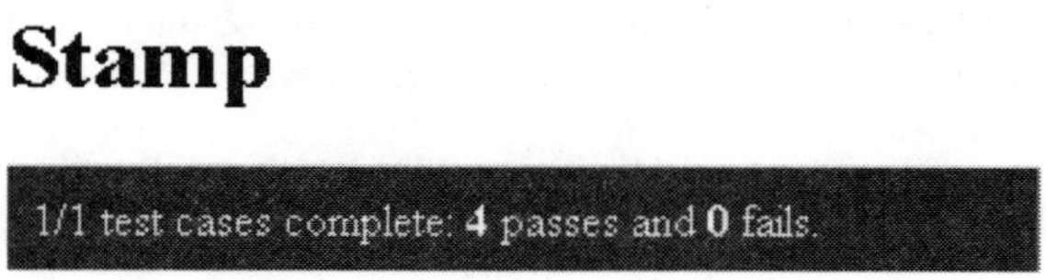

Stamp

1/1 test cases complete: **4** passes and **0** fails.

So far, so good. But what about the StampCollection class?

Mock Objects

One area of Unit Testing that you may be wondering about is dealing with situations where one class uses another. What about classes that make use of data from an external source, such as a database? These will surely require us to execute the tests in an environment in which there's a database with some sample data we can use, right? Well, not necessarily! In fact, one tenet of Unit Testing is that you should only test the particular unit in question—not other classes at the same time. In particular, the tests should be isolated, as much as possible, from external environments like databases. Otherwise, these external environments will reduce the scope of the test to a specific case. Testing against databases and other external data sources is more a part of the integration tests that happen as the next step in the test lifecycle.

To solve this problem, the answer is to use **mock objects**. Mock objects are objects that simulate the behavior of a real object. From the perspective of the API, they should be indistinguishable from the real thing as far as any other objects using the mock are concerned. Using mock objects with our test scripts, we can even do things like set up test data for the mock to return when a particular method is called.

Let's say, for example, that we have a class designed to fetch articles from our database; the class uses other classes to do the work of connecting to the database and fetching the result, as you've seen in Volume I, Chapter 3 with the `MySQL` and `MySQLResult` classes. Let's imagine we want to test the `Articles` class we created in Chapter 3 without having to make any real database connections. To do so, we'd create mock objects for the `MySQL` and `MySQLResult` classes, which we then give to the `Articles` class in exactly the same way as the real database objects would. The mock objects simulate connecting to and fetching data from the database without actually doing so. They have exactly the same API as the real thing, so the articles class has no idea that it's not getting real data back. We can thus create tests that focus purely on the `Articles` class, which is now independent of any other class on which it would normally rely.

Mock objects are extremely important for Unit Testing, as they allow you to break the dependencies between classes so you can test one at a time. Without mock objects, things can get pretty convoluted. For a fairly complex application, the class you're testing may depend on another class, which, in turn, depends on another class, and so on. You'll be uncertain if a bug you've found is really part of the class you're testing, or is caused by one of the other units on which the class directly or indirectly relies.

Before you groan about this meaning yet more work, SimpleTest makes the creation of mock objects extremely easy—in fact, they're created automatically! Let's turn back to our StampCollection class, and I'll show you how this works. StampCollection expects us to give it Stamp objects via the add method. To break the dependence of the StampCollection on the Stamp class, we need a mock object for Stamp. To give you an idea of how this works, here's an example that uses a hack to show you the mock object code generated by SimpleTest:

File: **10.php**

```php
<?php
if (!defined('SIMPLE_TEST')) {
  // Modify this line to point at your simpletest installation
  define('SIMPLE_TEST', '../../simpletest/');
}
require_once SIMPLE_TEST . 'unit_tester.php';
require_once SIMPLE_TEST . 'mock_objects.php';
require_once SIMPLE_TEST . 'reporter.php';
require_once '8.php';

echo '<pre>';
// Don't try this at home. _createClassCode is private!
echo Mock::_createClassCode('Stamp', 'MockStamp');
echo '</pre>';
?>
```

Note that, in this example, I called a private method provided by SimpleTest, namely _createClassCode. I can do this because I'm a trained PHP stunt man demonstrating how mock objects work! In other words, don't try this when writing your own tests—SimpleTest provides a public API for creating mock objects that we'll see in a moment.

Here's the code for the mock class, as it will be displayed by the above script:

```php
class MockStamp extends SimpleMock {
  function MockStamp(&$test, $wildcard = MOCK_WILDCARD) {
    $this->SimpleMock($test, $wildcard);
    $args = func_get_args();
    $this->_mockMethod("Stamp", $args);
  }
  function &stamp() {
    $args = func_get_args();
    return $this->_mockMethod("stamp", $args);
  }
}
```

The mock object class contains the same methods as the class it simulates—in the case of the Stamp class, this is simply the constructor, stamp. The mock object class, when instantiated as an object, now fully simulates the Stamp API (as the generated code is pretty complex, you may want just to take my word for this).

Now, let me show you how to create correctly a mock object like this for use in your testing:

File: **11.php (excerpt)**

```php
<?php
if (!defined('SIMPLE_TEST')) {
  // Modify this line to point at your simpletest installation
  define('SIMPLE_TEST', '../../simpletest/');
}
require_once SIMPLE_TEST . 'unit_tester.php';
require_once SIMPLE_TEST . 'mock_objects.php';
require_once SIMPLE_TEST . 'reporter.php';
require_once '8.php';

// Create a MockStamp
Mock::generate('Stamp');
```

Using the Mock::generate method, the mock object class is generated as above, and is then automatically made available for instantiation. Now, for the StampCollection test script:

File: **11.php (excerpt)**

```php
// Create the test class
class TestOfStampCollection extends UnitTestCase {
  function TestOfStampCollection()
  {
    $this->UnitTestCase('StampCollection');
  }

  // Test adding with the add method
  function testAdd()
  {
    // Create the MockStamp object
    $mockStamp = &new MockStamp($this);

    // Set the member variables
    $mockStamp->name = 'Penny Black';
    $mockStamp->price = 3500;

    // Create the StampCollection
```

```
$stampCollection = &new StampCollection();

// Add the MockStamp to the StampCollection
$stampCollection->add($mockStamp);

// Get a copy of the stamp back
$stampCopy = $stampCollection->fetch();

// Compare the names of the stamps
$this->assertEqual($stampCopy->name, $mockStamp->name);
    }
}
```

Here, we're basically performing a "round trip" with an instance of StampCollection. We create a MockStamp object, using the add method to add it to the StampCollection; then, we get a copy back with the fetch method. Finally, we use the assertEqual SimpleTest method to compare the values of the MockStamp and the copy we retrieved from StampCollection. What happens? Take a look at Figure 6.9.

Figure 6.9. Forgery Doesn't Pay

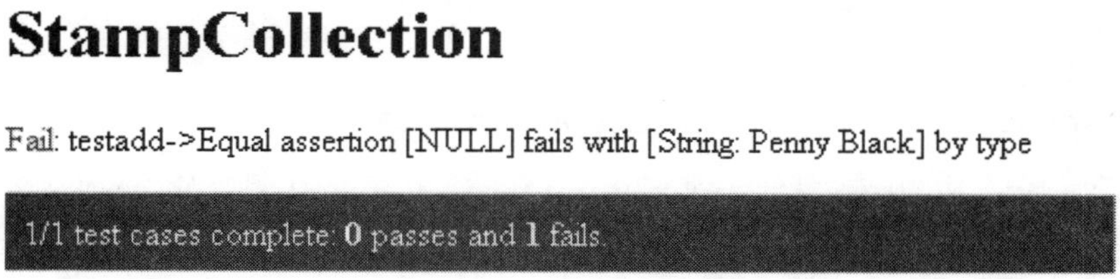

StampCollection

Fail: testadd->Equal assertion [NULL] fails with [String: Penny Black] by type

1/1 test cases complete: 0 passes and 1 fails.

Failure! How could such a simple operation have gone wrong? Time to take a close look at our StampCollection class. Here's the problem, in the add method:

```
function add($stamp)
{
  $this->collection[] .= $stamp;
}
```

It looks like we've mistakenly used the string append operator (.=) to add the stamp to the end of the array. We should have used the assignment operator (=) instead! This is a case where a serious logic bug slips through the cracks of PHP's error checking without so much as a warning message, but, thanks to SimpleTest, the bug could be found and fixed. What's more, we now have test scripts in place that we can rerun whenever we need to feel that warm glow of confidence that the code is stable and bug-free.

Of course, you can do a lot more with SimpleTest, and, thankfully, it's very well documented; in-depth tutorials are provided with the download, and there's more information on the author's site. Despite its alpha status, progress is being made very quickly and it's likely that SimpleTest will become a very important contribution to the wealth of freely available PHP code.

Further Reading

❏ *A HOWTO on Optimizing PHP*:
http://phplens.com/lens/php-book/optimizing-debugging-php.php

An excellent run down of many approaches to optimize PHP code and improve performance.

❏ *Effortless (or Better!) Bug Detection with PHP Assertions*:
http://www.sitepoint.com/article/1008

This article provides a lesson in the importance of testing.

❏ *PEAR::PHPUnit Tutorial*:
http://pear.php.net/manual/en/packages.php.phpunit.intro.php

Don't miss this quick overview of unit testing and examples with PEAR::PHPUnit.

❏ *Strong Typing vs. Strong Testing*: http://mindview.net/WebLog/log-0025

Bruce Eckel makes a fascinating argument that strong testing (i.e. Unit Testing) levels the playing field between dynamically typed languages (e.g. Python and PHP) and statically typed languages (such as C++ and Java) in this great article.

7

Design Patterns

With a grasp of object oriented programming under your belt, thanks to Volume I, Chapter 2, I'll bet you're wide-eyed and wondering what to do with all this great new stuff that's supposed to help you write maintainable, well-designed PHP applications, right? This is a common problem for developers coming to grips with the object oriented paradigm. It takes a long time to do anything really useful with OOP, many of their early attempts being no more than long sections of procedural code wrapped in a few class methods.

Thankfully, object oriented programming has been around for quite some time and is supported by many languages; overcoming such problems is well-trodden territory. More importantly, our OOP coding ancestors were kind enough to put together a catalog of best practices, known as **design patterns**, which worked over and over again, and could be readily applied to solving problems in a uniform manner. The landmark publication was the book, *Design Patterns* (Addison-Wesley, ISBN: 0-201-63361-2) by the "Gang of Four" (Erich Gamma, Richard Helm, Ralph Johnson and John Vlissides), which has become a modern classic in IT literature—if, indeed, such a thing is possible. Search Amazon for "Design Patterns," and you can't miss it. While you're browsing Amazon, it's also worth looking at Martin Fowler's *Patterns of Enterprise Application Architecture* (Addison-Wesley, ISBN: 0-321-12742-0), which provides further patterns, many of which relate directly to the problems developers encounter when building Web-based applications.

My own opinion of design patterns is that they provide a shortcut to discovering the way you'd probably *end up* solving a particular problem, provided you had enough time to experiment with all the possible ways you might structure your code. In other words, they're down-to-earth descriptions of how a group of programmers found they could best solve the problems they faced.

Talking about what design patterns *are* is something I generally prefer to avoid. It's like trying to explain the concept of snow to someone who's grown up in the Sahara desert; until you've seen snow for yourself, it's not going to make much sense. Reading the solutions in this chapter, which look at specific examples using real code, is, in my opinion, a far better way to grasp the concepts.

But, to give you a rough idea of where this chapter is headed, consider this: in your Web building experience, have you ever had a feeling of *déjà vu*? Have you ever said to yourself, "I've done this before," or, "I'm sure I saw a really good solution to this problem. Now, where was it?"

What the Gang of Four did with *Design Patterns* was identify twenty three common problems that give developers that *déjà vu* feeling, and provide guidelines for how we could best solve each. Time has shown that the Gang of Four (GoF) got it right; use of their solutions typically helps developers write applications that are easy to maintain, yet are able to cope with the special cases that occur in the real world. The adage "design is dead," often quoted these days in discussions of the visual design of Websites, can also be applied to object oriented programming, thanks to design patterns. If you can learn to spot the problem in the first place, the solution is just a matter of identifying and applying the right pattern.

A welcome side-effect of studying design patterns is that they often help people learn how to get the most out of the object oriented paradigm. In reading this chapter, you may find that object oriented PHP becomes much richer, rather than feeling overwhelmed by a whole load of new syntax that you have no idea what to do with.

Although the GoF laid out a catalog of twenty three patterns, we'll only cover the five that I've found to be used or useful in PHP 4, to give you a taste of what design patterns are about. A more in depth analysis of object oriented programming is beyond the scope of this book. This is not to say that other patterns[1] cannot be usefully applied in PHP, but I've included here the patterns that can be easily applied to any PHP application, and do not suggest some sort of framework that affects the structure of your application.

---

[1] The Model-View-Controller (MVC) pattern, the Command Pattern and the Template Method, to name a few.

There are a couple of factors that you should be aware of when considering which design patterns can be applied in PHP 4:

❑ Some of the problems the GoF were aiming to address simply never raise their heads in the development of Web-based applications for the Apache/PHP environment, where an application remains memory-resident for only as long as it takes to build a Web page. The Memento pattern is one such example.

❑ PHP 4 doesn't support some of the features found in other languages (e.g. Java), such as static class member variables. As such, trying to apply some patterns[2] results in awkward workarounds that often cause more problems than they solve. One of the main drivers behind PHP 5 was to make PHP well suited to design patterns.

Enough said. Time for some patterns!

The Factory Method

In most programming languages that support the object oriented paradigm, it's possible to use class methods or functions to create and return new objects. An example in PHP might be:

```php
<?php
// A PHP Function which creates an object
function &createSomeObject()
{
    return new SomeClass();
}

// Get an instance of SomeClass
$someObject = &createSomeObject();
```

It may be unclear why anyone would want to do what we've done in this example. Rest assured there are a number of specific problems that can be solved with this approach, which is known as the **factory method** pattern. The following situations and examples should make things clear.

Imagine that you're working on an application. Within it, you create objects from a given class in many places—including inside other classes. You're aware, however, that there may be a need to use a different class at some future time. If you use a function or class method to create the object for you, changing the class from

---

[2]The Singleton pattern, for instance.

which that object is created will require you to modify only the method that creates it.

For example, in Chapter 1 we developed the class Auth, which creates an instance of the Session class:

```
class Auth {
  function Auth(&$db, $redirect, $hashKey, $md5 = TRUE)
  {
    $this->db = &$db;
    $this->redirect = $redirect;
    $this->hashKey = $hashKey;
    $this->md5 = $md5;
    $this->session = &new Session(); // Session created
    $this->login();
  }
```

What happens if, instead, we use a function called createSession, to create the object for us? In that case, we can replace the Session class with some other class of a different name without having to modify the Auth class:

```
class Auth {
  function Auth(&$db, $redirect, $hashKey, $md5 = TRUE)
  {
    $this->db = &$db;
    $this->redirect = $redirect;
    $this->hashKey = $hashKey;
    $this->md5 = $md5;
    $this->session = &createSession(); // Fetch new object
    $this->login();
  }
```

This is particularly useful when writing unit tests that use mock objects (see Chapter 6). In this case, we can modify the behavior of the createSession function in the test script so that MockSession is used by Auth, rather than the real Session class.

Another problem to which the factory method can provide a solution occurs when the choice of class will depend on *runtime* circumstances that you can't predict in advance. You might wish to avoid writing conditional logic at the point at which the object is created, in order to help keep the code maintainable and allow the same conditions to be used elsewhere in your application. Using a factory method, you can separate the task of instantiating the objects from the code that needs to use them.

For example, let's say we want to analyze a text document to ascertain how many vowels and consonants it contains. We might parse the document, then create objects to represent the elements of the document in which we're interested. We can then go back and analyze these objects to get the statistics we're interested in.

To start, let's put together a class, TextStats, which will parse documents using a character by character approach, taking advantage of PHP's ability to treat strings as arrays:

File: **1.php (excerpt)**

```php
/**
 * Class for Analyzing Text
 */
class TextStats {
  /**
   * The document to analyze
   */
  var $doc;
  /**
   * An array of Vowel and Consonant objects
   */
  var $chars = array();

  function TextStats($doc)
  {
    $this->doc = $doc;
    $this->buildStats();
  }

  /**
   * Calls a factory method to get a Vowel or Consonant
   */
  function buildStats()
  {
    $length = strlen($this->doc);
    for ($i=0; $i<$length; $i++) {
      // Factory method called here
      if ($char = &CharFactory::getChar($this->doc[$i])) {
        $this->chars[] = $char;
      }
    }
  }
```

Of particular interest in the above section of code is the `buildStats` method, which statically calls the factory method, `getChar`, in the `CharFactory` class. Using this approach, we can leave to the factory method the task of working out what to do with the current character; this keeps the `buildStats` method very simple.

To finish off the `TextStats` class, we add a couple of methods to determine how many vowels and consonants the document contains:

File: **1.php (excerpt)**

```php
/**
 * Find out how many Vowels in document
 */
function numVowels()
{
  $vowels = 0;
  reset($this->chars);
  foreach ($this->chars as $char) {
    if (is_a($char, 'Vowel')) {
      $vowels++;
    }
  }
  return $vowels;
}

/**
 * Find out how many Consonants in document
 */
function numConsonants()
{
  $consonants = 0;
  reset($this->chars);
  foreach ($this->chars as $char) {
    if (is_a($char, 'Consonant')) {
      $consonants++;
    }
  }
  return $consonants;
}
}
```

Now, let's look at the factory method itself. It takes a single character as its argument and examines it first with a regular expression. Should it decide that the character is a letter of the alphabet, it then performs a second check to see whether the letter is a vowel. The factory method then creates an instance of either Vowel or Consonant, and returns it to the caller.

File: **1.php** (excerpt)

```php
/**
 * Factory for creating Vowel and Consonant objects
 */
class CharFactory {
  /**
   * The factory method
   */
  function &getChar($byte)
  {
    if (preg_match('/[a-zA-Z]/', $byte)) {
      $vowels = array('a', 'e', 'i', 'o', 'u');
      if (in_array(strtolower($byte), $vowels)) {
        $char = &new Vowel($byte);
      } else {
        $char = &new Consonant($byte);
      }
      return $char;
    }
  }
}
```

Finally, we define the Vowel and Consonant classes. Now, it's time to test drive our text statistics package on the home page of sitepoint.com.

File: **1.php** (excerpt)

```php
/**
 * Class representing a Vowel
 */
class Vowel {
  var $letter;
  function Vowel($letter)
  {
    $this->letter = $letter;
  }
}

/**
 * Class representing a Consonant
 */
class Consonant {
  var $letter;
```

```php
    function Consonant($letter)
    {
      $this->letter = $letter;
    }
}

// Get some document
$doc = file_get_contents('http://www.sitepoint.com/');

// Remove HTML tags
$doc = strip_tags($doc);

// Create a TextStats object
$ts = new TextStats($doc);
?>
Today at http://www.sitepoint.com/ there are
<?php echo $ts->numConsonants(); ?> consonants and
<?php echo $ts->numVowels(); ?> vowels. Amazing huh?
```

Viewed as a UML diagram, the collection of classes is as shown in Figure 7.1.

Figure 7.1. Learning to Spell with Factory Methods

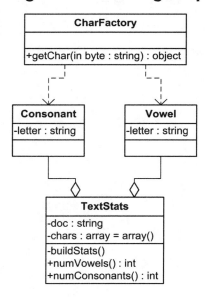

Although our factory method is only making a decision about which of two classes to instantiate, it's clear that we can easily modify it to create other objects, such as a `Number` or `Period` class, without having to modify the `buildStats` method. Without too much work, we can build a package that allows us to perform all sorts of statistical analyses of text documents, as the factory method allows us to add functionality in stages.

Now, imagine you've developed a package of classes that you've distributed to a group of users. Here, the factory method can help you provide those users with a simple API for getting to the "parts" of the package they need for their particular circumstances, and which allows them to switch "parts" with minimum effort.

A good example of this is the PEAR::DB package, which provides a database abstraction layer to help you write applications that can be used with different vendors' database software. When working with `DB`, you'll likely only work with one type of database at a time, so you'll only need to use the classes in PEAR::DB that relate to that database.

The `DB::connect` method does just this. It uses a factory method to give you objects with which you can access the database you're interested in; to create these objects, you simply provide the method an identifying string (the DSN). For example, we could use the following to connect to MySQL:

```
$dsn = 'mysql://harryf:secret@localhost/sitepoint';
$db = &DB::connect($dsn);
```

The `$db` variable now contains an instance of `DB_MySQL`. Were we to modify the `$dsn` variable to `pgsql://harryf:secret@localhost/sitepoint` to connect to PostgreSQL instead, we'd get back an instance of `DB_PgSQL`. The factory method `DB::connect` allows us to avoid dealing with the question of which class to instantiate; should we require our application to run on a database that's different from that for which it was originally designed, the modifications required should be reduced.

One final approach to applying the factory method pattern—an approach that seasoned programmers might regard as the "true" factory method—is to have multiple factory methods in an inheritance hierarchy of factory classes. This allows you to get back from the factory different objects, depending on which subclassed factory method was called.

To illustrate, let's imagine we use an email package in which the body of the email message is handled by separate classes, a plain text message and an HTML email each representing a single class. We want to be able to create instances of these classes without explicitly identifying them in our code, so that we can send emails to a list of customers based on whether they declared a preference for plain text or HTML emails. Using the strict, Gang of Four-approved approach to a factory method, the first step is to create a hierarchy of factory classes, each of which provides the method getBody. What happens upon any call to getBody will depend on which subclass of EmailFactory we're dealing with.

File: **2.php (excerpt)**

```php
/**
 * Base factory class
 */
class EmailFactory {
  function getBody($text)
  {
    // Abstract Factory Method
  }
}
/**
 * Factory for plain text emails
 */
class TextEmailFactory extends EmailFactory {
  function getBody($text)
  {
    return new TextBody($text);
  }
}
/**
 * Factory for HTML emails
 */
class HtmlEmailFactory extends EmailFactory {
  function getBody($text)
  {
    return new HtmlBody($text);
  }
}
```

Next, come the two classes that are *created* by the factory classes. The design pattern allows me to avoid identifying them by name outside of the factory classes.

File: **2.php (excerpt)**

```php
/**
 * The class created by TextEmailFactory::getBody()
 */
class TextBody {
  var $text;
  function TextBody($text)
  {
```

```
    $this->text = $text;
  }
}
/**
 * The class created by HtmlEmailFactory::getBody()
 */
class HtmlBody {
  var $text;
  function HtmlBody($text)
  {
    $this->text = $text;
  }
}
```

Next, we define the `EmailSender` class, which deals with sending the email to the recipient. Note that these classes don't do anything real (for instance, send an email); I'm just using them here to demonstrate a strict factory method. With `EmailSender` in place, we've set up some variables to demonstrate the factory methods in action.

File: **2.php (excerpt)**

```
/**
 * Class which "sends" and email
 */
class EmailSender {
  function sendMessage($email, $body)
  {
    echo "Sending email to $email with a " . get_class($body) .
      '<br />';
  }
}

// A dummy array of customers to send emails to
$customers = array(
  array('email' => 'jbloggs@yahoo.com',
        'emailpreferred' => 'html'),
  array('email' => 'jleno@cnn.com',
        'emailpreferred' => 'text'),
  array('email' => 'aleegator@reptiles.com',
        'emailpreferred' => 'html')
);

// The HTML and plain text versions of the email
$htmltext = 'This is an <em>HTML Message</em>';
$plaintext = 'This is plain text';
```

Finally, we loop through the array of customers, using a `switch` statement to *first* decide which factory class to use, then, secondly, to call the `addBody` method that's defined in whichever factory class has been created. Once we've stored an instance of either `HtmlBody` or `TextBody` in the `$body` reference, we simply pass it to the `$sender` to have the email sent to the customer.

File: **2.php (excerpt)**

```php
// Create the sender
$sender = &new EmailSender();

// Loop through the customers
foreach ($customers as $customer) {
  // Decide which factory class to create
  switch ($customer['emailpreferred']) {
    case 'html':
      // Create the factory
      $factory = &new HtmlEmailFactory();
      // Call the factory method
      $body = &$factory->getBody($htmltext);
      break;
    case 'text':
    default:
      // Create the factory
      $factory = &new TextEmailFactory();
      // Call the factory method
      $body = &$factory->getBody($plaintext);
      break;
  }
  // "Send" the message
  $sender->sendMessage($customer['email'], $body);
}
```

Viewed as UML, this implementation of a factory method is as shown in Figure 7.2.

Figure 7.2. The Spam Factory

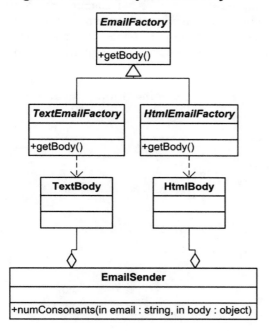

That should give you a feel for the types of problems factory methods can help you deal with, as well as the different approaches you can take to apply them. You should also have a better idea about what the concept of Design Patterns actually means; it's really nothing mysterious—just good sense.

The Iterator Pattern

Iterate, v. t. To utter or to do a second time or many times; to repeat.
—Webster's 1913 Dictionary

An **iterator** is an API (a group of methods) that makes it possible to access **collections** in a uniform manner. By collections, I mean data sets such as arrays, query result sets from MySQL, the lines in a file, or any other data structure that can be thought of as a group of data items. The common way to talk about an iterator in action is to say you're **iterating over a collection**.

What an iterator allows you to do is write code that accesses a collection in such a way that it doesn't actually matter what that collection contains. This description may sound vague, but think of it this way: imagine that you had a class that was able to build HTML tables from a database result set, an XML document, a text file, a directory, or just a plain old array *without needing to modify the code* of the table-generating class. Using iterators, such a thing is possible. Iterators allow you to write a table-generating class that could be reused to display many different types of data from different sources.

To begin with, let's consider the normal process of looping through an array:

File: **3.php**

```php
<?php
$colors = array('red', 'green', 'blue');

echo '<b>First iteration:</b><br />';
foreach ($colors as $color) {
  echo $color . '<br />';
}

echo '<b>Second iteration:</b><br />';
foreach ($colors as $color) {
  echo $color . '<br />';
}
?>
```

The `foreach` construct, which is built into PHP, effectively acts as a simple iterator. It steps through an array element by element, and, when it reaches the end of the array, it automatically returns to the start. This explains why it's possible to use `foreach` twice without needing to use PHP's `reset` function to reset the **array pointer** in the above example. Unfortunately, this won't work for an object for which you've defined your own data accessing methods.[3]

Here's an example that allows me to achieve the same result using a method that will perform the iteration for me:

File: **4.php (excerpt)**

```php
<?php
class Colors {
  // An array where the colors are stored
  var $colors;
  function Colors()
  {
```

---

[3]At least, not with PHP 4; with PHP 5, a new extension, known as the Standard PHP Library (SPL), will make it possible to access objects with `foreach`.

```
    $this->colors = array('red', 'green', 'blue');
  }
  // This method iterates over the colors array
  function fetch()
  {
    // Use the each() function to get the current value and step
    // forward
    $color = each($this->colors);

    // If $color wasn't false...
    if ($color) {
      // return the value
      return $color['value'];

    // $color is false (reached the end of the array)...
    } else {
      // Reset the colors array
      reset($this->colors);
      // Return false
      return FALSE;
    }
  }
}
```

Now, although the class doesn't do anything useful, as we'll see momentarily, the `fetch` method makes it possible to iterate over the contents of the `$colors` array in a very similar manner to a `foreach` loop.

Let's take a closer look at the `fetch` method. The first thing we do is use PHP's `each` function to pull the current element from the `$colors` array. The `each` function automatically moves an array pointer forward after it's returned the current value, which makes it a very handy function for iterating over arrays. The value returned from `each` is a little unusual, though; it's both an associative array with the keys `'key'` and `'value'`, and an indexed array in which element `0` is the key name and element `1` is the value. Here's what `each` returns for the first element of the `$colors` array:

```
Array
(
    [0] => 0
    [1] => red
    [key] => 0
    [value] => red
)
```

Note that if `each` finds itself at the end of the array, it returns `FALSE`, which explains this part of the `fetch` method:

```
// If $color wasn't false...
if ($color) {
  // return the value
  return $color['value'];
```

Then, if we find that `each` has returned `FALSE`, we use PHP's `reset` function to set the array pointer back to the start, while returning `FALSE` so that the code that's using the `fetch` method knows it has come to an end:

```
// $color is false (reached the end of the array)...
} else {
  // Reset the colors array
  reset($this->colors);
  // Return false
  return FALSE;
}
```

Here's how we can use the `fetch` method of the `Colors` class in a script:

File: **4.php (excerpt)**

```
// Instantiate the Colors class
$colors = new Colors();

// Iterate over it twice using a while loop and the fetch() method
echo '<b>First iteration:</b><br />';
while ($color = $colors->fetch()) {
  echo $color . '<br />';
}

echo '<b>Second iteration:</b><br />';
while ($color = $colors->fetch()) {
  echo $color . '<br />';
}
?>
```

Although we're using a `while` loop here, you can see that using the `fetch` method is very similar to using the `foreach` construct.

But, What's the Point?

That example gives you a rough idea of how a particular iterator functions. But you're probably wondering, "why bother?" Well, bear with me here. In this next example, we're going to start with a class that builds HTML tables and, bit by bit, all should become clear. One trick we're going to use here is to keep the table HTML itself very simple and rely on CSS to do the more complex parts of formatting the look and feel.

The table-generating class is shown here:

File: **UI/HTMLTable.php** (in **SPLIB**) (excerpt)

```php
<?php
// Class for building a table using an iterator
class HTMLTable {
  var $collection;
  var $idPre;
  var $table;
  function HTMLTable(&$collection, $idPre = '')
  {
    $this->collection = &$collection;
    $this->idPre = $idPre;
    $this->table = "<table id=\"" . $idPre . "Table\">\n";
  }
```

The constructor for the table takes two arguments; the first is a collection, which can be any object you want—a database query result, an array iterator, or a class for reading from a file—as long as it conforms to the iterator API that HTMLTable expects (see below). The other argument is a prefix for HTML id attributes, which helps me identify in the table elements for formatting through my CSS code.

The addHeadings method takes either a string or a one dimensional array and uses it to build the headings for the columns:

File: **UI/HTMLTable.php** (in **SPLIB**) (excerpt)

```php
  function addHeadings($headings)
  {
    $this->table .= "  <tr id=\"" . $this->idPre .
      "HeaderRow\">\n";
    if (is_array($headings)) {
      foreach ($headings as $heading) {
        $this->table .= "    <th id=\"" . $this->idPre .
          "HeaderCol\">" . $heading . "</th>\n";
      }
    } else {
      $this->table .= "    <th id=\"" . $this->idPre .
        "HeaderCol\">" . $headings . "</th>\n";
    }
```

```
    $this->table .= "  </tr>\n";
  }
```

It's in the `buildRows` method that the iteration occurs:

```
function buildRows()
{
  $alt = '1';
  while ($row = $this->collection->fetch()) {
    $this->table .= "  <tr id=\"" . $this->idPre . "Row" .
      $alt . "\">\n";
    if (is_array($row)) {
      foreach ($row as $col) {
        $this->table .= "    <td id=\"" . $this->idPre .
          "Col\">" . $col . "</td>\n";
      }
    } else {
      $this->table .= "    <td id=\"" . $this->idPre .
        "Col\">" . $row . "</td>\n";
    }
    $this->table .= "  </tr>\n";
    $alt = ($alt == 1) ? 1 : 2;
  }
}
```

Note the `while` loop (displayed here in bold). It expects that the collection I passed to the constructor will have a `fetch` method. The result returned from `fetch` can be either a string or a one dimensional array.

```
function render()
{
  return $this->table . "</table>\n";
}
}
?>
```

Finally, the `render` method completes the table and returns the HTML.

Now, obviously this class will work just fine if we pass it an instance of the `Colors` class above (try it yourself, if you like). But, let's see now how it bears up when we give it a database result set instead:

```php
<?php
// Include MySQL class
require_once 'Database/MySQL.php';
// Include HTMLTable class
require_once 'UI/HTMLTable.php';

// Instantiate MySQL
$db = &new MySQL('localhost', 'harryf', 'secret', 'sitepoint');
$sql = "SELECT title, author FROM articles LIMIT 0,5";

// Get a query result via factory method
$result = $db->query($sql);

// Pass result to HTMLTable on instantiation
$table = &new HTMLTable($result, 'Iterator_');

// Add the headings to the table
$table->addHeadings(array('Title', 'Author'));

// Build the rows
$table->buildRows();
?>
```

Essentially, all we've done here is perform a query as normal, before passing the result to the HTMLTable class for display.

The rest of the script displays the generated table in a simple HTML page, along with a little CSS code to format the table.

```html
<!DOCTYPE html PUBLIC "-//W3C//DTD XHTML 1.0 Strict//EN"
  "http://www.w3.org/TR/xhtml1/DTD/xhtml1-strict.dtd">
<html xmlns="http://www.w3.org/1999/xhtml">
<head>
<title> Iterator </title>
<meta http-equiv="Content-Type"
  content="text/html; charset=iso-8859-1" />
<style type="text/css">
  …CSS code omitted…
</style>
</head>
<body>
<?php echo $table->render(); ?>
```

```
</body>
</html>
```

Figure 7.3 shows the table that results.

Figure 7.3. Iterated Database Result

Title	Author
Build your own Database Driven Website using PHP & MySQL	Kevin Yank
Write Secure Scripts with PHP 4.2!	Kevin Yank
Advanced email in PHP	Kevin Yank
eZ publish: PHP's Killer App	Harry Fuecks

Still not impressed? Well, how about an iterator that lists directories?

File: **Iterators/DirIterator.php (in SPLIB)**

```php
<?php
class DirIterator {
  var $directory;
  var $dir;
  function DirIterator($directory)
  {
    $this->directory = $directory;
  }
  function fetch()
  {
    if (!$this->dir) {
      $this->dir = dir($this->directory);
    }
    if (($entry = $this->dir->read()) !== FALSE) {
      return $entry;
    } else {
      $this->dir->close();
      $this->dir = NULL;
      return FALSE;
    }
  }
}
```

```
}
?>
```

Again, this iterator has a `fetch` method that uses the in-built `dir` class that PHP provides.

Let's put this to the test:

File: **6.php**

```php
<?php
// Include MySQL class
require_once 'Iterators/DirIterator.php';
// Include HTMLTable class
require_once 'UI/HTMLTable.php';

// Instantiate the Directory Iterator
$iterator = &new DirIterator('c:/htdocs/phpanth/');

// Pass result to HTMLTable on instantiation
$table = &new HTMLTable($iterator, 'Iterator_');

// Add the headings to the table
$table->addHeadings('c:/htdocs/phpanth/');

// Build the rows
$table->buildRows();
?>
```

Skipping the HTML/CSS you've already seen, Figure 7.4 shows the output that results when I pass the `DirIterator` object to the `HTMLTable` class on my system.

Figure 7.4. Iterated Directory Listing

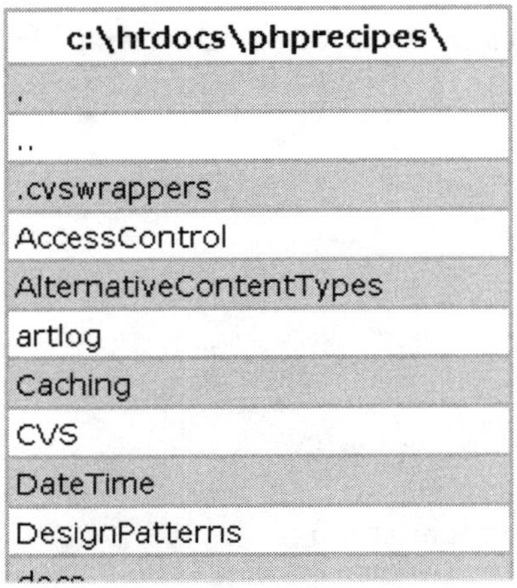

c:\htdocs\phprecipes\
.
..
.cvswrappers
AccessControl
AlternativeContentTypes
artlog
Caching
CVS
DateTime
DesignPatterns

What else? How about an iterator that reads lines from a file?

File: **Iterators/FileIterator.php (in SPLIB)**

```php
<?php
class FileIterator {
  var $filename;
  var $fp;
  function FileIterator($filename)
  {
    $this->filename = $filename;
  }
  function fetch()
  {
    if (!$this->fp) {
      $this->fp = fopen($this->filename, 'r');
    }
    if (!feof($this->fp)) {
      return fgets($this->fp, 4096);
    } else {
      fclose($this->fp);
      return FALSE;
    }
  }
}
?>
```

Using this requires only a minor modification to the class names we instantiate:

File: **7.php**

```php
<?php
// Include MySQL class
require_once 'Iterators/FileIterator.php';
// Include HTMLTable class
require_once 'UI/HTMLTable.php';

// Instantiate the File Iterator
$iterator = &new FileIterator('3.php');

// Pass result to HTMLTable on instantiation
$table = &new HTMLTable($iterator, 'Iterator_');

// Add the headings to the table
$table->addHeadings('PHP Source Code');

// Build the rows
$table->buildRows();
?>
```

Iterators make it all so easy. For typical PHP problems, the type of data you need to display in some form of HTML list (e.g. a table or a select menu) will usually be an array of strings, an array of arrays, or an array of objects. Our HTMLTable class is already prepared for the first two, so we can use it again and again with many different data sources.

The most important aspect of deciding when to apply iterators to your classes involves choosing the method naming scheme. In the examples above, we called all the iterator methods fetch. In the classes that use your iterators, you must also plan for the data types your iterators might return. With practice, you can make iterators one of your development habits and save yourself a considerable amount of time reproducing HTML-related code to output collections of data.

Iterator APIs

As anyone who's worked with Java will know, the iterator API we've proposed here—namely a single method called fetch—is very simple. I'd estimate that for around 90% of situations in which you need to iterate over a collection in PHP, this single-method iterator will be all you'll need. Be warned though—it's only intended for use with particular data structures. In particular, if you use this API to iterate over an array, some elements of which evaluate to false, the code using the iterator will stop prematurely, believing that it has come to the end of the collection.

This shortcoming, along with other requirements, such as being able to move backward and forward through the collection or performing multiple iterations over a collection simultaneously, creates the need for a more complex API. A general "profile" of a more advanced iterator looks like this:

```php
<?php
class Iterator {
  function Iterator() {…}

  // Resets the collection
  function reset() {…}

  // Moves the collection point forward one
  // (but typically returns no value)
  function next() {…}

  // Sometimes called isFinal() or isValid();
  // used to check for the end of the collection
  function hasMore() {…}

  // Gets the current value from the collection
  function current() {…}
}
?>
```

The above class shows the methods commonly provided by more advanced iterators. The detail (i.e. what actually happens inside the class) will vary between iterators, depending on the problem each is intended to solve.

If you're interested in exploring other types of iterators in PHP, the best approach is to examine open source class libraries that use them, such as Eclipse[1] and eXtremePHP[2].

The Strategy Pattern

The **strategy pattern** is used in situations in which there is a common problem that can be solved by one of many algorithms. It can help eliminate long-winded `if-else` or `switch` structures and, if the problem to be solved repeats itself within an application, also removes the need to reproduce the same code for each solution.

---

[1] http://www.students.cs.uu.nl/people/voostind/eclipse/
[2] https://sourceforge.net/projects/extremephp/

The real meaning of this explanation becomes clear when we consider a very common problem in PHP applications—validating the input from a form. Consider the following script:

File: **8.php (excerpt)**

```php
<?php
// Validate the form
if (isset($_POST['submit'])) {
  // A array to store errors
  $errors = array();

  // Check the incoming data
  if ($_POST['user'] < '6') {
    $errors[] = 'Username is too short';
  }
  if ($_POST['pass'] < '6') {
    $errors[] = 'Password is too short';
  }
  if ($_POST['pass'] != $_POST['conf']) {
    $errors[] = 'Passwords do not match';
  }
  if (!preg_match(
        '/^[a-z0-9._-]+@[a-z0-9.-]+\.[a-z]{2,4}$/i',
        $_POST['email'])) {
    $errors[] = 'Invalid Email address';
  }
}
?>
```

The above code is the validation routine for the form below, which represents a fairly typical PHP script.

File: **8.php (excerpt)**

```html
<!DOCTYPE html PUBLIC "-//W3C//DTD XHTML 1.0 Strict//EN"
  "http://www.w3.org/TR/xhtml1/DTD/xhtml1-strict.dtd">
<html xmlns="http://www.w3.org/1999/xhtml">
<head>
<title> Form </title>
<meta http-equiv="Content-Type"
  content="text/html; charset=iso-8859-1" />
</head>
<body>
<b>Please enter your details:</b><br />
<form action="<?php echo $_SERVER['PHP_SELF']; ?>" method="post">
Username: <input type="text" name="user" /><br />
```

```
Password: <input type="password" name="pass" /><br />
Confirm: <input type="password" name="conf" /><br />
Email: <input type="text" name="email" /><br />
<input type="submit" name="submit" value="Submit Form" />
</form>
<?php
if (isset($errors) && count($errors) > 0) {
  echo "<b>The following errors occurred:</b><br />\n";
  echo "<ul>\n";
  foreach ($errors as $error) {
    echo "<li>" . $error . "</li>\n";
  }
  echo "</ul>\n";
}
?>
</body>
</html>
```

A "common problem" to which we can apply the strategy pattern occurs in this script. The problem is that we need to validate the data in the form by taking a detailed look at the submitted values. There are a number of algorithms being used here to solve the problem—so this is a prime target for a strategy pattern!

To begin implementing the pattern, we need a base class that defines the basic behavior of *all* validation algorithms:

File: **Validators/Validator.php (in SPLIB)**

```php
<?php
/**
 * Validator base class for form validation
 * @abstract
 */
class Validator {
  /**
   * Stores validation error messages
   * @access private
   * @var array
   */
  var $errors;

  /**
   * Constucts a new Validator object
   */
  function Validator($validateThis)
  {
```

```php
    $this->errors = array();
    $this->validate($validateThis);
}

/**
 * Validation method for subclasses to provide
 * @abstract
 * @return void
 */
function validate($validateThis) {}

/**
 * Adds an error message to the array
 * @return void
 */
function setError($msg)
{
    $this->errors[] = $msg;
}

/**
 * Returns true if string valid, false if not
 * @return boolean
 */
function isValid()
{
    if (count($this->errors) > 0) {
        return FALSE;
    } else {
        return TRUE;
    }
}

/**
 * Iterator for fetching error messages
 * @return mixed
 */
function fetch()
{
    $error = each($this->errors);
    if ($error) {
        return $error['value'];
    } else {
        reset($this->errors);
        return FALSE;
    }
```

```
    }
}
?>
```

The general approach we've used here is to have an array of errors. To determine whether a particular piece of data is valid, the isValid method looks at the size of the errors array to ascertain whether any errors have been placed there. The fetch method provides an iterator to extract messages, which can then be displayed to a user.

With this foundation in place, we can extend the class using subclasses that deal with validating particular types of data. Here's how we'd validate user names:

File: **Validators/ValidateUser.php (in SPLIB)**

```php
<?php
require_once 'Validators/Validator.php';
/**
 *   Validates a username
 */
class ValidateUser extends Validator {
  /**
   * Validates a username
   * @access private
   * @return void
   */
  function validate($user)
  {
    if (!preg_match('/^[a-zA-Z0-9_]+$/', $user )) {
      $this->setError('Username contains invalid characters');
    }
    if (strlen($user) < 6) {
      $this->setError('Username is too short');
    }
    if (strlen($user) > 20) {
      $this->setError('Username is too long');
    }
  }
}
?>
```

When Validator is instantiated, it expects to be given a value to test for validity; it passes this value to the validate method. The work involved in writing subclasses like ValidateUser therefore focuses purely on the validate method, allowing you to concentrate on the problem at hand, while easily extending your set of validation classes to cater to new data types.

Here's another subclass for password validation:

```php
<?php
require_once 'Validators/Validator.php';
/**
 *  Validates a password
 */
class ValidatePassword extends Validator {
  /**
   * Validates a password
   * @access private
   * @return void
   */
  function validate($passwords)
  {
    $pass = $passwords[0];
    $conf = $passwords[1];
    if ($pass != $conf) {
      $this->setError('Passwords do not match');
    }
    if (!preg_match('/^[a-zA-Z0-9_]+$/', $pass)) {
      $this->setError('Password contains invalid characters');
    }
    if (strlen($pass) < 6) {
      $this->setError('Password is too short');
    }
    if (strlen($pass) > 20) {
      $this->setError('Password is too long');
    }
  }
}
?>
```

Here we have an additional issue. We must accept two fields: the password, and a value against which to confirm it. In order to preserve the API defined by the Validator class, the class accepts these two values in the form of an array.

One final validator deals with email addresses:

```php
<?php
require_once 'Validators/Validator.php';
/**
 *  Validates an email address
```

```
*/
class ValidateEmail extends Validator {
  /**
   * Validates an email address
   * Note that the regular expression used here will not allow
   * certain valid email addresses, such as
   * someone@195.11.25.34
   * @access private
   * @return void
   */
  function validate($email)
  {
    $pattern = '/^[a-z0-9._-]+@[a-z0-9.-]+\.[a-z]{2,4}$/i';
    if (!preg_match($pattern, $email)) {
      $this->setError('Invalid email address');
    }
    if (strlen($email) > 100) {
      $this->setError('Address is too long');
    }
  }
}
?>
```

Be warned that the regular expression for validating an email addresses will reject some valid addresses (in particular, addresses that include an IP address). The code here is meant as a simple example, rather than production-level script. *Mastering Regular Expressions* (O'Reilly, ISBN: 0596002890) defines a regular expression that's more than 6KB long (!), and which correctly validates every possible email address.

We've now defined all our validation classes, as shown in the UML diagram in Figure 7.5.

Figure 7.5. Validation Strategy

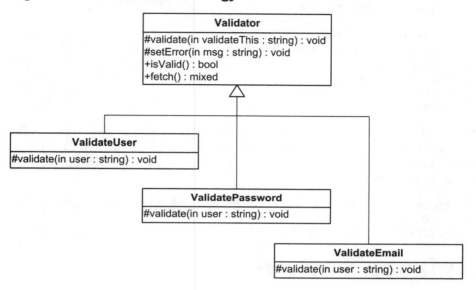

Using the validators to deal with the form submission we saw before, the code becomes:

File: **9.php (excerpt)**

```php
<?php

require_once 'Validators/ValidateUser.php';
require_once 'Validators/ValidatePassword.php';
require_once 'Validators/ValidateEmail.php';

// Validate the form
if (isset($_POST['submit'])) {
  // A array to store errors
  $errors = array();

  // Collection of validators
  $validators = array();
  $validators[] = new ValidateUser($_POST['user']);
  $validators[] = new ValidatePassword(array(
      $_POST['pass'], $_POST['conf']));
  $validators[] = new ValidateEmail($_POST['email']);

  // Iterate over the validators, validating as we go
```

```
foreach ($validators as $validator) {
  if (!$validator->isValid()) {
    while ($error = $validator->fetch()) {
      $errors[] = $error;
    }
  }
}
}
?>
```

The rest of the page remains unchanged, but we've made the code that handles validation far more flexible and modular. If we wanted to add a `Validator` to check a credit card number, for example, all we'd need to do would be to plug it into the `$validators` array:

```
$validators[] = new ValidateCreditCard($_POST['creditcard']);
```

The rest happens automatically!

The Adapter Pattern

One of PHP's greatest advantages as a language for building Web-based applications is the size and strength of its community—in particular, the wealth of open source code available as examples, and for use in your own projects. Developers simply need to head over to PHP Classes[3] to find examples of the solutions others have created to overcome the problem we're dealing with—perhaps the solution even slots neatly into our existing code, preventing us from having to reinvent the wheel.

While this is a big plus for PHP, it comes with a downside. Companies such as Sun and Microsoft are able to put together cohesive libraries of classes that integrate well, the whole being much greater than the sum of the parts. As it's not backed by any large software house, PHP lacks a library of components that compare with the likes of the Java or .NET class libraries. Much of the freely available PHP code was designed by developers working in a vacuum; a class may have been designed to work either alone or as part of a small library of classes that a particular developer uses. As such, attempting to slot someone else's class into your application may well highlight its incompatibility with your existing design.

[3] http://www.phpclasses.org/

Thankfully, that's where the **adapter pattern** comes in very handy. The essential purpose of the adapter pattern is to provide on top of an existing class API, an additional API that makes it compatible with other environments.

For example, we have a class for accessing MySQL; within this class, the method that executes a query is called `query`. All the code that uses the class expects to find the `query` method available for running SQL statements. Then one day, your application has to be ported at short notice to a PostgreSQL database; you need classes that are capable of dealing with PostgreSQL—fast! And you happen to know of a very solid open source library that offers just what you need. Unfortunately, instead of using a method called `query`, the library in question provides a method called `execute` for performing SQL statements. What can you do? Rewrite all your existing code to use `execute` instead of `query`?

The answer is an **adapter class**, which uses the PostgreSQL class but provides an API that's the same as your existing MySQL class. In other words, it maps the `execute` method to your `query` method.

Taking a specific example along the same lines, the `MySQL` and `MySQLResult` classes we developed in Volume I, Chapter 3 obviously tie you to using a MySQL database. This won't cause many issues if you're happy with MySQL, but, should your application be required to run on a different database server, you may run into difficulties. PHP has two well known database abstraction libraries, PEAR::DB[4] and ADOdb[5], with another, PEAR::MDB[6] in progress; this may become a successor to PEAR::DB eventually.

Let's take PEAR::DB as the example. How can we adapt it (without modifying the source code, of course—a bad idea, unless you fancy supporting your own hybrid version of PEAR::DB) to make it usable with the code that's currently geared to our `MySQL` class?

I'll assume here that you've used the PEAR::DB API before (and if you haven't, see the section called "Further Reading").

We're lucky in the way our `MySQL` class is implemented, as PEAR::DB also has a `query` method from which it returns a result object. Unfortunately, our `MySQLResult` class provides a `fetch` method, while, in PEAR::DB, the equivalent method is `fetchRow`. To deal with this, we need two adapter classes. The first wraps the main PEAR::DB class and provides a `query` method that "catches" the

---

[4] http://pear.php.net/package/DB
[5] http://php.weblogs.com/ADOdb
[6] http://pear.php.net/package/MDB

PEAR::DB result object and wraps it in the second class, which adapts `fetch` to `fetchRow`.

File: **Database/PEARDBAdapter.php (in SPLIB) (excerpt)**

```php
// Include PEAR::DB
require 'DB.php';

// Adapter for PEAR::DB MySQL connections
class PEARDBAdapter {
  // Instance of PEAR::DB
  var $db;

  function PEARDBAdapter($host, $dbUser, $dbPass, $dbName)
  {
    $dsn = "mysql://$dbUser:$dbPass@$host/$dbName";
    $this->db = &DB::connect($dsn);
  }

  // Query factory method
  function &query($sql)
  {
    // Call the PEAR::DB query() method
    $result = &$this->db->query($sql);

    // Wrap the result in a PEARDBResultAdapter
    return new PEARDBResultAdapter($result);
  }
}
```

The `PEARDBAdapter` class acts as a wrapper for the main PEAR::DB class, most importantly, providing a `query` method that catches the `DB_Result` object created by a query, and placing it inside a `PEARDBResultAdapter` (see below).

Here's the `PEARDBResultAdapter` class:

File: **Database/PEARDBAdapter.php (in SPLIB) (excerpt)**

```php
// Adapater for PEAR::DB Result
class PEARDBResultAdapter {
  // Instance of PEAR::DB Result
  var $result;

  function PEARDBResultAdapter(&$result)
  {
    $this->result = &$result;
  }
```

```
// Adapts the PEAR::DB Result fetchRow() method
function &fetch()
{
  // Call the PEAR::DB Result fetchRow() method
  if ($row = &$this->result->fetchRow(DB_FETCHMODE_ASSOC)) {
    return $row;
  } else {
    return FALSE;
  }
}
}
?>
```

The DB_Result fetchRow method is adapted within the fetch method to the API we require.

Compatibility Note

My own **MySQL** class automatically resets the result resource, allowing me to iterate over the result multiple times. PEAR::DB doesn't support this functionality, because some of the databases it supports provide no mechanism by which developers can perform multiple iterations over the same results. The code of this example will ignore this subtlety.

For full compatibility, we could modify fetch so that it re-executed the query to obtain a fresh result set for each new iteration, or we could cache the results in an array.

Now, let me show you how this adapter class works. First, here's a simple example that shows what I usually do with my own **MySQL** class:

File: **10.php**

```php
<?php
// Include MySQL class
require_once 'Database/MySQL.php';

// Instantiate MySQL connection
$db = &new MySQL('localhost', 'harryf', 'secret', 'sitepoint');

// Perform query
$sql = "SELECT title, author FROM articles LIMIT 0,5";
$result = &$db->query($sql);

// Display some results
while ($row = $result->fetch()) {
```

```
    echo '<b>' . $row['title'] . '</b> by ' . $row['author'] .
      "<br />\n";
}
?>
```

Here's the same thing, using the PEARDBAdapter class:

File: **11.php**

```
<?php
// Include the adapter classes
require_once 'Database/PEARDBAdapter.php';

// Instantiate PEARDBAdapter connection
$db = &new PEARDBAdapter('localhost', 'harryf', 'secret',
  'sitepoint');

// Perform query
$sql = "SELECT title, author FROM articles LIMIT 0,5";
$result = &$db->query($sql);

// Display some results
while ($row = $result->fetch()) {
  echo '<b>' . $row['title'] . '</b> by ' . $row['author'] .
    "<br />\n";
}
?>
```

Notice that all the code that appears after the PEARDBAdapter is instantiated is exactly the same as it was when I used my own MySQL class—even the constructor arguments are the same! All I needed to do was modify two lines of code (the include and the object creation); the rest of my application could happily keep on running. Now, with the power of PEAR::DB at my disposal, I can modify my application to run on any database it supports.[4].

As you can see, the adapter pattern offers a powerful technique to help you mould third party libraries for use in your own code—without your needing to rewrite anything. Adapters can even be useful if you're writing brand new code that uses a third party library, as they allow you to customize the API to your needs. The trick to using an adapter pattern is to find the commonalities between the API your code expects (or needs), and the API that the third party library provides, then use your adapter class as a translator between the two.

---

[4]The practical extent of this portability can depend on other factors. For example, different databases support different forms of SQL. For example, the LIMIT 0,5 in the query is not supported by most databases, although recent versions of PostgreSQL do allow it.

The Observer Pattern

The **observer pattern** is a useful solution for triggering events upon a specified occurrence within your application.

For example, you may have a back end administration tool that allows authorized users to add articles to your Website. When an article is published, a number of things may need to happen in addition to storing the content in the database; for instance, you may need to refresh the site's cached HTML files, send an email to subscribers to inform them of the new content, and perhaps update a static XML document that contains your site's RSS feed, which others use to stay up-to-date about the content you publish. The observer pattern makes triggering these additional features easy and modular.

The terminology of the observer pattern is that the object doing the work (in this case, perhaps it's a class called `Article`) is the **observable**, while the objects that respond to changes in the observable (i.e. the cache-, email-, and RSS-related classes) are known as **observers**. The general process of using the observer pattern is to attach the observers to the observable. Then, when changes occur in the observable, it notifies the observers, leaving them to take further action.

Understanding how the observer pattern works in practice can be a little confusing. Let's look at the base classes required to implement it, but don't worry if this doesn't make sense at first glance; using the observer pattern is a lot easier that understanding it!

First, let's look at the base `Observable` class:

File: **Observer/Observable.php (in SPLIB)**

```php
<?php
/**
 * Base Observerable class
 * @abstract
 */
class Observable {
  /**
   * Array of Observers
   * @access private
   * @var array
   */
  var $observers;

  /**
```

```
 * Constructs the Observerable object
 */
function Observable()
{
  $this->observers = array();
}

/**
 * Calls the update() function using the reference to each
 * registered observer, passing an optional argument for the
 * event - used by children of Observable
 * @return void
 */
function notifyObservers($arg = NULL)
{
  $keys = array_keys($this->observers);
  foreach ($keys as $key) {
    $this->observers[$key]->update($this, $arg);
  }
}

/**
 * Attaches an observer to the observable
 * @return void
 */
function addObserver(&$observer)
{
  $this->observers[] = &$observer;
}
}
?>
```

Let's take a moment to review the methods here. addObserver is used to register an observer object with the observable, and add it to the internal array of observers. This is used before the observable class does anything, and sets the scene for the observers to respond to events.

The notifyObservers method is used by the observable to tell all the observers that something has happened. It takes an optional argument, so that, if need be, the observable can tell observers something about the event efficiently. This method calls the update method for each observer, passing a reference to the observable along with the argument:

```
$this->observers[$key]->update($this, $arg);
```

The `update` method is part of the `Observer` base class, which all observers must extend:

File: **Observer/Observer.php (in SPLIB)**

```php
<?php
/**
 *  Base Observer class
 */
class Observer {
  /**
   * Abstract function implemented by children to respond to
   * to changes in Observable subject
   * @abstract
   * @return void
   */
  function update(&$source, $arg) {}
}
?>
```

The `update` method doesn't do anything for the base class, but in subclasses it should be overridden to respond to events.

With the base classes in place, let's see how the pattern works with some skeleton classes that would allow articles to be published, and deal with cache, email notification and RSS issues.

File: **12.php (excerpt)**

```php
<?php
// Include the Observable and Observer base classes
require_once 'Observer/Observable.php';
require_once 'Observer/Observer.php';

class Article extends Observable {
  // To publish an article
  function publish()
  {
    echo 'Publishing article.<br />';
    // Perform query here that updates the database
    $this->notifyObservers('published');
  }
  // To delete an article
  function delete()
  {
    echo 'Deleting article.<br />';
    // Perform query here that deletes an article
```

```
    $this->notifyObservers('deleted');
  }
}
```

The `Article` class is the observable, inheriting from the `Observable` class. It provides two (skeleton) methods, which publish and delete an article. After the database update has been performed, each of these methods calls the `notifyObservers` method, passing an argument to indicate to the observers the nature of the event.

Here are the observer classes:

File: 12.php (excerpt)

```php
class Cache extends Observer {
  function update(&$source, $arg)
  {
    switch ($arg) {
      case 'published':
      case 'deleted':
        echo 'Refreshing cache<br />';
        break;
    }
  }
}

class Subscribers extends Observer {
  function update(&$source, $arg)
  {
    switch ($arg) {
      case 'published':
        echo 'Notifying subscribers by email<br />';
        break;
    }
  }
}

class RSSFeed extends Observer {
  function update(&$source, $arg)
  {
    switch ($arg) {
      case 'published':
      case 'deleted':
        echo 'Updating the RSS Feed<br />';
        break;
    }
```

```
    }
}
```

Each observer provides an `update` method that's called by the observable when the `notifyObservers` method is used. Within each `update` method, the observer decides what to do next based on the argument received from the observable. Note that the `Subscribers` class reacts only to the `'published'` argument, because we don't want subscribers notified if an article is deleted. `RSSFeed` and `Cache`, however, respond to both the `'published'` and `'deleted'` states.

To clarify, the UML class structure in this example is shown in Figure 7.6.

Figure 7.6. Article Observers

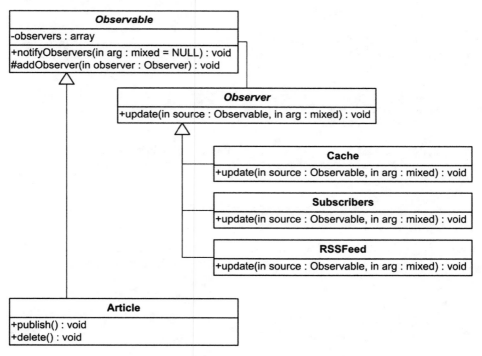

With the classes ready, we instantiate them before adding all three observers to the observable object, `$article`:

File: **12.php (excerpt)**

```
// Create the observers
$cache = &new Cache();
```

```
$subscribers = &new Subscribers();
$rssfeed = &new RSSFeed();

// Create the observable
$article = &new Article();

// Add the observers to the observable
$article->addObserver($cache);
$article->addObserver($subscribers);
$article->addObserver($rssfeed);
```

A simple form demonstrates the interaction of the objects:

File: **12.php (excerpt)**

```
if (isset($_POST['publish'])) {
  $article->publish();
} else if (isset($_POST['delete'])) {
  $article->delete();
} else {
?>
<form action="<?php echo $_SERVER['PHP_SELF']; ?>" method="post">
<textarea cols="50" rows="5">
This is a sample article
</textarea><br />
<input type="submit" name="publish" value="Publish Article"><br />
<input type="submit" name="delete" value="Delete Article"><br />
</form>
<?php
}
?>
```

If we click the Publish button, our code executes the Article class's publish method; behind the scenes, the observers respond to the event, displaying:

```
Publishing article.
Refreshing cache
Notifying subscribers by email
Updating the RSS Feed
```

The observer pattern is a powerful but easy-to-use mechanism for executing multiple routines without specifically calling them in our code. We can add or remove observers easily, without making serious modifications to the main logic of the application. More importantly, it's easy to reuse the observers on other observables, and add their capabilities to other parts of our site, such as a forum.

You can even register a single observer with multiple observables, so that it reacts to events from any of them!

A hybrid form of the observer pattern is commonly used when parsing XML documents with SAX. Rather than a single `update` method, the observer classes have multiple methods, such as `startElementHandler` and `endElementHandler`, which are called on the basis of their context within the XML document. PEAR::Log[7] also uses a form of observer pattern to allow the triggering of events on log updates.

It's likely that the observer pattern will become more widely used in PHP applications. Much like Java, PHP 5 provides **interface classes**, which can be **implemented** by a class that already has a parent it extends. This allows the observable and observer APIs to be implemented without disturbing an existing class hierarchy.

Further Reading

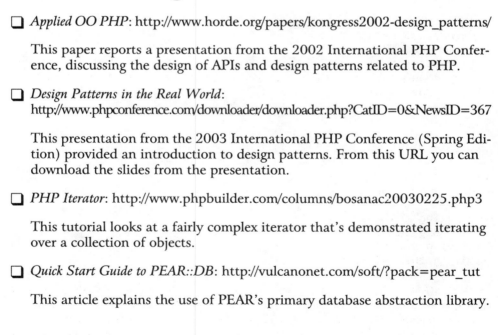

❑ *Applied OO PHP*: http://www.horde.org/papers/kongress2002-design_patterns/

This paper reports a presentation from the 2002 International PHP Conference, discussing the design of APIs and design patterns related to PHP.

❑ *Design Patterns in the Real World*:
http://www.phpconference.com/downloader/downloader.php?CatID=0&NewsID=367

This presentation from the 2003 International PHP Conference (Spring Edition) provided an introduction to design patterns. From this URL you can download the slides from the presentation.

❑ *PHP Iterator*: http://www.phpbuilder.com/columns/bosanac20030225.php3

This tutorial looks at a fairly complex iterator that's demonstrated iterating over a collection of objects.

❑ *Quick Start Guide to PEAR::DB*: http://vulcanonet.com/soft/?pack=pear_tut

This article explains the use of PEAR's primary database abstraction library.

---

[7] http://pear.php.net/package/Log

Appendix A: PHP Configuration

This is a quick reference to configuring PHP that covers the most important general settings you need to be aware of, either when running applications in a live environment, or because they impact security or the way you write code.

Configuration Mechanisms

The primary mechanism for configuring PHP is the `php.ini` file. As the master file, this provides you with control over all configuration settings. Entries generally take the format:

```
setting = value
```

Be sure to read the comments provided in the file before making changes, though. There are a few tricks, such as `include_path` using a colon (`:`) as a seperator on Unix, and a semicolon (`;`) on Windows.

Most Web hosts will not provide you access to your `php.ini` file unless you have root access to the system (which is typically not the case if you're using a cheap virtual hosting service). Your next alternative is to use `.htaccess` files to configure PHP (assuming the Web server is Apache).

An `.htaccess` file is a plain text file that you place in a public Web directory to determine the behavior of Apache when it comes to serving pages from that directory; for instance, you might identify which pages you'll allow public access to. Note that the effect of an `.htaccess` file is recursive—it applies to subdirectories as well.

To configure PHP with `.htaccess` files, your hosting provider must have the Apache setting `AllowOverride Options` or `AllowOverride All` applied to your Web directory in Apache's main `httpd.conf` configuration file. Assuming that is done, there are two Apache directives you can use to modify PHP's configuration:

php_flag
> used for settings that have boolean values (i.e. on/off or 1/0) such as register_globals

php_value
> used to specify a string value for settings, such as you might have with the include_path setting

Here's an example .htaccess file:

```
# Switch off register globals
php_flag register_globals off

# Set the include path
php_value include_path ".;/home/username/pear"
```

The final mechanism controlling PHP's configuration is the group of functions ini_set and ini_alter, which let you modify configuration settings, as well as ini_get, which allows you to check configuration settings, and ini_restore, which resets PHP's configuration to the default value as defined by php.ini and any .htaccess files. Using ini_set, here's an example which allows us to avoid having to define our host, user name and password when connecting to MySQL:

```
ini_set('mysql.default_host', 'localhost');
ini_set('mysql.default_user', 'harryf');
ini_set('mysql.default_password', 'secret');

if (!mysql_connect()) {
  echo mysql_error();
} else {
  echo 'Success';
}
```

Be aware that PHP provides for some settings, such as error_reporting, alternative functions that perform effectively the same job as ini_set. Which you prefer is a matter of taste.

Note that certain settings, such as register_globals, can only be usefully modified by php.ini or .htaccess, because such settings influence PHP's behavior *before* it begins executing your scripts.

Furthermore, some configuration settings can be changed *only* in php.ini, such as extension_dir, which tells PHP the directory in which PHP extensions can be found. For a complete reference on controlling settings, refer to the PHP Manual[1].

---

[1] http://www.php.net/ini_set

Key Security and Portability Settings

Table A.1 shows the most important PHP settings that relate to the security and portability of your PHP scripts.

Table A.1. Key Security and Portability Settings

Setting	Notes
`register_globals` (default: `off`)	Automatically creates global variables from incoming HTTP request variables, such as GET and POST. For security and portability, it is highly recommended that you switch this off. See http://www.php.net/register_globals for more details.
`magic_quotes_gpc` (default: `off`)	Automatically escapes quotes in incoming HTTP request variables with a backslash, helping prevent SQL injection attacks. If you know what you're doing, it's usually better to switch this functionality off and handle this escaping yourself when inserting into a database, given the problems this feature can cause you with forms, as well as the performance overhead they introduce. See Volume I, Chapter 1 for information on making your scripts compatible with this feature.
`call_time_pass_reference` (default: `off`)	Allows you to use variable references at call time (e.g. `htmlentities(&$string)`). To keep code clean and understandable, and to ensure portability, keep this functionality switched off.
`short_open_tag` (default: `on`)	Allows you to start a block of PHP code with just `<?` instead of the longer `<?php`. Also lets you write out PHP expressions with `<?=`, which is identical to `<?php echo`. While convenient, these shortcuts are not XML compliant, and can cause the PHP processor to become confused when it encounters XML processing instructions such as `<?xml version="1.0"?>`. Many people have `short_open_tag` switched off, so, for maximum portability, avoid the shortcuts and switch this feature off during development.

Setting	Notes
asp_tags (default: off)	Allows ASP style tags (<% … %>) as an alternative to the PHP open and close tags (<?php … ?>). Few people use these, so, for maximum portability, it's best to avoid them, and switch this feature off during development.
error_reporting (default: E_ALL & ~E_NOTICE)	When developing, and for maximum portability, it's best to set this to E_ALL, so that PHP will inform you of situations where, for example, a $_GET variable your code relies upon has not been initialized. This forces you to write code that is more secure and contains fewer logic errors, in order to avoid warnings. This also ensures that your code will run neatly on other servers configured this way.
display_errors (default: on)	Determines whether PHP sends error messages to the Web browser. When running your application in a live environment, it's generally better to switch this off, instead using PHP's logging mechanism to capture errors to a file, for example.
open_basedir (default: not set)	Allows you to restrict all PHP file operations to a given directory or below. This can be a good idea to prevent a script that is used to display the contents of files, for example, from being used to access sensitive files elsewhere on your server.
allow_url_fopen (default: on)	Allows you to specify remote file locations for use with functions like fopen (e.g. fopen('http://www.sitepoint.com/','r');). It's a handy tool but is also potentially a security risk for a badly written script. Switch it off if you know you don't need it.

Includes and Execution Settings

Table A.2 shows the most important PHP settings that relate to includes, and how well your PHP scripts run.

Table A.2. Includes and Execution Settings

Setting	Notes
include_path (default: '.')	Allows you to specify relative and absolute paths that PHP should search when you use one of the include related commands. Make sure you have at least the current directory (.) specified, or most third party scripts will fail to work. On Unix systems, the list of directories is separated by colons (:), while on Windows the separator is a semi colon (;).
auto_prepend_file (default: not set)	PHP will execute the file(s) specified *before* executing any requested script. Useful for performing site-wide operations such as security, logging, defining error handlers, stripping backslashes added by the magic quotes feature, and so on. Useful for applications that you're sure you will only use yourself, but unsuitable for use in code you intend to distribute. Those unable to modify php.ini settings with .htaccess files will be unable to use such code. The list separator is the same as that used for the include_path setting.
auto_append_file (default: not set)	The twin of auto_prepend_file, executed *after* a requested script is executed.
max_execution_time (default: 30)	Specifies the maximum execution time (in seconds) for which a PHP script run via a Web server may be allowed to execute. Generally, it's best to leave this as the default setting and use the set_time_limit function to extend the limit on a per-script basis. A value of 0 for either removes any limitations on script execution time.
memory_limit (default: 8M)	The amount of memory PHP has available to it at runtime. Usually, the default is fine, but when handling very large XML documents, for example, or dealing with images, you may need to increase it. The bigger this value, and the more memory a script actually uses, the less memory is available for other applications running on your server.

Setting	Notes
post_max_size (default: 8M)	The maximum amount of data that PHP will accept via an HTTP POST (e.g. a form that uploads an image). You may need to increase this if you have an application that will allow users to upload bigger files.

Error-Related Settings

Table A.3 shows the most important PHP settings that relate to the way PHP handles errors, in addition to display_errors and error_reporting, which are described in Table A.1.

Table A.3. Error-Related Settings

Setting	Notes
log_errors (default: off)	Allows you to log errors to a text file, in conjunction with error_log (below). Useful for a live site where you've switched off the display of errors to visitors.
error_log (default: not set)	A filename to which errors are logged when log_errors is switched on.
ignore_repeated_errors (default: off)	Using this, if the same error occurs from the same PHP script on the same line, the error will only be reported once per script execution. Helps prevent massive log files resulting from errors that occur in loops, when logging to a text file.
ignore_repeated_source (default: 30)	Similar to ignore_repeated_errors, but, in this case, it suppresses repeated errors of the same type *throughout* a PHP script.
report_memleaks (default: on)	Make sure this is switched on, especially if you're using experimental versions or non-stable releases of PHP, otherwise you may end up crashing your server once leaked memory has eaten up all available space. error_reporting must be set to report warnings for this setting to apply.

Miscellaneous Settings

Table A.4 shows additional important settings that you should be aware of in your PHP configuration.

Table A.4. Miscellaneous Settings

Setting	Notes
session.save_path (default: /tmp)	If storing sessions in files on a Windows-based system, you will need to modify this setting to an available directory to which PHP can write session files.
session.use_cookies (default: 1)	Use cookies to store the session ID on the client, rather than placing the session ID in the URL (which can present a greater risk to security).
extension_dir (default: './')	The path under which compiled PHP extensions can be found. On Windows-based systems, it might be something like this: `extension_dir = C:\php-4.3.2\extensions\`
extension	On Windows based systems only, this is used to identify all the extensions which should be loaded. The extensions specified should reside in the extension_dir path (above). For example: `extension = php_xslt.dll`

Appendix B: Hosting Provider Checklist

PHP, and, more generally, the LAMP combination of Linux, Apache, MySQL and PHP/Perl/Python, is widely available via literally thousands of Web hosts at very affordable prices. You can easily get quality Web hosting that will suit 90% of your needs for under $10 a month per site. That said, all PHP installations are not created equal, and depend largely on the configuration settings defined in `php.ini` as well as the extensions the host has installed for you. There are also a number of general issues relating to the amount of control you're given over your own environment, and these are important if you don't want big trouble later on.

This is a summary of the key issues you should investigate before paying for a hosting service. Contact potential providers and have them respond on each of these points. Follow up by asking for opinions from other people who know/have used the service in question. There are many online forums where you'll find people who are able to offer advice. Be aware, though, that the ratio of "knowledgable" to "ignorant" is stacked highly in favor of ignorance; gem up on technical detail so you're able to verify that the answers you were given were actually well-informed.

Some of the points I've provided here may seem a little extreme, but once you've been around the block a few times, you'll probably want to get value for your money, rather than spending your Saturday mornings fixing the problems your host made for you on Friday night.

General Issues

❏ **Require Linux and Apache (1.3)**

From the point of view of performance and reliability, this is the best combination. Avoid any host using Apache 2.x (it's not yet completely stable with PHP). Ask for details of the Linux distribution. Although Red Hat and Suse are popular, you may find hosts using Debian (or, better yet, Rock Linux) know more about what they're doing.

❏ **Does the host provide you with SSH access to the server?**

SSH gives you a secure connection to the server to perform tasks from the Linux command line or transfer files with SCP (secure copy). Avoid any host who allows you to use telnet (a fundamentally insecure way to connect to a server over the Internet). For Windows users, Putty[1] makes an excellent command line tool over SSH, while WinSCP[2] provides a secure file transfer mechanism using an SSH connection. Oh, and don't transfer files with ftp—it's as insecure as telnet.

☐ **Is the host a reseller or do they maintain the server themselves?**

Resellers can provide significant value if you need help at a basic technical level (if, for example, you call yourself a newbie), but they generally have the same level of control over the server as you. Going "straight to the source" means you won't have to deal with delays when there are system problems, as you'll likely be dealing directly with those who maintain the server. The down side is that they tend to be less "newbie tolerant" so you may get answers—but not ones you can understand

☐ **To what degree does the host "overload" the server?**

Many Web hosting companies create far more accounts on a server than the maximum for which the system is specified. The best metric is the uptime command (to which you require access); this will tell you the server load averages over 1, 5 and 15 minutes. Ideally, the server should never have load averages above 1. Obviously, the problem isn't as simple as this, but once you see your server hit averages in excess of 5, you'll begin to experience significant delays in your PHP-based applications.

☐ **What is the hosting provider's policy on running scripts and programs from the command line?**

MySQLDump is a very handy tool for backing up your database, but it's no good if you can't run it. Some hosts automatically kill any command line application that executes for longer than a given time.

☐ **Does the host provide you access to cron, the Unix utility that allows you to schedule batch jobs?**

If so, make sure the host allows command line scripts to be executed. Some hosts have taken to implementing cron so that it executes scripts via a Web

---

[1] http://www.chiark.greenend.org.uk/~sgtatham/putty/download.html
[2] http://winscp.sourceforge.net/eng/

URL. This is no use if the script in question uses the MySQLDump application to back up your database—a PHP script executed via Apache will typically run as a user, which will not have the correct permissions required for the job.

PHP-Related Issues

❑ **Can you see the output of `phpinfo` on the server you will actually be assigned to?**

Some hosts may claim this is a security risk, but expert hosts know that security by obscurity is no substitute for *real* security. The information provided by `phpinfo` is *not* a security risk to hosting providers that know what they're doing, and have Linux, Apache, and firewalls correctly set up. What `phpinfo` tells you is the best way to confirm the facts.

❑ **Is PHP installed as an Apache module (not the CGI variant)?**

This provides much better performance.

❑ **Is the Apache setting AllowOverride set to Options or All?**

This will let you modify `php.ini` settings with `.htaccess` files.

❑ **Is PHP Safe Mode disabled?**

The `safe_mode` option in `php.ini` is, in theory, a way to make PHP secure, and prevent users from performing certain tasks or using certain functions that are security-sensitive. Safe Mode is nothing but a large headache if you're doing any serious work in PHP.

❑ **Check the upgrade policy of your host.**

Ask the host how much warning you will get before upgrades are performed. Check that they will provide you with a copy of the `php.ini` file they'll be using for the upgrade (before it happens). The number of hosts that, overnight, switch from `register_globals = on` to `register_globals = off` is considerable. Make sure you test your applications on your development system against the new version before the host performs the upgrade.

❑ **Ask for a list of installed PHP extensions.**

Confirm that these extensions match the requirements of your applications. Few hosts, for example, bother to provide the XSLT extension. Confirm also that the host guarantees all extensions will remain available between PHP upgrades.

☐ **Will PHP be available for use from the command line?**

If not, you might alternately require access to Perl or Python, or the ability to run shell scripts, if you're happy with those languages. Usually, running a serious Website will require that you have the ability to run routine batch jobs (with cron), for tasks like backups, mailing you the PHP error log, and so on.

☐ Last but not least, throw in one or two questions that will test your hosting providers' knowledge of PHP. Although it may not be their job to write PHP code, when you find yourself in the position of knowing a lot more about PHP than your host, the end result is depressing. It's important to have a host that understands your needs.

Appendix C: Security Checklist

Given that online PHP applications are exposed to essentially anyone and everyone, security should be one of, if not *the* top concern as you develop your applications. To some extent, the ease with which PHP applications can be developed is also one of its greatest weaknesses, in that, for beginners who aren't aware of the possible dangers, it's very easy to deploy an application for which the line of security resembles swiss cheese.

Make sure you're informed, and, if in any doubt, ask. The Open Web Application Security Project (OWASP)[1] is a corporate-sponsored community focused on raising awareness of Web security, and is an excellent source of information on potential dangers. They recently published a "Top 10" list of common security flaws in Web applications, the relevant points of which I've summarized here.

The Top Security Vulnerabilities

❑ **Unvalidated data**

Never trust anything you get from a Web browser. The browser is completely outside of your control, and it's easy to fake values like the HTTP referrer. It's also easy to fake a hidden field in a form.

More importantly, when dealing with forms, for example, validate the data carefully. Use a "deny all, permit a little" policy. For example, if a registration form has a field for the user name, allow only alphabetical characters and perhaps the numbers 0–9, rather than simply rejecting particular special characters. Use regular expressions to limit data to exactly what you require. Packages like PEAR::QuickForm, as you saw in Volume I, Chapter 9, provide built-in mechanisms for validating forms and do a lot to help cover weaknesses you might otherwise neglect.

Also, where things like include files are concerned, watch out for logic like this:

```
include($_GET['page']);
```

Make sure you check the value of $_GET['page'] against a list of files your code is designed to include:

---

[1] http://www.owasp.org/

```
$pages = array(
  'news.php', 'downloads.php', 'links.php'
);

if (in_array($_GET['page'], $pages)) {
  include $_GET['page'];
} else {
  include 'not_found.php';
}
```

Without such checks, it's very easy for an attacker to use code similar to this to execute other PHP scripts—even ones you didn't write.

☐ **Broken access control**

Fundamental logic of this form is easy to get wrong if you don't know what you're doing. For example, often, developers check a user name/password combination against a database using logic like this:

```
if ($numRows != 0) {
  // allow access ...
}
```

That means they let users in even if they found *more than one* matching entry in the database, which, if your site also has security holes like command injection flaws (see below), may provide attackers access to a lot more than you were expecting. It's easy to make mistakes in situations you think are secure when, in fact, the logic can be bypassed easily. In general, use respected third party libraries such as PEAR::Auth[2] and PEAR::LiveUser[3] wherever possible. Also, investigate Web testing frameworks such as SimpleTest[4], which provide the ability to test your site from the point of view of a Web browser.

☐ **Session and Cookie Vulnerabilities**

Watch out for session hijacking possibilities. On sites where you really need secure authentication (e.g. ecommerce sites), use SSL to serve the site to the browser, to ensure the conversation is encrypted and that no one is listening in. If you're passing session IDs via the URL, as you will for WML-based sites, make sure that you're not placing the session ID in URLs that point to remote sites. Also, when passing visitors to a remote site, forward them via an intermediate script that strips out any possible HTTP referrer information that

[2] http://pear.php.net/package/Auth
[3] http://pear.php.net/package/LiveUser
[4] http://www.lastcraft.com/simple_test.php

contains the session ID. In general, it's better to handle sessions with cookies. If you're working with your own cookie-based authentication, store an identifying session ID in the cookie only, not the user name and password.

❏ Cross Site Scripting (XSS)

By using the legitimate mechanisms your site provides, it's possible for attackers to post on your site, for example, JavaScript that results in other users giving away their session IDs, thereby allowing the attacker to hijack their session. Less serious, but equally embarrassing, is simply posting HTML that "scrambles" the layout of your page, perhaps closing a `table` tag prematurely. Use a "deny all, permit a little" approach, or, better yet, employ a separate markup language such as BBCode (see Volume I, Chapter 5), while eliminating HTML with PHP functions like `strip_tags` and `htmlentities`. If you really want to allow HTML to be posted, consider building a filter based on PEAR::XML_HTMLSax[5] (see Chapter 2).

❏ Command Injection

Command injection occurs when an attacker is able to influence the way PHP interacts with external systems, such as the file system or a database. An SQL injection is a prime example, which occurs when an attacker uses a form or URL to modify a database query. This was discussed in some detail in Volume I, Chapter 3. The bottom line is: escape all data you receive from a user before you use it in a query.

❏ Error Handling

An experienced attacker will be able to gain a lot of important information about your system from your error messages. Although this comes under the heading of "security by obscurity" (which is no substitute for having a *really* secure application), for a live site, it's a good idea to instruct PHP to log error messages to a file, rather than display them to the browser. See Volume I, Appendix A for details.

❏ Insecure Use of Cryptography

First of all, when it comes to cryptography, don't roll your own. Second, remember that if it's an algorithm that's meant to be decoded, then someone (other than you) is also capable of decoding it. Remember that, strictly speaking, MD5 is not an encryption algorithm (i.e. you cannot decrypt an

---

[5] http://pear.php.net/package/XML_HTMLSax

MD5 string to obtain the original data); it's a message digest algorithm. But if you don't need to decrypt a value then use MD5, which is available through PHP's md5 function. This allows you to compare the encrypted versions of two pieces of data (e.g. a stored password and that entered by a user), which avoids the risks involved in working with encrypted values that could possibly be decrypted by an attacker.

❏ **Administration Flaws**

Allowing an attacker to gain the same access you have to your site is clearly bad news. Avoid FTP and telnet in favor of SCP/SFTP and SSH, respectively. Linux distributions usually have the required client tools pre-installed. For Windows, check out putty[6] for SSH access and WinSCP[7] for SCP/SFTP. FTP and telnet expose your password to network sniffers. Make sure that any Web administration tools your host provides are used only over an SSL connection. If you're using third party software, such as phpBB, change the default administrator password immediately, and stay informed about potential security flaws.

❏ **Configuration and Patching**

When installing PHP, the configuration file `php.ini-recommended` makes the best starting point to make sure you've got the package configured correctly.

If you're using a hosting company, they should take care of most of the issues for you, such as patching software as vulnerabilities are announced. Still, it's worth staying up to date on your own, using sites like Security Focus[8] and others listed at DMOZ[9].

More information is available at PHP Advisory[10] although, sadly, the site is no longer being maintained.

---

[6] http://www.chiark.greenend.org.uk/~sgtatham/putty/
[7] http://winscp.sourceforge.net/eng/
[8] http://www.securityfocus.com/incidents/
[9] http://dmoz.org/Computers/Security/Mailing_Lists/
[10] http://www.phpadvisory.com/

Appendix D: Working with PEAR

PEAR[1], the **PHP Extension and Application Repository**, is the brainchild of Stig Bakken, and was inspired by Perl's CPAN[2].

As a project, it was originally conceived in 1999 and reached its first stable release in January 2003. It serves two purposes. First, it provides a library of PHP classes for solving common "architectural" problems, a number of which you've seen in this book. Second, under the title "PECL" (PHP Extension Code Library), PEAR provides a repository for extensions to PHP. PECL was originally intended to store "non standard" extensions that lay more on the fringes of PHP, but it has since evolved into the default repository for all extensions not included in the core PHP distribution. Here, I'll be concentrating on the PHP classes that PEAR provides.

Those who submit work and maintain the PEAR repository are all volunteers. Originally a small community of developers, the release of the first stable version of PEAR has seen their numbers grow significantly, and receive a greater focus from the PHP community as a whole. There's still a lot of work to be done to raise the standards to that of PHP itself, documentation being a key area in which there's still much room for improvement. If you're struggling, a good place to start is PHPKitchen's list of PEAR Tutorials[3]. That said, PEAR already offers significant value in terms of reducing the effort required in developing PHP applications.

But what does PEAR actually mean to you? Considering the capabilities of PEAR::SOAP, which was covered in Chapter 2, attempting to write your own SOAP implementation first, *then* writing the "application" code that will use it is clearly a waste of time. Browsing the list of packages[4], you'll see that PEAR provides you many more classes, categorized by subject, to help prevent you having to reinvent wheels. It's important to understand the focus of PEAR classes is *architectural* issues, not application-level classes. In other words, PEAR is not Hotscripts; you won't find complete applications there; rather, you'll find code that can be reused in many different applications. Also important is that the PEAR developer community does its best to maintain and support the library, compared to, say, projects available via SourceForge[5], which are often individual

[1] http://pear.php.net/
[2] http://www.cpan.org/
[3] http://www.phpkitchen.com/staticpages/index.php?page=2003041204203962
[4] http://pear.php.net/packages.php
[5] http://www.sourceforge.net/

endeavours and come to a sudden end once the individuals in question stop contributing their time. Otherwise, there is some emphasis on maintaining a degree of standardization throughout the library. For example, all error handling should be performed using PEAR::Error, and the code should be documented using the PHPDoc standard, which means you should be able to extract the API documentation using PHPDocumentor[6] (see Chapter 6) if you can't find it on the PEAR Website.

Be warned: the degree of integration between the packages within PEAR is currently fairly low when compared to, say, the Java class library. This means, in some cases, that you'll be confronted with decisions like whether to use PEAR::HTML_QuickForm's validation functionality, or PEAR::Validate, or both. It's a good idea to invest some time investigating which fits your development style up-front, rather than jumping straight in and using a PEAR class for a critical part of your application, only to discover later that it wasn't the best fit for the problem.

One important point to be clear on is that referring to "PEAR" can actually mean one of two things: the repository as a whole, or the PEAR front end (also known as the package manager), which provides tools for installing and upgrading the PEAR packages you use.

Note that it's *not* a requirement that you use the PEAR package manager to install PEAR packages. If you need to, you can download them directly from the PEAR Website and manually extract them to your PHP's include path. Make sure you check the dependencies listed on the site (these being other required packages) and be aware that most packages implicitly require PEAR "base" package[7] for tasks like error handling.

Installing PEAR

These days, the foundations of PEAR are provided with PHP distribution itself, but Web hosts typically fail to provide customers with their own default PEAR installation, so it's worth knowing how to go about doing this from scratch. The process can differ slightly between Unix and Windows based systems.

Step one is to make sure you can run PHP scripts via the command line. This is always possible if you type the full path to the PHP binary. For a Unix based system, you'd use the following:

---

[6] http://www.phpdoc.org/
[7] http://pear.php.net/package/PEAR

```
/usr/local/bin/php /home/username/scripts/my_script.php
```

For Windows, you'd use something like this:

```
c:\php\cli\php.exe c:\scripts\my_script.php
```

Note that in the Windows path above, we used the executable in the `cli` (command line interface) subdirectory of the PHP installation, this executable behaving slightly differently from that used by Apache to handle Web pages. PHP binary releases for Windows since 4.3.0 place the `cli` version of the PHP executable in this directory.

It's possible to make PHP much easier to use from the command line, though, by making some changes to your system's environment variables. For an in-depth discussion see *Replacing Perl Scripts with PHP Scripts*[8] on PHPBuilder[9].

Next, point your browser at http://pear.php.net/go-pear, where you'll see a PHP script. This script is used to install the PEAR package manager—the basis you'll need in order to install other PEAR packages. Download this to your computer (File, Save As) as `go-pear.php`. From here, you have a number of options.

Storing `go-pear.php` somewhere under your Web server's document root directory will allow you to run the script as a Web page. This behavior is still experimental, though, so there are no guarantees it'll work correctly. If you do use this approach, make sure that the script is not publicly available!

Better is to execute the `go-pear.php` script via the command line, for example:

```
/usr/local/bin/php /home/username/pear/go-pear.php
```

Or, on Windows:

```
c:\php\cli\php c:\pear\go-pear.php
```

This will start an interactive command line interface, which will ask you questions about how you would like PEAR installed. Note that the "installation prefix" is the directory in which PEAR (as well as any packages you install later) will be installed, and is referred to as `$prefix`, while `$php_dir` is the path to your PHP installation (in which `go-pear.php` will put PEAR-related documentation by default, unless you specify otherwise). Windows users should be aware that

---

[8] http://www.phpbuilder.com/columns/jayesh20021111.php3
[9] http://www.phpbuilder.com/

changing the installation prefix pops up a Windows "Browse" dialog box, through which you can specify the required directory.

With the installation options set to your requirements, the go-pear.php script will connect to the PEAR Website, and download all the packages required to set up the package manager (it also asks if you require additional packages, which are well worth having). Packages are installed in a subdirectory pear of the directory you specified as the installation prefix (so, in the above examples you'd end up with c:\pear\pear or /home/username/pear/pear).

Finally, if you let it, the go-pear.php installer will attempt to modify your include_path in php.ini. To do this manually, assuming you used the directories above, you'd specify the following:

```
include_path = ".:/home/username/pear/pear"
```

For Windows users, the path is as follows:

```
include_path = ".;c:\pear\pear"
```

Finally, to use the PEAR package manager from the command line, you need to set up some environment variables. For Windows users these can be automatically added to your Windows registry by right clicking on the file PEAR_ENV.reg and choosing Run. They may also be manually configured as environment variables via the Windows Control Panel. Users with Unix-based systems can configure them to be set up every time you log in, by editing the file .profile in your home directory (/home/*username*):

```
# Envinment variables
export PHP_PEAR_SYSCONF_DIR=/home/username/pear
export PHP_PEAR_INSTALL_DIR=/home/username/pear/pear
export PHP_PEAR_DOC_DIR=/home/username/pear/pear/docs
export PHP_PEAR_BIN_DIR=/home/username/pear
export PHP_PEAR_DATA_DIR=/home/username/pear/pear/data
export PHP_PEAR_TEST_DIR=/home/username/pear/pear/tests
export PHP_PEAR_PHP_BIN=/usr/local/bin/php
```

Finally, you need to add the PEAR command line script to your system path, which, on Windows, can be achieved through the System Control Panel application (on the *Advanced* tab, click Environment Variables), by appending ;c:\pear to the PATH variable.

On Unix-based systems, add the following to your .profile script:

```
export PATH=$PATH;/home/username/pear
```

Once you've done all that, you're ready to move on and use the package manager in one of its many incarnations.

The PEAR Package Manager

Assuming you set PEAR up correctly, you can now use the command line interface to the PEAR package manager to install packages. For example, from the command line, type:

```
pear install HTML_Common
```

That will install the package HTML_Common from the PEAR Website. The package names for the command line are the same as those on the Website.

The PEAR Package Manager uses XML_RPC to communicate with the PEAR Website. If you're behind a proxy server or firewall, you will need to tell PEAR the domain name of the proxy server with:

```
pear config-set http_proxy proxy.your-isp.com
```

To unset the variable at some later stage, simply use:

```
pear config-set http_proxy ""
```

Now to add QuickForm to the installed PEAR packages, you simply need to type:

```
pear install HTML_QuickForm
```

Should another release of QuickForm be made after you've installed it, you can upgrade the version with:

```
pear upgrade HTML_QuickForm
```

If, for some reason, you later decide you don't need QuickForm any more, you can remove it using:

```
pear uninstall HTML_QuickForm
```

For a list of all PEAR commands, simply type **pear**.

Now, if you don't like command lines, there's also an (experimental) Web-based front end to PEAR (as well as a PHP-GTK front end, which is beyond the scope of this discussion). To use it, you first need to install it from the command line (note that if you executed `go-pear.php` through your Web server, the Web-based front end is also installed for you). Type the following commands:

```
pear install Net_UserAgent_Detect
pear install Pager
pear install HTML_Template_IT
pear install PEAR_Frontend_Web
```

Note the first three packages are required by PEAR_Frontend_Web. With that done, you can launch the front end from your Web server using the following simple script:

```php
<?php
// Optional if include path not set
# ini_set('include_path', 'c:\htdocs\PEAR');

require_once 'PEAR.php';

// For Windows users
# $pear_user_config = 'c:\windows\pear.ini';
// For Unix users
$pear_user_config = '/home/username/pear/pear/PEAR/pear.conf';

$useDHTML = TRUE; // Switch off for older browsers

require_once 'PEAR/WebInstaller.php';
?>
```

Installing Packages Manually

It's possible to install packages manually (although this involves more work), but it's important to watch the include paths carefully when doing so. First of all, create a directory that will be the base of all the PEAR classes you install. This directory *must* be in your include path. Next, install the main PEAR package[11]—download the latest *stable* version and extract it directly to the directory you've created, so that `PEAR.php` is in the root of this directory.

Installing further packages can be completed in more or less the same fashion, but you need to be careful which directory you extract to. For example, looking at PEAR::DB, the main `DB.php` file goes alongside the `PEAR.php` file in the root of the PEAR class directory, while further PEAR::DB-related files go in the subdirectory `DB`. The best way to check is to look at the `package.xml` file that comes

[11] http://pear.php.net/package/PEAR

with every PEAR package. This contains an element called `filelist`, which lists all the files contained in the package and the location at which they should be installed. For each `file`, check the `baseinstalldir` attribute which, if specified, tells you where, relative to the root PEAR class directory, the file should be placed. The `name` attribute specifies the path and filename *relative* to the `baseinstalldir` (or just the root PEAR class directory if there's no `baseinstalldir` attribute), where each file should be placed.

Index

This index covers both volumes of *The PHP Anthology*. Page references in another volume are prefixed with the volume number and appear in italics (e.g. *I-123* refers to page 123 of Volume I).

Symbols

A

B

custom error pages, *I-333*
custom session handlers, 10
custom tags (see BBCode)

D

Data Access Objects (DAO), *I-104*
database indexes, *I-96*
database persistence layers (see persistence layers)
databases, *I-65*, *I-216*
   (see also MySQL)
   backing up (see backing up MySQL databases)
   storing dates in, *I-172*
dates
   day of the week, *I-182*
   day of the year, *I-186*
   days in month, *I-183*
   first day in the month, *I-187*
   leap years, *I-185*
   number suffix, *I-188*
   storing in MySQL, *I-172*
   week of the year, *I-183*
dates and times
   in HTTP, 264
DELETE queries
   counting rows affected, *I-93*
derived data, 226
design patterns, *I-21*, xiii, 311
   adapter pattern, 190, 342
   factory method, 313
   iterator pattern, 323, 333
      (see also iterators)
   observer pattern, 25, 347
   strategy pattern, 334
development techniques, xiii
directories
   reading, *I-123*
dispatch maps, 160
doc tags (see @ doc tags)
DocBlocks, 294

Document Object Model (DOM), 80, 102, 110, 112, 114
   (see also XPath)
DOM (see Document Object Model (DOM))
DOM inspector, 79
downloads (see files, downloads)
drop-down menus, *I-299*

E

echo statements, 201, 245, 246
Eclipse PHP library, 290, 334
ECMAScript (see JavaScript)
email, *I-237*, 29
   attachments, *I-239*
   complex messages, *I-238*
   embedded images, *I-240*, *I-243*
   HTML, *I-243*
   mailing lists, *I-251*
   multipart, *I-245*
   multiple recipients, *I-245*
   PHP setup, *I-237*
   receiving, *I-247*
email addresses
   temporary, 25
encapsulation, 286
encryption, *I-275*, 46, 51
   (see also MD5 digests)
enctype attribute, *I-280*
enterprise application architecture, *I-21*
entity references (see XML entity references)
environment errors, *I-10*, *I-319*
error reporting levels, *I-321*, *I-322*
   (see also errors, levels)
error_reporting directive, *I-321*, *I-322*
   (see also error reporting levels)
errors, *I-320*, *I-324*, *I-325*
   (see also environment errors)
   (see also logic errors)
   (see also semantic errors)

processing instructions (see XML processing instructions)
proxy servers, 224
pseudo-cron, *I-205*
    (see also cron)
public methods, *I-39*

Q

QuickForm (see PEAR, PEAR::HTML_QuickForm)
quotes (see code optimization, quotes)
quotes in SQL statements, *I-83*, *I-84*

R

R&OS PDF, 170
raw data, 226
RDF (see RSS)
realms, 6
redirection, 20
    (see also HTTP headers, location)
refactoring, *I-28*
reference counting, *I-48*
references, *I-20*, *I-39*, *I-45*, 276
    (see also call-time pass-by-references)
    (see also passing by reference)
    improving performance with, *I-47*
    in PHP 5, *I-48*
    returning from functions/methods, *I-46*
    to new objects, *I-46*
register_globals directive, *I-18*, 11, 18
registering users (see user registration systems)
regular expressions, *I-153*, *I-158*, 44, 340
REPAIR TABLE queries, *I-103*
repairing corrupt MySQL databases, *I-103*
require, *I-12*
    (see also include)
require_once, *I-12*, *I-14*, *I-17*, 276, 283
    (see also include_once)

reserved characters, *I-144*
resource identifiers, *I-74*
RESTORE TABLE queries, *I-101*
result pagers (see paged results)
return commands
    in constructors, *I-31*
return values, *I-5*
    for constructors, *I-31*
reusable code, *I-20*, *I-23*
rich clients, 215
RLIKE operator, *I-96*
robots (see visitor statistics, excluding search engines)
RSS, 79, 85, 102
    aggregation, 122
    generating, 114
    validation, 122
RTFM, *I-2*
    (see also PHP manual)

S

SAX (see Simple API for XML (SAX))
Scalable Vector Graphics (SVG), 169, 200
    rendering with PHP, 205
scope, *I-34*
script execution time (see timing PHP scripts)
search engine friendly URLs, *I-307*
search engine queries, 236
searching and replacing text in strings, *I-149*
searching MySQL databases, *I-95*
    (see also FULLTEXT searches)
Secure Socket Layer (SSL), 1
security, *I-3*
SELECT queries, *I-80*
    aliases, *I-91*, 62
    counting rows returned, *I-89*, *I-92*
        with MySQL, *I-90*
        with PHP, *I-89*